WHERE THE WILD BOOKS ARE

Where the

Jim Dwyer

Wild Books Are

A FIELD GUIDE TO ECOFICTION

UNIVERSITY OF NEVADA PRESS  RENO AND LAS VEGAS

University of Nevada Press, Reno, Nevada 89557 USA
Copyright © 2010 by University of Nevada Press
All rights reserved
Manufactured in the United States of America
Design by Kathleen Szawiola

Library of Congress Cataloging-in-Publication Data
Dwyer, Jim, 1949–
    Where the wild books are : a field guide to ecofiction / Jim Dwyer.
p. cm.
    Includes bibliographical references and index.
    ISBN 978-0-87417-811-1 (pbk. : alk. paper)
    1. Ecofiction—History and criticism. 2. Ecology in literature.
3. Ecocriticism. I. Title.
    PN3448.E28D89 2010
809.3—dc22   2009052482

The paper used in this book is a recycled stock made from 100
percent post-consumer waste materials, certified by FSC and meets
the requirements of American National Standard for Information
Sciences—Permanence of Paper for Printed Library Materials, ANSI/
NISO Z39.48-1992 (R2002). Binding materials were selected for
strength and durability.

FIRST PRINTING
19   18   17   16   15   14   13   12   11   10
5   4   3   2   1

CONTENTS

PREFACE

In the early 1970s a veritable fusillade of new fiction emanating from the environmental movement exploded onto the American literary scene. As with the new feminist fiction, these books weren't mere escapism, even though many were action-packed and entertaining. As critics joined the ranks of readers, a new term emerged: ecofiction. A look back at the literature reveals that ecologically oriented fiction had existed over a century previously, and that it can be considered an important precursor to contemporary ecofiction.

Where the Wild Books Are is a guide to the growing fields of ecofiction. It is intended for use as a reader's advisory and reference work for scholars, fiction aficionados, and librarians. Librarians can use it as both a reference and collection development tool. It can also be used as a textbook or for supplemental reading in college courses on literature and the environment. Professors, librarians, and reading group leaders can use it to develop their curricula and reading lists. This is not intended to be "the last word" in ecofiction, simply the most complete and best research guide to date. It is intended to encourage reading, discussion, and debate.

Selecting the works and authors covered in this book was a painstaking process involving the application of objective criteria tempered by my own subjective reactions. (Did I learn something, gain a new perspective, or have a strong emotional reaction?) The background research for *Where the Wild Books Are* included reading over a thousand novels, several thousand reviews, and hundreds of critical works, attending conferences, and directly consulting other authors and critics over the course of a quarter century. The people mentioned in the acknowledgments and many others helped shaped my definition of ecofiction, deepen my understanding of it, relate it to literary movements, and identify both central and more obscure authors and works.

My criteria for determining whether a given work is ecofiction closely parallel Lawrence Buell's: "1. The nonhuman environment is present not merely as a framing device but as a presence that begins to suggest that human history is implicated in natural history. 2. The human interest is not understood to be the only legitimate interest. 3. Human accountability to the environment is part of the text's ethical orientation. 4. Some sense of the environment as a process rather than as a constant or a given is at least implicit in the text" (1995, 6).

Chapter 1 is a discussion of exactly what ecofiction is. Please note that the debate on this issue is ever evolving and there are many valid and varied perspectives.

Chapter 2 defines and analyzes ecofiction, tracing its history from its emergence in the mid-nineteenth century to the present day.

Contemporary ecofiction is incredibly complex and varied. Chapter 3 is an attempt to categorize it.

Almost all the books evaluated in this study were written in English or are available in English translation, but just as the natural environment and its problems do not recognize political or linguistic borders, neither does art. Therefore, a rather lengthy chapter is devoted to ecofiction from around the world. A great deal of ecofiction in other languages, particularly Asian and African languages, remains to be translated into English. The scope of further research on ecofiction should be broadened in four directions: geographically/linguistically, ethnically, inclusion of children's literature, and by format, including feature films, television programs, and the growing body of fiction found exclusively on the Internet.

Since environmental concerns have become ever more common in the broad genres of romance, western Americana, speculative fiction, and mysteries, they are covered in separate chapters. An individual author or work may fall into several categories, creating considerable overlap. Dana Stabenow, for example, is an Alaskan Inuit ecofeminist author who has written both mysteries and science fiction.

Rather than interspersing many bibliographies throughout the book, a single author bibliography is provided. Each entry includes author, title and subtitle, and publication information. Whenever possible, an edition in print or at least a recent edition was chosen, and that publication date is listed. The original publication date for each work is included parenthetically in the discussion of the books in the text and at the beginning of the bibliography entry, if a later edition is listed. Please note that this book is not intended as a comprehensive bibliography for every author covered, since such a book would be thousands of pages long. The bibliography is limited to works of fiction. Many of the authors included have also written poetry, personal essays, nonfiction, literary criticism, and, in some cases, drama. These works are excluded.

For more complete bibliographic histories, ISBNs for specific editions, and so on, consult critical works about the authors, large online catalogs such as the Library of Congress or Melvyl (the catalog of the University of California Libraries), and reference works such as *Contemporary Authors.* The World Wide Web is an increasingly important scholarly tool and publication medium, but for reasons of brevity and because of frequently changing Web addresses, the only Web sites listed are the ones referred to in the endnotes. Scholars are encouraged to visit the Web sites of professional organizations such as the Association for the Study of Literature and the Environment and the Western Literature Association and sites for individual authors.

HOW TO USE THIS BOOK

To select a good book to begin with or an important author to study, start with the appendix's list of 100 best books. Authors, titles, and where they appear in this book are indicated.

I made my selections by determining how well a book was received by its audience, books that had a powerful impact on the reader and on other writers, raised awareness of an issue or position on an issue, and met the highest literary standards. The one exception on the list is *Ecotopia* by Ernest Callenback, which isn't terribly well written, but was enormously influential on readers, other writers, and the environmental movement itself. I also chose books based on subjective criteria, those with the most emotional impact on me—inspiring, exciting, and inciting me to read and especially to do more. Many of the authors are famous, while others are rather obscure. It is interesting to note that these books span many different time periods, genres, and countries.

For work written before the 1970s (approximately), see chapter 2.

For genre fiction, see chapters 6–9.

For work from various countries, see chapter 5.

For the work of a single author, consult the bibliography.

For books on a specific subject or place, use the subject index. An extremely broad topical approach is also provided in the "Contemporary Ecofiction" chapter, separating the works into the categories of Philosophical/Spiritual, Animals, Ecofeminist, Environmental Action/Ecodefense, Food and Drink, Ecotopias, the Contemporary Pastoral, and Cautionary and Dystopian.

Example: "Dams" in the subject index identifies entries for *From the River's Edge* by Elizabeth Cook-Lynn, *Wind from an Enemy Sky* by D'Arcy McNickle, *The Monkey Wrench Gang* by Edward Abbey, *Dancers in the Scalp House* by William Eastlake, *People of the Valley* by Frank Waters, and so on. The bibliography entries reveal that the works of Abbey, Eastlake, and Waters can be found in the history and contemporary chapters, and that Cook-Lynn and McNickle are discussed in the Native American chapter.

ACKNOWLEDGMENTS

My deepest and most sincere thanks to:
Margaret Dalrymple, Joanne O'Hare, and the late Trudy McMurrin of the University of Nevada Press.

Jo Ann Bradley and Flora Quinn of the California State University, Chico, Meriam Library Interlibrary Loan Department (ILL) and ILL staff from other libraries for providing me with hundreds of books and articles, some highly obscure. All my colleagues at Meriam Library for their continuing encouragement and advice, particularly Colleen Power for her expert assistance with the speculative fiction chapter and James Tyler for proofreading and editorial assistance. The late Lawrence Clark Powell, university librarian at UCLA and Arizona, author of over forty books, and a champion of western American literature was the quintessential librarian/literary scholar and my primary role model and inspiration.

Other librarians who were particularly helpful include Fred Stoss, SUNY-Buffalo; Brian Aveney, librarian emeritus and speculative fiction expert; Maria Anna Jankowksa, University of Idaho, and editor of *Electronic Green Journal;* Kristin Ramsdell, romance fiction expert, California State University, Hayward; David Laird, librarian emeritus and keeper of the Frank Waters flame; Donna Seaman, *Booklist;* Barbara Hoffert, *Library Journal;* Roy Conant, Book House; and Chris Dodge, *Utne Reader.* Thanks to former Meriam Library Director Carolyn Dusenbury and Head of Library Collections Julie Clarke for administrative support.

The California State University, Chico, English department, especially professors Andrea Lerner, Susan Aylworth, Sarah Emily Newton, Peter Hogue, and Robert O'Brien, and Lisa Emmerich of the history department. Colleagues at other universities, including Karla Armbruster, Webster University; Charles Bergman, Pacific Lutheran University; Frank Bergon, Vassar College;

Susan Bernardin and Charlotte Zoe Walker, SUNY Oneonta; Michael Branch, David Fenimore, Cheryll Glotfelty, Ann Ronald, and Scott Slovic, University of Nevada; Linda Helstern, North Dakota State University; Melody Graulich, Utah State University; Ursula Heise, Stanford University; Terry Heller, Coe College; Michael Kowalewski, Carleton College; Paul Lindholdt, Eastern Washington University; Glen Love, University of Oregon; Tom Lynch, University of Nebraska; Patricia Monaghan, DePaul University; Patrick D. Murphy, University of Central Florida; Steve Norwick, Sonoma State University; Diane Quantic, Wichita State University; Harold Simonson, University of Washington; Steve Tatum, University of Utah; Bron Taylor, University of Florida; O. Alan Weltzien, University of Montana-Western; Nick Witschi, Western Michigan University. Scott Slovic deserves particular thanks for assistance on the international chapter and for demanding the highest scholarly standards.

Authors Rick Bass, Linda Gunnerson, Thomas King, Barbara Kingsolver, Kent Nelson, the late Louis Owens, Marina Schauffler, Joan Slonczewski, and especially Brenda Peterson who has been a constant font of encouragement and good advice. Pat Schuman, Charles Harman, and Margo Hart of Neal-Schuman Publishers, publishers of my first Book, *Earth Works: Recommended Fiction and Nonfiction about Nature and the Environment for Adults and Young Adults,* in 1996.

My late parents Bill and Ellen Dwyer for their encouragement to read and to appreciate nature, and my brother Billy for the books he recommended and for reality checks. High school English teachers Cale Campbell and Jan DeVries for encouraging my writing aspirations, and scoutmaster Chuck Furstenburg, who introduced me to the study of natural history and instilled a deep conservation ethic.

All of the people listed above and many of the authors whose work is considered here have inspired, encouraged, or assisted me in the course of this long project. Any errors are mine.

WHERE THE WILD BOOKS ARE

1

Ecocriticism and Ecofiction

DEFINITIONS AND ANALYSES

O ne of the most significant developments in literary criticism over the
previous quarter century is the proliferation of an ecocritical approach
to literature. Cheryll Glotfelty notes a curious disconnection between previous literary scholarship and the real world: "If your knowledge of the outside
world were limited to what you could infer from the major publications of the
literary profession, you would quickly discern that race, class, and gender were
the hot topics of the late twentieth century, but you would never suspect that
the earth's life support systems were under stress. Indeed, you might never
know there was an earth at all."[1]

Although definitions of ecocriticism vary, it might be simply described as
a critical perspective on the relationship between literature and the natural
world, and the place of humanity within—not separate from—nature. Ecocriticism arose from the development of a greater understanding of ecological
processes, concern over the intensification of global environmental degradation, deep ecological philosophy, the green movement, ecofeminism, and the
emergence of scholars whose formative years occurred during a time of great
political, social, and environmental ferment in the 1960s and 1970s. Some of
their immediate precursors such as Glen Love, Ann Ronald, Wallace Stegner,
Thomas Lyon, and Joseph Meeker, who were already studying the relation-

ship between nature and literature, also embraced a more specifically ecological approach. Their work, in turn, had been informed by classic nature writers such as Henry David Thoreau, John Muir, John Burroughs, Mabel Osgood Wright, Mary Austin, and Aldo Leopold, among many others.[2]

In his essay "Literature and Ecology: An Experiment in Ecocriticism," William Rueckert coined the term "ecocriticism" and championed a new direction for literary scholarship. "There must be a shift in our locus of motivation from newness, or theoretical elegance, or even coherence, to a principle of relevance. . . . I am going to experiment with the application of ecology and ecological concepts to literature, because ecology has the greatest relevance to the present and the future of the world we live in. . . . I am going to try to discover something about the ecology of literature, or try to develop an ecological poetics by applying ecological concepts to the reading, teaching, and writing about literature."[3]

William Howarth has proposed "Some Principles of Ecocriticism," noting that "*Eco* and *critic* both derive from Greek, *oikos* and *kritis,* and in tandem they mean 'house judge,' which may surprise many lovers of green, outdoor writing. . . . [An ecocritic is] a person who judges the merits and faults of writings that depict the effects of culture upon nature, with a view toward celebrating nature, berating its despoilers, and reversing their harm through political action."[4] While this definition with its call for activism has been subject to much debate, it serves as a useful touchstone for the definition(s) of ecofiction that follow. Ecocriticism seems to be inherently interdisciplinary, cross-cultural, syncretic, holistic, and evolutionary in its nature.

Although most any text can be analyzed ecocritically, some are more inherently ecological than others, including many works of contemporary fiction. Fiction that deals with environmental issues or the relation between humanity and the physical environment, that contrasts traditional and industrial cosmologies, or in which nature or the land has a prominent role is sometimes called ecofiction. The earliest use of "ecofiction" I have encountered is as the title of a seminal 1971 anthology containing both science fiction and mainstream stories. Perhaps because of ecocriticism's relative infancy, there is not even consensus on spelling. It is usually spelled as one word, but sometimes hyphenated or split into two words: "eco-fiction" and "eco fiction." (Most database searches of "eco fiction," though, will retrieve articles about the Italian author and semiotician Umberto Eco.) The terms "environmental fiction," "green fiction," and "nature-oriented fiction" are sometimes used interchangeably with "ecofiction," but might better be considered as categories of ecofiction.

Ecofiction is a composite subgenre made up of many styles, primarily modernism, postmodernism, realism, and magic realism, and can be found in many genres, primarily mainstream, westerns, mystery, romance, and speculative fiction. Speculative fiction includes science fiction and fantasy, sometimes mixed with realism, as in the work of Ursula K. Le Guin.

Ecofiction has deep literary roots and a rich and growing canopy of branches. Extending this arboreal analogy, one might consider this book to be a sort of silvicultural analysis and survey of fiction. In the literary old-growth mixed forest, we find that there are many different species (genres and subgenres) that have coevolved and are interdependent. It is also not uncommon for ecologically oriented authors to write in many different forms: poetry, fiction, literary or philosophical essays, environmental activism, and natural history. Edward Abbey, Mary Austin, Jim Harrison, Barbara Kingsolver, Rick Bass, and Leslie Marmon Silko are good examples of nature-oriented authors who have mastered many forms.

Mike Vasey defines ecofiction as "stories set in fictional landscapes that capture the essence of natural ecosystems. . . . [They] can build around human relationships to these ecosystems or leave out humans altogether. The story itself, however, takes the reader into the natural world and brings it alive. . . . Ideally, the landscape and ecosystems—whether fantasy or real—should be as 'realistic' as possible and plot constraints should accord with ecological principles."5 It should be noted that magic realism and speculative fiction, however, frequently employ fantastic elements to provide readers with a different perspective on the nature of reality itself, as in Kim Stanley Robinson's Three Californias or Mars trilogies.

Ecofiction is also a component of two related literary phenomena that Patrick D. Murphy terms "nature oriented literature" and "environmental literature." "Nature oriented literature is limited to having either nonhuman nature itself as the subject, character, or major component of the setting, or to a text that says something about human-nonhuman interaction, human philosophies about nature, or the possibility of engaging nature by means of or in spite of human culture."[6] Murphy observes that environmental literature "does not stop at describing the natural history of the area, but instead, or in addition, discusses the ways in which pollution, urbanization, and other forms of human intervention have altered the land or environment. It treats human action in defense of, or in behalf of, wild and endangered nature."[7] Advancing Murphy's argument one step, one might term fiction that focuses on environmental action or the green movement as "green fiction." The purpose of such texts is "to propel people back into the rest of nature with new perspectives and frames of reference."[8]

According to Diane Ackerman, "Often in fiction nature has loomed as a monstrous character, an adversary dishing out retribution for moral slippage, or as a nightmare region of chaos and horror where fanged beasts crouch ready to attack. But sometimes it beckons as a zone of magic, mysticism, inspiration, and holy conversion."[9]

This distinction raises the issue of "true" versus "false" ecofiction. Some disaster novels, like *Jaws,* are a good example of the latter because they "emphasize our separateness from nature, our vulnerability to the great and morally blank forces of the universe. . . . False ecofiction is based on the fear that something will go wrong. . . . But true ecofiction is based on an integrative view of reality. It is emotionally oriented toward creating a whole world. The true ecofictionist wants to play God. The false ecofictionist wants to play Satan."[10] Although this may be an oversimplistic distinction, given the philosophical complexity of authors such as Jim Crace, Frank Waters, or Octavia Butler, ecofiction does tend to be optimistic in the face of daunting challenges.

One person's true or false ecofiction may not be another's. Patricia Greiner acknowledges that ecofiction "advocates actions of various kinds, *some liberal, some radical, in defense of the wild*, and aligns itself with other liberal *and radical* causes in its rejection of traditional sources of power and authority, such as national government, the military and big business."[11] One might be surprised, therefore, by her seemingly contradictory contention that "false ecofiction . . . stems from its emphasis on conflict, usually between environmentalists and despoilers, or between human beings and a nature which has become hostile to them in its own defense."[12] She labels Edward Abbey's *The Monkey Wrench Gang*, arguably the most significant single work of ecofiction, as "false," even though that book is widely considered a perfect example of "radical action in defense of the wild." Many ecocritics and green authors would agree with Lawrence Buell's Abbey-like assertion that "environmentalism of any sort cannot hope to achieve even modest reforms unless *some* take extreme positions advocating genuinely alternative paths: rejection of consumer society, communitarian anti-modernism, animal liberation."[13]

One method to determine if a book is "true ecofiction" is to consider the author's agenda and the intended effect on readers. *Greenwar* (1997) by Steven Gould and Laura J. Mixon, for instance, becomes a rejection of "environmental extremism" after an "ecoterrorist" bombs an offshore facility producing "green foods." While most activists and critics would condemn terrorism, the authors tar a wide range of environmental activists and activities with the "terrorist" brush. It should also be noted, however, that the author's intention is not always clear, that differences in opinion over these distinctions reflect a broader debate on the relationship between art and activism, and that some critics might reject this distinction entirely as a specious one.

A third perspective is offered by Patricia D. Netzley, who divides ecofiction not between the "true" and "false," but into three categories: "works that portray the environmental movement and/or environmental activism, works that depict a conflict over an environmental issue and express the author's beliefs . . . and works that feature environmental apocalypse."[14] One might also argue that some apocalypse and disaster novels are good examples of false ecofiction, for example, Samuel Butler's novel *Erewhon* (1872), which refutes the theory of evolution, as does some contemporary Christian fiction. *Erewhon,* and the works of Jules Verne and (later) Edgar Rice Burroughs (featuring fantastical characters like Tarzan who dominate nature rather than find a balance within it) reflect a pre-environmental consciousness. The thorny issue of the disaster novel is considered in greater depth in the "Cautionary and Dystopian Fiction" section of chapter 3.

Less controversial is Netzley's claim that "all works of environmental fiction have one element in common: the author's desire to promote environmentalism among the general public."[15] One important way that it does so is by engaging "the reader's sensitivity to the work's illumination of the basic tenet of ecology—the pattern of relationships among organisms, including human beings, and their relationship to the environment as a whole."[16]

Ecofeminism has also had a strong impact on literature. Elizabeth Englehardt uses the term "ecological feminism," which she describes as meeting four criteria: humans are part of nature and not separate from or superior to it, the nonhuman community has agency to consider and act, activism must be based on long-term sustainability and be related to social justice and equality, and "women are not necessarily united in sisterhood, nor or they equally oppressed, not are they the only gender to have a role in enacting justice. . . . Race matters, gender matters, class matters, and all of us have complicated identities."[17] Karen J. Warren reaffirms and expands upon this definition, asserting that "there are important connections between how one treats women, people of color, and the underclass on one hand and how one treats the nonhuman natural environment on the other."[18]

Why should one read fiction in addition to, or even in place of, other forms? Garry Peterson notes that "how people use and relate to nature is determined in large part by the models, theories, and stories that people use to describe how human society and nature work. These concepts provide the mental infrastructure that underpins much of human action. Stories can help people reflect on their own models, and perhaps help them better understand their own ways of thought as well as those of other people.[19]

Seaman observes that "there are places where even the most supple nonfiction cannot enter, regions of the psyche rife with ambiguity, paradox, and perversity, the deep, shadowy caves and fathomless waters in which we struggle with the conflicting demands of instinct and reason, altruism and greed. These realms are best suited for the unfettered form of fiction."[20] Fiction not only speaks to both the head and heart more directly than non-fiction, it also speaks more deeply *about* them.

A primary distinction between nonfiction and fiction is the degree to which the imagination is invoked. According to Jonathan Bate, "The dream of deep ecology will never be realized upon the earth, but our survival as a species may be dependent on our capacity to dream it in the works of the imagination."[21] Lawrence Buell observes that acts of "the environmental imagination . . . potentially register and energize at least four types of engagement with the world."[22] They can connect people with the experience and suffering of other beings, including animals, with places they have been or where they may never go, with alternative futures, and with a sense of caring for the planetary environment. Imaginative literature is best suited to engaging people intellectually *and* emotionally, providing them a greater personal stake in the text itself, and making them care. Fiction is frequently less didactic and more nuanced than nonfiction, delivering its messages by implication. Personal engagement minus didacticism equals inspiration. Just ask a group of environmental activists whether they were more influenced by Ed Abbey or by green theoreticians and philosophers. Stories are powerful.

Action springs from consciousness, sensitivity, concern, optimism, and inspiration. Much modern American fiction is labeled "apolitical." However, one might argue that "apolitical" art is actually quite political in that it tends to support the status quo and provide an escape from environmental, social, and political realities. Ecofiction is frequently highly political. Barbara Kingsolver insists that "the artist's maverick responsibility is sometimes to sugarcoat the bitter pill and slip it down our gullet, telling us what we didn't want to know."[23] Noting that political literature is more commonplace in Europe, Asia, and Latin America than in the United States, Kingsolver rejects the false dichotomy between "pure" and "political" art: "Good art is political, whether it means to be or not, insofar as it provides us the chance to understand points of view alien to our own."[24] Art, in whatever form, can provide a different lens to view the world and an impetus to action.

This study is intended to raise awareness of many fine, and in some cases unjustly overlooked texts, their interrelation and to a much smaller extent their interpretation, to occasionally suggest guidance as to appropriate audiences and uses, to expand the canon of ecofiction, and to further popularize it. Read on!

2

Ecofiction's Roots and Historical Development

Ecofiction's roots are as ancient as pictograms, petroglyphs, and creation myths. Nature forms the very core of Native American, Australian Aboriginal, pagan, Celtic, Taoist, and many other cosmologies and their associated oral and written literature. These legends and the values they represent are echoed in contemporary ecofiction by indigenous and white authors alike. They can be found in classical literature such as Ovid's *Metamorphoses* and Latin pastoralism. Animal legends, human-animal metamorphoses, and pastoralism are common to many oral traditions and much written folklore.

Medieval European literature is rich in naturalistic content and tone, as evidenced by Arthurian lore, the *Chanson de Roland, Beowulf, Sir Gawain and the Green Knight,* the works of St. Francis of Assisi, and others. The "green Shakespeare" includes at least *The Tempest, King Lear, A Midsummer Night's Dream, A Winter's Tale,* and *As You Like It.* Contemporary green adaptations of Shakespeare include Gloria Naylor's *Mama Day* (1988), Jane Smiley's *A Thousand Acres* (1991), and Jonis Agee's *Strange Angels* (1993).

The focus on nature in Romanticism, traditional pastoralism, and transcendentalism influenced ecofiction, but critics tend to disagree about whether the fiction associated with these movements is truly ecological. One might argue that such books are precursors because they precede the development of modern ecological science and the related consciousness that emerged in the late nineteenth century, but most lack the activist quality of much ecofiction. Despite the environmental ravages of the Industrial Revolution, an awareness of environmental crisis was only beginning to emerge. By the turn of the twentieth century, however, political and literary resistance to industrialism emerges. The animal heroes in Kenneth Grahame's *The Wind and the Willows* (1908), for instance, actually *do* something about their plight, making it a truly activist pastoral.

Even though they themselves did not write fiction, the nature and philosophical writing of nineteenth-century essayists such as Ralph Waldo Emerson, Henry David Thoreau, John Burroughs, Margaret Fuller, and particularly John Muir has had a strong influence on modern ecological thought, environmentalism, and ecofiction.

NINETEENTH CENTURY

Although ecofiction is primarily a literary phenomenon of the twentieth and early twenty-first centuries, there are several works from the nineteenth that warrant inclusion in the canon.

Susan Warner's *The Wide, Wide World* (1850) foreshadowed a spate of fiction incorporating both environmentalism and feminism in the late nineteenth and early twentieth centuries.

Herman Melville's most famous work, *Moby Dick* (1851), engenders controversy among critics, some of whom consider it merely another example of human domination over nature, while others cite Ahab's failure as an illustration of the futility and folly of such attempts. Lacking an ecological consciousness, Ahab not only fails to understand nature and his own nature, but even the *need* to understand them. Glen Love notes that Melville "virtually overwhelms the reader with natural science in the cetology chapters only to question science's capacity to reveal—or the human mind to encompass—the limitless dynamism of nature. . . . Melville's myriad explorations of cetology and the natural sciences serve to reprove Ahabian anthropocentrism."[1]

Although not as famous, Melville's Polynesian trilogy (1846–49) is equally fascinating and may be more inherently ecological. It consists of *Typee: A*

Peep at Polynesian Life (1846), *Omoo: A Narrative of Adventures in the South Seas* (1847), and *Mardi and a Voyage Thither* (1849). *Typee* is a thinly veiled autobiographical adventure based on jumping ship, becoming lost in a cloud forest, and being taken in by supposedly barbaric cannibals who turn out to be gentle and earth-oriented, a stark contrast to the "civilization" that dispatched ships to slaughter whales for oil. *Omoo* is a more comical account of the mutiny and jailbreak on Tahiti that Melville participated in. The "Long Ghost" in the account is the ship's doctor, a rational, scientific man who becomes increasingly feral as he moves from analyzing nature to experiencing it directly. *Omoo* is also an indictment of the deleterious effects of colonialism and particularly Christian missionaries on the Polynesian environment and culture. *Mardi* is a darker and more complex philosophical allegory and inquiry into the themes raised in the first two books. A quest for beauty and innocence ends in disaster. *The Encantadas, or Enchanted Isles,* is a novella about the Galapagos that appears in Melville's *Piazza Tales* (1856).

Disappointed by the failure of the Brook Farm commune, Nathaniel Hawthorne rejected early agrarian communalism in *The Blithedale Romance* (1852). William Morris's *News from Nowhere* (1890) is a more optimistic portrayal of an ecologically oriented socialist society that prefigures Ernest Callenbach's *Ecotopia* by over eighty years.

Mark Twain's masterpiece *The Adventures of Huckleberry Finn* (1884) has an environmental aspect: the rather wild Huck and the slave Jim find freedom from civilization's laws and constraints by escaping downriver. *Roughing It* (1872) is a semifictionalized account of Twain's early adventures in the West, blending autobiography and tall tale. Although he praises nature and condemns the social and environmental damage wrought by mining, his bemused reaction to starting a massive forest fire is a powerful example of the myth of the West as a source of boundless bounty.

The Island of Dr. Moreau (1896) by H. G. Wells, with its theme of the dangerous folly of trying to modify mature, is thought by some to be the first green science fiction. It was preceded, however, by *After London: or, Wild England* (1885) by Richard Jefferies, which describes what England would be like if a cataclysm returned it to a wild state. Jefferies was a prolific pastoralist who broke away from the constraints of his typical style to write this unusual disaster novel-jeremiad-pastoral.

Bird conservationist W. H. Hudson wrote both ornithology books and romantic nature fiction set in South America. *A Crystal Age* (1887) depicts a peaceful, nature-oriented, loving utopia. The similar *Green Mansions: A Romance of the Tropical Forest* (1904) and *The Purple Land* (1885) were international best-sellers.

Literature, nature, spirituality, and ethics were the primary concerns of Hamilton Wright Mabie. In *A Child of Nature* (1901) he considers the spiritual and healing aspects of nature.

Hamlin Garland (*Main Traveled Roads*, 1891, and many others) rejected the myth of agrarian utopias, but cited existing political and economic forces, not nature, as sources of poverty and hardship. His *Cavanagh, Forest Ranger* (1910) was one of the earliest environmental action novels and ecoromances. Frank Norris's *The Octopus* (1901) is based on the Mussel Slough massacre of 1880, when the railroads and banks that dominated California politics double-crossed settlers out of the land they had so laboriously brought into production. The protagonist evolves from being a tenderfoot dilettante to a radical firebrand, but in the end his radicalism is tempered by conversations with a lowly shepherd and with the owner of the railroad.

Sarah Orne Jewett, a feminist transcendentalist environmentalist, is the veritable grandmother of ecofeminism. *The White Heron and Other Stories* (1886) and *The Country of Pointed Firs* (1896) are true classics, as relevant and readable now as they were then. In the preface to *The Best Stories of Sarah Orne Jewett* (1925), editor Willa Cather enthused that "the *Pointed Fir* sketches are living things caught in the open. . . . They melt into the life of the land until they are not stories at all, but life itself."[2]

The characters in Jewett's first collection, *Deephaven* (1877), value a traditional way of life, understanding and working with nature despite the hardships it sometimes presents. They embody transcendentalism by finding not just sustenance but divinity in nature, and by forming a caring community based on the premise that they are part of a grand unity.

In "A White Heron," a shy nine-year-old meets a young ornithologist who tries to enlist her aid in finding a rare white heron that he wishes to shoot as a specimen. Sylvia must choose between his friendship (and a large reward) and the bird's life. Although she wavers, she keeps the location of the nest a secret. One can understand nature better by accepting it and being part of its unity than by separating oneself from it to kill and dissect it.

The Country of the Pointed Firs is Jewett's masterpiece, the only novel in which she sustained the quiet intensity and luminous language of her best short stories. Mrs. Almira Todd, a folksy middle-aged widow, is a brilliant herbalist and healer whose remedies treat a variety of physical and emotional ills. Along with her potions, she spreads gentle love and the positive moral influence of nature. She thus unifies wild and cultivated nature with the human community. Todd's holistic, sustainable approach to life is subtly contrasted with the technological and economic forces that were damaging New England's natural environment while its economy continued to decline.

EARLY TWENTIETH CENTURY

Around the turn of the twentieth century the Appalachians proved to be fertile ground for several proto-ecofeminists, among them Mary Noailles Murfree (aka Charles Egbert Craddock), Grace MacGowan Cooke, Lucy Furman, Emma Bell Miles, Louise R. Baker, Marie Van Vorst, Amélie Rives Troubetzkoy, and Alice MacGowan. Cooke's *The Power and the Glory* (1910), Miles's *The Spirit of the Mountains* (1905), and Murfree's *In the Tennessee Mountains* (1884) and *His Vanished Star* (1894) in particular attained both popular and critical success, and all but *Spirit of the Mountains* are still in print a century later.

In her time, Charlotte Perkins Gilman was best known for "The Yellow Wallpaper" (1899), a short story about a woman who goes insane when her neurologist husband isolates her in a room as a cure for melancholia. The 1979 republication of her 1915 ecofeminist science fiction novel, *Herland*, created an instant classic. *Herland* is a nurturing, utopian society living in balance with nature. The more didactic *With Her in Ourland: Sequel to Herland*, was serialized in the journal *Forerunner* in 1916, but wasn't published separately until 1997.

Mary Austin's first book, *The Land of Little Rain* (1903), a classic work of creative nature writing, has been recognized by many critics as her finest, but she was also a prolific novelist and short-story writer whose work was published in dozens of periodicals, four collections, and one posthumous collection, *The Mother of Felipe and Other Early Stories* (1950). A more recent anthology (*Western Trails,* 1987) contains stories from all five books, periodicals, previously unpublished stories, and illuminating commentary by editor Melody Graulich. Austin's stories synthesize Indian and Mexican legends, tall tales, other myths, and nature writing in a highly oral and poetic style that is best read aloud. The stories in *Lost Borders* (1909) serve as meandering trails deep into the desert. Although they resemble Indian legends and frontier tall tales in some ways, they are informed by a consciousness that regards the desert as a woman. Austin wrote two short-story collections for children. In *The Basket Woman* (1910), a boy overcomes his prejudice against Indians by listening to a chisera, that is, a female ethnobotanist/basketmaker/healer/storyteller. The exhibits in a museum literally come alive and lead two children deep into the desert in the imaginative *Trail Book* (1918).

Austin's *The Ford* (1917) is a semiautobiographical novel based on oil development in Inyo and Kern counties in the 1890s and the Owens Valley water controversy of 1905, with the scene of the latter moved from the eastern to the western side of the Sierras. The socialists and reformers therein may be righteous but lack the practicality and resources to deal effectively with capitalists. The male concept of the wilderness as a female to be exploited must be superseded by a more ecofeminist consciousness based not on a transplanted European socialism, but a native version of sustainable development. *Desert Rose* was written in 1927 but not published until 1988, purportedly due to structural problems but more likely because it was too critical of so-called progressives. When Grant Arliss travels to the desert to rest and reconsider his political program, he meets Dulcie Adelaid, who doesn't believe in marriage but is committed to three things: loving relationships, the land, and living according to one's ideals. Gard Sitwell, the protagonist of *Starry Adventure* (1932) finds meaning in the natural and cultural aspects of the Southwest, a stark contrast to the artificial drawing-room culture of the East.

John Fox Jr.'s mountain trilogy, set in the Appalachians, has an unusually strong ecological perspective for its time, presenting a wide variety of people as strong stewards of God's creation (*The Little Shepherd of Kingdom Come*, 1903; *The Trail of the Lonesome Pine*, 1908; *The Heart of the Hills*, 1913). *The Little Shepherd* may have been the first million seller in America.[3]

Arthur Conan Doyle may be best known for Sherlock Holmes, but he also created Professor Challenger, who explored for prehistoric animals in *The Lost World* (1911) and survived the passage of the Earth through *The Poison Belt* (1912). The latter has a subtle environmental moral, as does the short story "When the World Screamed," which can be found in *The Complete Professor Challenger Stories* (1989).

Four radical writers of the early twentieth century, Jack London, D. H. Lawrence, B. Traven, and Upton Sinclair, are as notable for their adventurous lives as they are for their writing. Lawrence challenged how people thought about sex, nature, politics, religion, and philosophy. Traven raised a political and literary ruckus, first in Germany and then in the Chiapas jungle. See chapter 5 for Lawrence and Traven.

Muckraker Upton Sinclair was a champion for social justice in American industries such as meatpacking (*The Jungle*, 1907), coal (*King Coal*, 1917), and oil (*Oil!* 1927). Brutal environmental conditions faced by workers were just one aspect of the horror of their jobs.

As a socialist, outdoorsman, and environmentalist, Jack London was a new, activist writer for a new century. The relation between the individual, society, and nature and appreciating the inner wildness of humans are two of London's key literary themes. These are frequently reiterated in three short-story collections, *The Son of the Wolf* (1900), *The God of His Fathers* (1901), and *Children of the Frost* (1902), and his oft-anthologized "To Build a Fire" (1908). His first novel, *A Daughter of the Snows* (1902), includes a heroine whose values and actions prefigured ecofeminism, much like a character in one of his later works, *Smoke Bellew* (1912).

London's most popular book, *The Call of the Wild* (1903), features Buck, a domesticated dog who overcomes human cruelty and deeply bonds with a more humane owner in the Klondike gold fields before being separated from him. Buck then becomes the leader of a pack of wolves. London inverts the story in *White Fang* (1906), in which a wolfdog is slowly domesticated. London provides both an implicit psychological message that we are all a mixture of the wild and the civilized, and a political one that cooperation and socialism are preferable to competition and capitalism. *The Sea-Wolf* (1904) and *Martin Eden* (1909) address these ideas more explicitly. His three Sonoma novels, particularly *The Valley of the Moon* (1913), are about personal and societal restoration by consciously reinhabiting the land. This literary utopia was a stark contrast to the failure of his own ranch and his frustrating final years.

London also dabbled in science fiction. *Before Adam* (1906) inverts the macho, imperialist myths of the jungle books of Kipling, Haggard, and Burroughs. Its prehistoric protagonist, Big Tooth, is superior in many ways to the civilized man who has visions about him. His last major work, *The Scarlet Plague* (1915), is a cautionary tale about the end of civilization.

Although it is considered primarily a work of psychological or philosophical fiction, Franz Kafka's novella *The Metamorphosis* (*Die Verwandlung*, 1915) can also be read as a totemic parable, as Paul Goodman notes: "Now, the totemic identification of beast and man is both symbolical and literal; unless we keep in mind both these aspects, we cannot understand the play and nightmares of children, nor the wonderful tales of Kafka."[4]

Willa Cather's dozen novels and four short-story collections tend to revolve around one of two basic themes: the relationship between the individual and the land or the artistic temperament. The first was introduced in her debut novel, *Alexander's Bridge* (1912). A bridge builder's underestimation of the Saint Lawrence River's power and his overestimation of the power of technology lead to his demise as the bridge fails and he is swept to a watery grave.

Two of Cather's most critically acclaimed books are set on the Nebraska prairie. In *O Pioneers!* (1913), the children of settlers are conflicted between Alexandra's love for the land and use of natural farming practices and her brothers' short-term profit orientation. "Crazy Ivar," an old mystic hermit, is ridiculed by the boys, but Alexandra considers him a font of wisdom. An immigrant woman seems to be a personification of Mother Earth in *My Ántonia* (1918).

The Song of the Lark (1915) successfully blends Cather's two primary themes. A talented young Swedish singer escapes provincial Colorado society to become an opera star in Chicago, but later she returns to the West to gain a deeper sense of her own nature in a more natural setting. *The Professor's House* (1925) is Cather's most explicitly ecological work. A professor who feels alienated from his ostentatious house and materialistic wife in particular, and from modern society in general, remembers a former student who had unsuccessfully attempted to save cliff dwellings in Colorado. Even though the efforts were futile, the memories inspire the professor to seek a more authentic way of life. *Obscure Destinies* (1932) consists of three stories about the prairie as told by an elderly settler. Most of her later fiction is less nature oriented.

Frank Waters was inspired by a combination of transcendental, Native American, and Oriental philosophies, and is best known as the transcriber/editor of the enormously influential nonfiction *Book of the Hopi* (1963). His first novel, *Fever Pitch,* was written in 1925, published in 1930, and reprinted under Waters's original title, *The Lizard Woman,* in 1984. It is a bildungsroman about Lee Marston, a young engineer who, like Waters, experiences a growing awareness of one's inclusion in a grand totality that may be evoked by intimately experiencing a specific place but encompasses all space and time. *The Wild Earth's Nobility* (1935), *Below Grass Roots* (1937), and *The Dust Within the Rock* (1940) make up an autobiographical trilogy that was rewritten and published as *Pike's Peak: A Family Saga* in 1971. This multigenerational mining saga explores conflicting attitudes about our relation to the land and one another. In *People of the Valley* (1941) Waters abandoned autobiographical fiction to create one of his most fascinating characters. Doña Maria Del Valle, an aged Latina/Indian seer, personifies the concept that people belong to the land, not vice versa.

Martiniano, in *The Man Who Killed the Deer* (1942), returns to the Pueblo reservation from boarding school as a carpenter, but since his skills are little in demand he also farms and hunts. When he kills a deer two days after the end of the government-imposed hunting season without first asking the deer's permission, he violates both tribal and white law. His resistance to white hunting laws begins a process that encourages tribal leaders to reassert claims to their sacred lake. Eventually 48,000 acres, including the lake, are returned to the tribe.

The Woman of Otowi Crossing (1966) is based on one of Waters's friends, Edith Warner, fictionalized as Helen Chalmers. A variety of perspectives are examined: Facundo's quiet wisdom, Chalmers's growing mysticism, the expanding consciousness of atomic scientist Edmund Gaylord, the humanistic but sentimental editor Jack Turner, and the strict rationalism of Helen's daughter, anthropologist Emily Chalmers. Emily asserts that Pueblo and Aztec ceremonies were linked through a series of seven physical caves, but Helen refutes her literalism, maintaining that the caves are a powerful parable representing humanity's evolutionary journey.

Laurence Manning wrote ecologically based science fiction in the 1920s and 1930s. His were among the first space exploration stories to focus on social and ecological aspects rather than hard science and action. Five related stories were published posthumously as *The Man Who Awoke: A Classic Novel from the Golden Age of Science Fiction* (1975). In one story, the protagonist emerges from suspended animation to find one society living in balance with nature and, prophetically, another one obsessed by and subservient to computers.

Henry Miller is best known for his "Tropic" books written in the 1930s (*Tropic of Cancer, Tropic of Capricorn*), but one of his last works, *Big Sur and the Oranges of Hieronymus Bosch* (1957) is of greater ecocritical interest. In Big Sur, a then-wild and remote area south of Carmel, a literary bohemian finds a sort of paradise in an isolated and primitive but intellectually sophisticated community.

Josephine Johnson wrote several nature-oriented novels, the most famous of which was her Pulitzer Prize-winning debut *Now in November* (1934). The daughter of a Midwestern farmer tells of the tribulations of the Dust Bowl and Depression years balanced by the wonders of nature. It is reminiscent of Cather's work. As a Quaker, Johnson was a pacifist, environmentalist, and champion of social justice. These concerns are expressed very effectively in her nonfiction book *The Inland Island* (1969).

Florida's contributions to ecofiction began with two women who were journalists, fiction writers, and powerful environmental activists: Marjorie

Kinnan Rawlings and Marjory Stoneman Douglas. Rawlings published the children's classic *The Yearling* in 1938 and the autobiographical novel *Cross Creek* in 1942. A collection of her short stories was published by the University of Florida Press in 1994. Douglas is best known for a work of nonfiction, *The Everglades, River of Grass* (1947), but she also wrote short stories that appeared in the *Saturday Evening Post* and other popular periodicals in the 1920s through the 1940s and have been collected in two volumes, *Nine Florida Stories* and *A River in Flood*.

Zora Neale Hurston was Florida's first well-known African-American writer. In the 1930s, she worked for the WPA to collect "Negro folklore," which she did, but in the process she also wrote about social ecology and nature, particularly the earth consciousness of older black women. Her 1937 novel *Their Eyes Were Watching God* contains detailed evocations of the Florida landscape and of people living close to the land, including a vivid depiction of living through a hurricane.

Few writers so brilliantly evoke both character and place as William Faulkner. Much of his work is set in the fictitious Yoknapatawpha County, which resembled his own Mississippi Delta home. The relation of the rural Indians, blacks, and whites to the land and to each other is an underlying theme. Of particular ecocritical note are *Go Down, Moses* (1942), which links the destruction of the land with slavery, racism, and poverty, and the magic realist novella *The Bear* (1942). The latter is also included in *Big Woods* (1955), a collection of hunting stories that explore the relation between human exploitation and the balance of nature.

What Faulkner was to Mississippi, John Steinbeck was to California, albeit in a more overtly political manner. Steinbeck's first novel about the relation between people and the land was *To a God Unknown* (1933). *In Dubious Battle* (1936), a fictionalized account of an actual apple pickers strike, demonstrates that integrity and strength of character are essential, but that the individual must be part of a larger, organized group in order to maintain that integrity and just compensation. This theme is reiterated in his most famous work, *The Grapes of Wrath* (1939), in which a family of Oklahoma farmers escapes the devastation of the Dust Bowl only to find that in the "golden land" of

California the workers work the land while the owners get the gold. *Cannery Row* (1945) and its sequel *Sweet Thursday* (1954) tell the tales of a group of working-class and unemployed men living in Monterey in the 1930s. The depictions of the Central California coast and tide pool ecology are very vivid. Steinbeck wrote two green novellas that are appropriate for readers of all ages. In *The Red Pony* (1937) a nine-year-old boy's relationship with his pony teaches him to love and respect animals and himself. *The Pearl* (1947) is an adaptation of a Mexican folktale in which a fisherman finds a huge pearl that causes unexpected misfortunes for his family when it is removed from the sea.

Aldous Huxley was concerned about the misapplication of technology, particularly its dehumanizing aspects and environmental consequences. The Savage, a rare natural-born child in the *Brave New World* (1932) of engineered babies, becomes alienated by the shallowness of a mechanized, soulless society. In the convoluted *Ape and Essence* (1948), a movie director finds a script set in 2108 America, which has been ravaged by nuclear war and inhabited by devil-worshipping mutants. In *Island* (1962) an oilfield developer tries to overthrow the antitechnological native government of an idyllic *island* but then realizes that his life has been empty and miserable compared to that of the inhabitants.

Huxley may have influenced two other famous dystopian British authors, George Orwell and William Golding. Orwell's two most famous cautionary novels, *Animal Farm* (1945) and *Nineteen Eighty-Four* (1949), are best known for their political and psychological aspects, but they also have an environmental subtext wherein uncontrolled nature is a source of rebellion. In Orwell's *Coming Up for Air* (1939), a middle-aged man returns to his childhood home to discover it destroyed by industrial waste and pollution. In Golding's powerful *Lord of the Flies* (1954) and *The Inheritors* (1955), human nature becomes absolutely barbaric in totally natural settings lacking the restraints of civilization. Ursula Heise, though, posits that the ecological visions of Huxley and Orwell are clouded by anthropocentrism: "population growth . . . is perceived as problematic when it raises physical and social problems for humans themselves, but not when it exerts intense pressure on natural ecosystems and the survival of other species."[5]

Wallace Stegner was not just a powerful and prolific author of fiction and nonfiction alike, but one of America's leading conservationists and a very significant teacher as the founder of Stanford University's prestigious writing program. His semiautobiographical frontier novel *The Big Rock Candy Mountain* (1943) marked the beginning of a bright literary light that shone for fifty years. Despite its promising title, the first sequel, *Second Growth* (1947), is not particularly ecofictional. The long-delayed second sequel, *Recapitulation* (1979), is more nature oriented.

The first direct fictional expression of Stegner's penchant for both natural and cultural preservation is *A Shooting Star* (1961), in which two women work to ensure that the family land being developed will include a large park. In *All the Little Live Things* (1967), two retirees from the East Coast move to California only to find their tranquility disturbed by a "hippie developer." (Given that "hippie developer" is an oxymoron, this book should be taken with a large grain of organic sea salt.) A much-improved sequel, *The Spectator Bird* (1976), won a National Book Award. Two senior citizens continue to seek their roots, their place in society, and their place in the natural world. The themes of friendship, aging, and the ways nature and people shape each other are recapitulated in Stegner's final novel, *Crossing to Safety* (1987).

The Pulitzer Prize-winning *Angle of Repose* (1971) is Stegner's most famous and most controversial work. He utilizes parallel story lines of an aging, disabled historian attempting to maintain his independence as he writes a book about his grandmother, and of the grandmother's narrative itself. The book depicts the negative effects of a boom-and-bust extractive economy on people and on the environment. The brilliance of Stegner's accomplishment was tarnished when it was revealed that he had extensively plagiarized the journals of Mary Hallock Foote. On the positive side, this led to the publication of Foote's excellent memoir, *A Victorian Gentlewoman in the Far West* in 1992. The controversy was dramatized in *Fair Use* (2000), a play by Sands Hall.

The Hobbit (1938) by J. R. R. Tolkien depicts an alternative, nature-based

English mythology related to Norse and Celtic myth. The nature-loving hobbits create something of an ecotopia. They must save it in *The Lord of the Rings* series (*The Fellowship of the Ring*, 1954; *The Two Towers*, 1954; *The Return of the King*, 1955), a multilevel fantasy saga pitting the evil Sauron against the Captains of the West for control of Middle Earth and of nature itself. The humble hobbits manage to survive as more "heroic" figures on the quest, as others rise and fall around them. As the world was becoming disenchanted by World War II, the Cold War, and early awareness of the current ecological crisis, Tolkien re-enchanted humanity and nature. The books are more philosophical, poetic, and contain a much stronger ecological context than the movie versions.

George R. Stewart considered four works of fiction as his ecological novels, using "ecology in the older sense, that is, all the things that go to make a place."[6] *Storm* (1941) may be the first novel to feature a natural phenomenon as protagonist. Each chapter covers a day in the life of the raging rainstorm, revealing how natural elements combine to create and shape it, how officials respond to it, and how the unprepared become its victims. *Fire* (1948) is an account a massive forest fire, containing asides about history, ecology, meteorology, forestry, and related topics. Two rangers serve as personifications of the opposing views of John Muir and Gifford Pinchot on the appropriate roles and uses of national forests, a conflict that continues to this day.

When graduate student Isherwood Williams (aka "Ish") is bitten by a rattlesnake in the remote Sierra Nevada in Stewart's classic *Earth Abides* (1949), he becomes immune to a plague that has exterminated most of humanity. Ish meets Em, an African-American woman, with whom he has children and eventually forms a small community with other survivors. Although most of "the Tribe" is still happy scavenging by the year 2002, Ish insists on a return to literacy, domestication of animals, and farming, but the Tribe becomes increasingly feral. *Earth Abides* is a classic cautionary novel that set a high literary and philosophical standard for a spate of similar books published shortly thereafter, such as Ray Bradbury's *Martian Chronicles*, Clifford Simak's *City*, and Arthur C. Clarke's *Childhood's End*. *Earth Abides* may be the first novel to use the word "ecology" and feature an ecologist. Although less famous than

Earth Abides, Sheep Rock (1951) is a more complex, experimental, and fully realized work of literature. Frederick Waage considers it "the best 20th century novel in this realm, in which the landscape itself is the protagonist."[7]

A small, depressed Maine fishing village is the setting for Ruth Moore's *Spoonhandle* (1946), in which some citizens are willing to overfish and violate the land while others live and work according to a higher moral code.

The Dollmaker (1954) by Harriette Louisa Simpson Arnow chronicles a family's move from a Kentucky farm to a Detroit defense plant, contrasting the divergent lifestyles and describing the spiritual and emotional pain of leaving the land.

The preponderance of postwar fiction trumpeted the benefits of technology, but Clifford Simak, Jack Vance, Ray Bradbury, Kurt Vonnegut, and many other science fiction authors were more cautionary voices. Much of the ecofiction of the 1950s was science fiction that analyzed the misapplication of science.

Simak questioned the relentless pursuit of technological progress for its own sake while seeking for the true meaning of humanity's existence. *City* (1952) is a collection of tales supposedly written by dogs after they become the dominant species and a peaceable kingdom with respect for all life-forms emerges. *City* foreshadows such developments as back-to-the-land hippies, cocooning high-tech yuppies, and the animal rights movement. In *Way Station* (1963), a provider of aid to galactic travelers and a deaf woman with strong psychic-naturalistic communication and healing powers convey a message of respect for different species and different kinds of people. Most people suddenly vanish from the earth in *A Choice of Gods* (1972). In the next five thousand years the remaining people expand their minds instead of their technology, and even the robots that remain from the earlier times begin to serve God.

According to Robert Silverberg, Jack Vance's *The Dying Earth* (1950) "is only a metaphor for decline, loss, decay, and, paradoxical though it may sound, also a return to a lost golden age, a simple and clean time of sparse population and unspoiled streams, of wizards and emperors, of absolute values and the clash of right and wrong."[8]

In *The Martian Chronicles* (1950) by Ray Bradbury, Mars is colonized and destroyed by earthlings who cannot adapt to its environment and therefore try to change it. Many of his other novels warn of the loss of freedom in an increasingly technologically oriented world, particularly *Fahrenheit 451* (1953), in which people's lives are dominated by wall-size televisions and firemen burn books to extinguish independent thinking.

With his first novel, *Player Piano* (1952), Kurt Vonnegut evinced a distrust of technology that is consistent throughout his work. *Cat's Cradle* (1963) and *Slaughterhouse Five* (1969) express it most effectively. In *Galapagos* (1985), what begins as "the nature cruise of the century" alters the course of evolution as the new "humans" grow fins, lose the human "big brains" that caused the planet so much trouble, and return to the sea.

Isaac Asimov's Foundation series is an exploration of what would later be called the Gaia hypothesis. Representatives of the technological First Foundation and the mentalic Second Foundation arrive on Gaia, a planet where all organisms are separate individuals sharing the overall consciousness of the planet itself. Asimov contrasts the violence, pettiness, and arrogance of other worlds against the peaceful higher consciousness of Gaia.

The Space Merchants (1953) by Frederik Pohl and Cyril Kornbluth is a satirical exploration of a planet ruled by advertising. The expansionist nature of advertising hastens overpopulation, resource depletion, and pollution. For Pohl's later work, see chapter 8.

In John Christopher's *No Blade of Grass* (1957), a Chinese rice virus creates a famine and a UN-developed isotope to cure it is worse than the disease. Chaos and violence develop most places, but a small group in England begins to develop a more ecologically based society. Grass is also a key component in Ward Moore's *Greener Than You Think* (1947), in which a new lawn fertilizer brings dead Bermuda "devil grass" to life. It grows at amazing speed, takes over everything, and stymies every attempt to stop it.

The literary fallout from the development of nuclear weapons consisted of some militaristic "space operas," some political fiction, and some books that were purely apocalyptic. A few books, though, considered the environmental aspects of nuclear weapons development along with the psychological, social, and political ones. *The Accident* (1955) by Dexter Masters depicts the last eight days of a scientist's life before he dies from radiation poisoning. This groundbreaking cautionary tale about the effects of nuclear testing and development is still powerful and relevant forty years later. Leigh Brackett's *The Long Tomorrow* (1955) depicts a post-apocalyptic America becoming a pastoral ecotopia where cities of more than a thousand people and new technology are illegal. Nevil Shute's *On the Beach* (1957) is a less optimistic cautionary tale set in Australia. In Walter M. Miller's *A Canticle for Leibowitz* (1960), monks have preserved scraps of the world's knowledge after a nuclear war has rendered Earth a wasteland. Miller leaves the reader wondering whether the knowledge that could revive technology might also lead to further wars. The last inhabitants of a fallout shelter rebel against crowding, fear, and the specter of a degraded environment in Mordecai Roshwald's *Level 7* (1959). In Philip Wylie's *Triumph* (1963), after most of the world is devastated by nuclear war, the survivors must overcome both environmental hazards and their own fears and prejudices to create a more peaceful, racially harmonious world. Pat Frank's *Alas Babylon* (1959) initially appears to be a standard nuclear holocaust novel, with civil defense totally ineffective against mass destruction, radiation, and social collapse, but it takes an optimistic turn when a group of survivors emerge to form a pastoral society.

Three philosophical novelists who emerged in this period included environmental considerations in some of their works. John Hersey is best known for his books about World War II, but he has also written on other subjects. In *The Marmot Drive* (1954), a Welsh farmer decides that all varmints must be moved off his farm, with disastrous results. *My Petition for More Space* (1974) is a cautionary tale about a near-future society where people must wait in long lines for permission to have a baby, protein, or more than the bare minimum of living space. *Blues* (1987), a blend of fiction and nonfiction about the Florida bluefish, is a consideration of the web of life, as are some of the stories in *Key West Tales* (1994). Saul Bellow's *Henderson the Rain King* (1959) is among other things the account of a millionaire's attempt to find himself through natural encounters and participation in a rain-making ceremony in the African wilderness. In John Barth's *The Sot-Weed Factor* (1960), an early

American tobacconist discovers the disparities between the heroic images and the hardscrabble realities of pioneer life.

Arguably the most important and enduring new green voices to emerge from this period were those of Peter Matthiessen and Edward Abbey. Although Matthiessen's short stories began appearing in literary magazines and anthologies in 1950, the only collection, *On the River Styx and Other Stories,* was not published until 1989. His first long fiction to reflect his environmental activism was *At Play in the Fields of the Lord* (1965), in which a variety of forces engage in religious, cultural, environmental, and military conflict in the jungles of the western Amazon. *At Play in the Fields of the Lord* is highly poetic, dramatic, and exciting, painfully poignant, challenging, and philosophically complex. It is a clarion call for the preservation of natural environments and indigenous cultures and thus the salvation of our own souls.

Matthiessen's *Far Tortuga* (1975) is based on an actual sea turtle fishing expedition he accompanied in 1967. The fishers persist in trying to maintain a traditional fishery and lifestyle against the odds, despite a sense of doom about the voyage and their very lives. This powerful, poignant sea story has been likened to Joseph Conrad's and Herman Melville's best work. For Matthiessen's later trilogy of mysteries about the Kurtz-like Edgar Watson, *Shadow Country,* see chapter 9.

Edward Abbey's first novel, *Jonathan Troy* (1954), is a semiautobiographical bildungsroman about a rebellious young man. Several of Abbey's lifelong themes emerge: the dehumanizing aspects of modern society, the industrial desecration of nature, the importance of individuality and anarchy, and the West as a land of new possibilities. In *The Brave Cowboy* (1956), Jack Burns rides his horse into Duke City (Albuquerque) and is jailed in an attempt to free a draft resister. Burns's adversary is not just the police or the military but the forces of consumerism and technological "progress." In the first edition, Burns appears to die, but Abbey later changed the ending, making Burns's demise ambiguous. In *Fire on the Mountain* (1962), rancher John Vogelin resists the air force's attempts to obtain his land for a missile base. Abbey endows Vogelin with the attributes of the classic western hero while simultaneously deconstructing the myths of the Old West: the air force wants to steal the land from the ranchers, but they stole it from the Indians, who stole it from the coyotes. Vogelin dies and the ranch is lost, but his grandson Billy and the remaining southwestern wilderness represent hope for natural and personal renewal. *Black Sun* (1971) is a bittersweet pastoral romance that contains some of Abbey's most vivid evocations of nature, and the romantic elements reveal greater sensitivity and less sexism than is sometimes the case in his work. For *The Monkey Wrench Gang* and Abbey's later work, see the "Environmental Action/Ecodefense" section of chapter 3.

Jack Kerouac is best known for *On the Road,* but *Big Sur* (1962) and *The Dharma Bums* (1958) are better presentations of the nascent environmental consciousness of the Beat Movement. (Daniel Duane's mountaineering novel *Looking for Mo* (1998) resembles a *Dharma Bums* for a new generation.) Although later associated with the hippie movement, Ken Kesey's two best books, *One Flew over the Cuckoo's Nest* (1962) and *Sometimes a Great Notion* (1964), are written in a modernist style influenced by Stegner, one of his teachers at Stanford. R. P. McMurphy, the protagonist of *Cuckoo's Nest,* seems like a classic independent western hero, an almost animalistic wild man who struggles against the authoritarian technocratic domain represented by Nurse Ratched. Kesey's later ecodefense novel *Sailor Song* (1992) is an entertaining romp. Richard Brautigan provided a literary bridge between the Beat and hippie periods with two works of ecofiction, *A Confederate General from Big Sur* (1964) and *Trout Fishing in America* (1967).

Wendell Berry, a prolific novelist, essayist, and poet, and also one of Stegner's students, appeared on the scene around 1960. His work harks back to the first half of the twentieth century in Kentucky, contrasting it to the present day. Farming, family, community, taking responsibility for one's actions, and living in a simple, nonwasteful manner are consistent themes in his work. Berry examines seven generations of a farm family in his Port William series, which began with *Nathan Coulter* (1960) and currently runs through *Andy Catlett* (2007). Although his writing style is much simpler than Faulkner's, the exploration of communities and nature over a long period in the Port William series is reminiscent of Faulkner's chronicles of Yoknapatawpha County.

Ecofiction in all genres truly flourished in the 1970s, which might be considered the "década de oro." It was heralded by John Stadler's groundbreaking anthology *Eco-Fiction* (1971), which contains science fiction and mainstream stories written primarily in the 1940s through 1960s, although earlier stories by Poe and Jewett are also included. James Agee's "A Mother's Tale" is particularly notable as a precursor of the animal rights movement. According to the editor, "It is a collection which seeks to make the reader think about his relationship with his natural environment. These are stories about ecology (though that may have been far from some of the writers' intents) to entertain, instruct, and disturb the reader. . . . Solutions, like the problems themselves, may have their beginnings in the small and simple acts of individual men."[9]

Many books published during the 1970s were very effective in exploring environmental and related social problems and/or influential in raising the environmental consciousness of other writers and the general public. They include:

1970: Frank Herbert, *Dune Messiah;* James Dickey, *Deliverance;* Stanislaw Lem, *Solaris;* Margaret Atwood, *The Edible Woman;* Joy Chant, *Red Moon and Black Mountain*

1971: Jim Harrison, *Wolf;* John Gardner, *Grendel;* Thomas McGuane, *The Bushwhacked Piano;* Wallace Stegner, *Angle of Repose;* Ursula K. Le Guin, *The Lathe of Heaven;* James D. Houston, *A Native Son of the Golden West;* Tom Robbins, *Another Roadside Attraction*

1972: Richard Adams, *Watership Down;* Rudolfo Anaya, *Bless Me, Ultima;* John Brunner, *The Sheep Look Up;* Le Guin, *The Word for World is Forest;* Andre Norton, *Breed to Come;* Atwood, *Surfacing*

1973: Harrison, *A Good Day to Die;* McGuane, *Ninety-two in the Shade;* Wilma Dykeman, *Return the Innocent Earth*

1974: John Nichols, *The Milagro Beanfield War;* Le Guin, *The Dispossessed;* James Welch, *Winter in the Blood;* Margaret Laurence, *The Diviners;* Suzy

McKee Charnas, *Walk to the End of the World;* Len Fulton, *The Grassman;*
Brenda Brown Canary, *Home to the Mountain;* Lem, *The Futurological
Congress;* John Hersey, *My Petition for More Space*
The banner year for ecofiction was 1975: Ernest Callenbach, *Ecotopia;*
Edward Abbey, *The Monkey Wrench Gang;* William Eastlake, *Dancers in
the Scalp House;* Harrison, *Farmer;* Nasnaga, *Indian Summer;* Peter Mat-
thiessen, *Far Tortuga;* Joanna Russ, *The Female Man;* Lisa Alther, *Kinflicks;*
Russell Hoban, *Turtle Diary;* Fulton, *Dark Adam Dreaming;* Gerald
Haslam, *Okies;* Farley Mowat, *The Snow Walkers*
1976: Marian Engel, *Bear;* Marge Piercy, *Woman on the Edge of Time;*
Stegner, *The Spectator Bird;* Frederick Manfred, *Manly-Hearted Woman;*
Herbert, *Children of Dune;* Kate Wilhelm, *Where Late the Sweet Birds
Sang;* Robbins, *Even Cowgirls Get the Blues*
1977: Leslie Marmon Silko, *Ceremony;* Adams, *The Plague Dogs;* Manfred,
Green Earth; Chant, *The Grey Mane of Morning;* Philip José Farmer,
Lavalite World; John D. MacDonald, *Condominium;* D'Arcy McNickle,
Wind from an Enemy Sky;
1978: Houston, *Continental Drift;* Nichols, *The Magic Journey;* Jack Schaefer,
Conversations with a Pocket Gopher; Wilbur Smith, *Hungry as the Sea;*
Vonda N. McIntyre, *Dream Snake;* Charnas, *Motherlines;* Gerald Vizenor,
Darkness in Saint Louis Bearheart; Geary Hobson, ed., *The Remembered
Earth*
1979: Harrison, *Legends of the Fall;* Atwood, *Life Before Man;* Wilhelm, *Juni-
per Time;* Herbert, *The Jesus Incident.*

. What spurred this sudden and rapid development? The primary causes
include accelerated population growth and the development of previously
untrammeled land; resistance to the Vietnam War and the growth of the
peace movement; the greening of the counterculture; popularization of the
environmental movement; burgeoning of feminism, particularly ecofeminism; Native American and Chicano activism; and the emergence of a "small
is beautiful" philosophy and deep ecology.
Gerald Haslam asserts that "the Vietnam war changed everything. Brack-

eted by a painful civil rights movement and an enlightened ecological crusade—vital developments both—the national agony over America's Asian conflict was central to revisioning our national experience. The war, and the domestic upheaval that attended it, symbolizes well the two decades of dizzying change that have led to hard-edged maturity in western American letters. Westerners, like Americans generally, have been unable to see themselves or their nation in quite the same naïve way they had prior to the 1960s, and contemporary western writing reflects an unwillingness to respect old boundaries, coupled with an enriched view of literary possibilities. If present trends are counter-cultural, they are counter-cultural in a generative sense, expanding limits, testing values, seeking the universal in the particular."[10]

With the exception of the science fiction, the majority of the books listed above were written by western American and Canadian authors, primarily from California, Arizona, and New Mexico. This is particularly true in the case of ecodefense and other environmental action novels. Susanne Bounds and Patti Capel Swartz have observed that "the Southwest has been, and often remains contended and contentious."[11] Resistance arose against changes wrought by the rapid population growth in areas that have naturally low carrying capacities. California and the Southwest were relatively lightly populated areas with spectacular biodiversity until the mid-twentieth century. According to the U.S. Census, the states of Arizona, New Mexico, Utah, and Nevada doubled in population between 1950 and 1975, from a combined total of only 2,300,000 people to 4,600,000. Today the population of Maricopa County, Arizona, alone is greater than the 1950 population for the entire region. The qualitative change has been even greater: urban sprawl (in Tucson alone, twenty-four acres are developed daily), the pollution-spewing Four Corners Power Plant, the strip mining of sacred Black Mesa, the damming of the Colorado and creation of Lake Powell, aka "Lake Foul," greatly increased levels of air and water pollution and of soil erosion, the introduction of what Edward Abbey termed "industrial tourism," and the continuing marginalization of Native American and Hispanic cultural values.

Abbey, Nichols, and Eastlake all moved from the East to the Southwest during this period and were angry eyewitnesses to these changes. Their resistance took three forms: nonfiction, fiction, and action, which included monkey-wrenching of construction equipment and burning highway billboards.

Meanwhile, in California, Callenbach was laying a literary blueprint for a new, peaceful, ecologically based, cooperative society in *Ecotopia* (1975) and *Ecotopia Emerging* (1981). For more on Callenbach, see chapter 8. Alas, it would seem that ecodefense and ecotopias have flourished in literature to a far greater extent than they have in society. These authors announced a revolution, but what happened instead was more political contention over development and environmental degradation, and the evolutionary mainstreaming of environmentalism and feminism, which have become better integrated into daily life today than they were thirty years ago. To offer a gastronomic analogy, there may not be as many vegetarian restaurants now as there were then, but there are far more restaurants where a vegetarian has a wider selection of choices.

3

Contemporary Ecofiction

Most of the authors from the 1970s were in the beginning or middle of their careers, and have continued to write. Over the past quarter century, many new authors have emerged and a wide variety of ecofiction continues to be written. This chapter will consider the major subdivisions of contemporary ecofiction.

PHILOSOPHICAL/SPIRITUAL

Many books by Native Americans have a strong philosophical/spiritual tradition. Indian cosmology is also reflected in the works of non-Native authors, most notably Frank Waters. See chapter 4, "Native American and Canadian Fiction," for many others. Other novelists draw on a wide variety of philosophical and religious traditions both ancient and modern. Although some of their works are ruminative, many others are exciting and action packed.

The Testament of Yves Gundron (2000) by Emily Barton takes place on a medieval European island. When Yves invents the harness and then the two- and the four-wheeled cart, agriculture is revolutionized, but unanticipated consequences occur as greed, envy, and doubt upset the islanders' formerly impoverished but relatively stable lives. The situation is further complicated when an airplane from the future carrying an anthropologist crashes on the island.

Set in a very different time and place, Buffalo at the turn of the twentieth century, Lauren Belfer's *City of Light* (1999) is another fascinating consideration of technological progress versus natural and cultural preservation.

Pantheism and activism commingle in Rick Bass's fiction. His first collection, *The Watch* (1989), introduces the themes of crossing the internal and external boundaries between civilization and wildness; predatory relationships, captivity, escape, and quests; characters with incredible speed, power, and endurance; and the inherent magic of nature, often expressed in luminescence. In *Platte River* (1994) his fiction becomes more complex and fantastic. The story "Mahatma Joe" is about an evangelist whose faith is extended to the vegetables he raises to ship to Africa. The title novella introduces a theme that might be called "the human animal." Several stories in *In the Loyal Mountains* (1995) explore what Alan Weltzien terms "the interstices between wilderness-wildness and domesticity-tameness."[1] *The Sky, the Stars, the Wilderness* (1997) consists of three highly varied novellas. In "The Myth of Bears," Trapper, the human equivalent of an old hunting dog, tracks his escaped, elk-like wife Judith through a harsh Yukon winter. The heart is the primary locus of "Where the Sea Used to Be," in which a geologist falls in love with the land, flying, and a woman. Myth and magic are intertwined with natural history and family relationships in the title novella, the story of a near-wilderness ranch in West Texas. In the novel *Where the Sea Used to Be* (1998), the scene shifts to a fictionalized version of Bass's Montana home, "Swan Valley." Mel, a wolf biologist, muses on the limitations of science, which must be fused with spirituality to tell the whole truth. Geologist Wallis learns to love the valley and decides not to reveal his oil discoveries, but his boss, old Dudley, finds his map and the drilling proceeds. The novel echoes *Moby Dick*, with Dudley as Ahab, but instead of just Ishmael being saved by a floating coffin, the entire valley is saved with the departure of Dudley's flaming coffin downriver in a Viking-style funeral. *Fiber* (1998), an amalgam of story and essay, is Bass's shortest but most experimental and challenging book. After describing the first three phases of his life as geologist, artist, and activist, Bass explains that he can no longer be sure how much of any story is fiction and how much is activism. The title story in the collection *The Hermit's Story* (2002) describes a dog trainer's wondrous surprise as a hole in the ice becomes a passage not to watery death but to a crystalline ice cavern that saves her. Bass turns to historical fiction in *The Diezmo* (2005), a powerful account of the psychological, social, and, to a lesser extent, environmental horrors of war. He returns to ecofiction in the short-story collection *The Lives of Rocks* (2006).

R. M. Berry's *Leonardo's Horse* (1997), whose locale shifts between Renaissance Italy and modern America, considers similar issues. *The Plague Years* (1997) by Ann Benson takes a similar approach, alternating between the fourteenth-century Black Death and 2005 when the world is suffering from "the Outbreaks."

Douglas Coupland, one of the leading "Generation X" writers, chronicles the angst, meaninglessness, and separation from nature of technologically oriented lives in *Generation X: Tales for an Accelerated Culture* (1991) and *Microserfs* (1995).

Jim Crace writes philosophical and political fiction, often with a strong environmental element, particularly the relationship between traditional and modern cultures in *Continent* (1986) and *A Gift of Stones* (1988). *Continent* describes the flora, fauna, tribes and communities, lore and superstition, sexuality, conflicts and predicaments, and changes over time on an imaginary ecotopian seventh continent. *Arcadia* (1991) and *Signals of Distress* (1995) introduce an element of ecodefense. (See chapter 6 for Crace's unusual romance *Being Dead*).

James Dickey probes the link between the male psyche and wilderness in two very different novels. In *Deliverance* (1970), four men test their masculinity on a river trip, but are confronted by vicious rednecks. In *To the White Sea* (1993), an American flyer shot down over Japan during World War II calls on the skills and attitudes he developed in the Alaskan wilderness to survive.

Rikki Ducornet writes sensuous, surrealistic, mythic, complex, subtly philosophical fiction. Nature abounds, and pro-environmental sentiments are slipped between the shimmering lines in her Tetralogy of Elements series: *The*

Stain (1984), *Entering Fire* (1984), *The Fountains of Neptune* (1989), and *The Jade Cabinet* (1993). *Entering Fire* includes a cautionary subplot about cloning. In *The Jade Cabinet,* a woman leaves an industrialist who has abused both nature and her. *Phosphor in Dreamland* (1995) is her most overtly ecological book. She mourns the passage of an imaginary Caribbean island's last loplop birds, and of Birdland's past, preserved only by the glass plates of a camera obscura.

Percival Everett has a critical reputation as one of America's most creative and diverse authors, dissecting and satirizing such subjects as race, education, culture, politics, personal identity, and sometimes the environment. *Zulus* (1989) is a dark fantasy about the last fertile woman on Earth after a nuclear war. In *Watershed* (1996), when an African-American hydrologist discovers a clandestine toxic dump and a dam to divert contaminated water into an Indian reservation, he reluctantly becomes involved in a struggle between AIM activists and the FBI. A big-game hunter sets his sights on the Grand Canyon as a site for commercial hunting, but he is thwarted by an unexpected alliance of Native American shamans, Zen masters, his own son, and Mother Nature herself in *Grand Canyon, Inc.* (2001).

Richard Grant takes a cosmic trip with *Tex and Molly in the Afterlife* (1996), in which the spirits of two dead hippies unite with shape-shifters to thwart a corporation's attempt to replant a clear-cut forest with artificial trees. *In the Land of Winter* (1997) is about an earth-spirited Wiccan's attempt to regain her elflike daughter after fundamentalist Christians accuse them both of Satanism.

Jim Harrison calls himself a "Zennist." In *Wolf: A False Memoir* (1971), a man reconsiders his life during a weeklong expedition in the deep woods, hoping to see a wolf. He rails against the destruction of the forest and moves from words to action when he pours sand in the gas tank of a bulldozer. Quests to find wildness within and beyond oneself, brilliant evocations of nature, rough-and-tumble adventure by an ordinary man, sex and sexual fantasies, direct religious experience, and returning to one's home are consistent themes in his work. The first of three novellas that make up *Legends of the Fall* (1979), "Revenge," is a violent vendetta. The more complex title piece is a miniature epic wherein Colonel William Ludlow is horrified by the effects of civilization on Montana: Indian genocide, mass slaughter of buffalo and other wildlife, destructive ranching practices, ruthless federal agents, and organized crime. The third novella, "The Man Who Gave Up His Name," is a gentle tale about a man in midlife crisis who has a transcendent moment while sitting on a stump and simplifies his life by moving to Florida, living in a one-room cabin, and watching the water and sky. *Warlock* (1981) is Harrison's only spoof, satirizing both detective fiction and his own work. In *Sundog: The Story of an American Foreman, Robert Corvus Strang, as Told to Jim Harrison* (1984), Strang justifies his career building massive dams by invoking improved public health. He evinces an understanding of natural processes and expresses his love of nature's healing properties, but acknowledges the unintended consequences of a water project in Brazil. *Dalva* (1988) is a multigenerational saga. Great-grandfather's journals reveal that he had originally come to the Sioux as a missionary but was eventually converted to Native American values as a ghost dancer. The themes of people being shaped by their landscapes and of the restorative value of nature are explored in depth, this time with a female protagonist named Dalva. Her quest is to meet her son Nelse, whom she was forced to give up for adoption. The saga continues in *The Road Home* (1998), with Dalva's grandfather, Nelse, Uncle Paul, and Dalva herself filling holes in the family history and providing varying interpretations. These interlinked novels explore transitions: land from hunting and gathering, to farming, to agribusiness, to Nelse's natural farming; family through a series of tragedies and triumphs; consciousness from mysticism to reductionism to one embodying both; and personal transitions throughout life and unto death.

The Woman Lit by Fireflies (1990) contains three tales of individual resistance to oppressive social forces. In "Brown Dog," anthropologist Shelley Newkirk wheedles the site of a secret burial mound from the title character in exchange for sex. Although Brown Dog's good intentions are sometimes sabotaged by impulsiveness, hormones, or alcohol, he is capable of living each day genuinely and without hidden agendas, unlike the self-serving academics. "Sunset Limited" centers on the reunion of five friends who destroyed draft files in the sixties. The title character in "The Woman Lit by Fireflies" revolts by fleeing from her oppressive husband at a highway rest stop and has a transformative experience while lost in the fields at night. *Julip* (1994) profiles three individuals coping with adversity whose relationships to animals help heal them from the psychic imbalances of modern life. Julip Durham, a young dog trainer who had been a lust slave for three middle-aged men fishing in Florida, attempts to get her brother transferred from prison to a mental hospital after he shoots, and barely wounds, "the Boys" for defiling his sister. In "The Seven-Ounce Man," Brown Dog joins a Red Power group in a comic assault on Shelley's latest dig. In "The Beige Dolorosa," a professor suffers psychic damage after being set up for a contrived sexual harassment charge. His equilibrium slowly returns during a stay at an Arizona ranch where he learns to ride a horse and begins a project to poetically rename the birds of America.

Harrison spins more variations on the themes of masculinity and the relation between self, civilization, and nature in *The Beast God Forgot to Invent* (2000). The title novella contrasts two men, a semiretired rare book and real estate dealer and a brain-damaged youth who experiences the world anew every day. The wealthy writer of superficial biographies in "Never Went to Spain" visits his ex-wife, now a grower of heirloom flowers, to shake him out of his rut. "Westward Ho" is a sly critique of Hollywood film culture and wannabe Indians in which Brown Dog tracks down the fake Indian activist who stole his totemic bear. In *True North* (2004) David Burkett IV is consumed by an urge to reveal the damage his ancestors had done to the forests of northern Michigan in order to expiate his guilt about it. Burkett slowly rejects his harsh, Calvinistic attitudes for a sexier form of spirituality and realizes that the people/nature divide is a false dichotomy. *The Summer He Didn't Die* (2005) consists of the title novella featuring Brown Dog, the hilarious *Republican Wives,* and *Tracking,* a memoir. For Harrison's *A Good Day to Die,* see the "Environmental Action/Ecodefense" section of this chapter. For his romance, *Farmer,* see chapter 6.

The Operator's Manual for Planet Earth (1997) by D. Trinidad Hunt is a New Age parable in which benevolent spirits communicate nine "Matos Mantras" to raise consciousness so people can begin to heal the damaged earth.

Richard Powers's complex *The Gold Bug Variations* (1991), a postmodern meditation on complexity and ecological philosophy, might be considered an operator's manual for the entire universe. Powers's *Gain* (1998), in which a woman dies of cancer from pollution from a soap factory, is a consideration of the relation between individuals and corporations and the ethics, or lack thereof, of the latter.

Still Life with Insects (1989) by Brian Kiteley chronicles an amateur entomologist's nervous breakdown and recovery. He intersperses insect sightings with observations on family, life, and nature. Michael Ventura's *The Zoo Where You're Fed to God* (1994) has a similar theme.

In Jim Lynch's *The Highest Tide* (2005), fourteen-year-old marine biology prodigy Miles O'Malley's discoveries of extremely unusual creatures in Washington State's Skookumchuck Bay, his resuscitation of a seemingly dead dog, and his offhand comment that nature is trying to tell us to pay attention make him a media darling and the subject of attention by a New Age cult. Miles's friendship with a psychic elderly neighbor deepens his insights and commitment to nature.

In B. W. Powe's *Outage: A Journey into the Electric City* (1995), a man becomes "wired" into electronic media and more estranged from the rest of his life. Likewise, the stories in Nick Arvin's *In the Electric Eden* (2003) are a consideration of the relationships between humans, technology, and nature.

Daniel Quinn espouses a radical deep ecological outlook that civilization took a wrong turn with the invention of agriculture and must return to nature and tribal modes to survive even another century. In *Ishmael* (1992) and *My Ishmael* (1997), a telepathic gorilla engages the human narrator in a Socratic dialogue about greed, humanity's refusal to share with the other animals, and the inevitable disaster to come unless people change their ways. *The Story of B* (1996) is a similar dialogue between a priest and an expatriate radical preacher. Quinn utilizes the graphic novel format in *The Man Who Grew Young* (2001), in which human life and history both travel backward to the beginning of civilization.

George Saunders's *Pastoralia* (2000) is a collection of short stories whose unusual protagonists (a fish, a caveman re-enactor, a male stripper, a self-help addict, etc.) are lovable losers whose dreams contrast sharply with the increasingly dystopic corporate America. The stories in *In Persuasion Nation* (2006) focus on the cycle of greed, waste, competitiveness, and conformity in a world driven by advertising and consumption.

Poet Terese Svoboda's fiction debut, *Cannibal* (1994), is set in modern Africa. Through encounters with people of other races and creatures of other species her protagonist learns to reject the whole concept of the self versus the other to perceive the underlying unity of society and nature. In *A Drink Called Paradise* (1999) Svoboda seems to refute this position, as a woman fails in her attempt to go native and is then hauled away after she may have been exposed to radiation from a bomb test or accident.

Elizabeth Marshall Thomas provides an animal's-eye view of the nativity of Christ in *Certain Poor Shepherds* (1996), which begins: "On the First Christmas, so say the Christians, a redeemer was born to save our kind from the consequences of our greed, waste, pride, cruelty, and arrogance. No redeemer appeared for the animals; however, none was needed."[2] A dog and a goat also follow the star to Bethlehem, where they are transfigured not by the baby Jesus, but by a new awareness of their inner spirituality. Thomas concludes that "perhaps our best hope of redemption lies in the fact that we are animals, not that we are people."[3] For other books by Thomas, see the "Prehistory" section of chapter 8.

In Harry Thompson's epic eight-hundred-page sea story *To the Edge of the World* (2005), young Charles Darwin's discoveries lead him to question the Christian fundamentalist worldview held by Captain Robert FitzRoy.

An ecologist visiting a Himalayan Buddhist monastery meets Gaia herself speaking through a computer in Michael Tobias's *Voice of the Planet* (1990).

Ramparts: Unseeing Eyes (1993) by Turf (full name) and Joel Mouclier is a graphic novel about deep ecology.

In John Updike's *Toward the End of Time* (1997), a dying man ruminates about how people from earlier civilizations related to one another, to society, and to nature after the Sino-American War of 2020 has left much of America a radioactive wasteland.

William T. Vollmann's *You Bright and Risen Angels* (1987) pits insects and environmental activists against utility corporations in an allegory of nature versus technology. His epic Seven Dreams: A Book of North American Land-scapes series is a gritty but thoughtful account of encounters between Native Americans and explorers/exploiters from the time of the Vikings forward. Technology is used primarily for conquest, making harmony with the inhabitants or the possibility to learn from them virtually nil. (Published to date: vol. 1: *The Ice Shirt*, 1990; vol. 2: *Fathers and Crows*, 1992; vol. 6: *The Rifles*, 1994; vol. 3: *Argall: The True Story of Pocahontas and Captain John Smith*, 2001).

Charles Walters's *The Beast of Muddy Brain* (2009) offers a deep ecology perspective on environmental ethics and the philosophy of nature.

East Garrison (2009) by G. M. Weger is a consideration of human ecology, habitat ecology, and the psychological effects of war.

W. D. Wetherell's novels and stories "often combine a love of nature and the conventional outdoor activities of boyhood with a darker and more mythic, almost magic-realist sensibility."[4] They include *Hyannis Boat, and Other Stories* (1989), *The Wisest Man in America* (1995), and *Wherever That Great Heart May Be* (1996).

In *Lowboy* (2009) by John Wray, a sixteen-year-old paranoid schizophrenic believes that the only way to cool down the world is to cool down his own body and the only way to do that is to find a girl willing to love him.

ANIMALS

Tales about animals or relations between people and other animals are very common. Human records as ancient as cave drawings depict humanity's fascination with animals. They have frequently appeared in art, folklore, and literature ever since, and are well represented in the works of many Native American authors discussed in chapter 4 and Australian Aboriginal authors in chapter 5.

Literary anthologies for all ages include *The Voice of the Wild*, *The Bear Went Over the Mountain*, *The Company of Animals*, *A Wondrous Menagerie*, and *A Bestiary*.

In Our Nature: Stories of Wildness (2000) is about the human animal. Editor Donna Seaman observes that "in spite of our machines, our plastics, and our artificial ingredients, we are as much a part of nature as any other animal.

. . . Enmeshed in the web of life, we identify strongly with our fellow creatures both domestic and wild."[5]

For books about wildlife conservation or animal rights, see the "Environmental Action/Ecodefense" section of this chapter. Also see chapter 8 for animal-oriented science fiction by David Brin, Vonda N. McIntyre, Andre Norton, and others, and chapter 6 for romances by Alina Reyes, Peter Høeg, and Rhoda Lerman.

Some authors are incredibly accurate in their depictions of wildlife. Griffing Bancroft's *Vanishing Wings* (1972) is so accurate that the Library of Congress classified it as nonfiction, but it is actually a compelling novel. Paleontologist Rob T. Bakker takes us back to the time of the dinosaurs in *Raptor Red* (1995). Ben Gadd provides a raven's-eye view of life in *Raven's End* (2003). Brian Clarke's *The Stream* (2000) views stream ecology from the perspective of trout, mayflies, and other denizens.

Three naturalists who have written many books for young adults and children have also written fiction for adults. Ewan Clarkson's *Ice Trek* (1987) and *Flight of the Osprey* (1996), Allan W. Eckert's *The Silent Sky* (1965) and *Song of the Wild* (1980), and R. D. Lawrence's *Cry Wild* (1991) and *The White Puma* (1990) are appropriate for all readers.

One author stands above the rest in his nuanced portrayal of animals, the human animal, and nature in general: naturalist Barry Lopez. Although Lopez is best known for his nonfiction (e.g., *Of Wolves and Men,* 1978) he also writes almost luminous fictional narratives that range between realism and magic realism (*Desert Notes: Reflections in the Eye of a Raven,* 1976; *Giving Birth to Thunder, Sleeping with His Daughter,* 1978; *River Notes,* 1979; *Winter Count,* 1981; *Crow and Weasel,* 1990; *Field Notes,* 1994; *Lessons from the Wolverine,* 1997; *Light Action in the Caribbean,* 2000). Lopez once stated that "I think if you can really see the land, if you can lose your sense of wishing it to be what you want it to be, if you can strip yourself of the desire to order and to name and see the land entirely for itself, you see in the relationship of all its elements the face of God. And that's why I say the landscape has an authority."[6]

Richard Inglis Hopper's *Strong Feather: The Story of the Last Covey in Indian Bend Wash* (2006) is a tale of quails, habitat conservation, friends, and family.

Seth Kantner's *Ordinary Wolves* (2004) is an incredibly accurate evocation of a young man growing up Inuit-style in a remote region of Alaska. The hardships of mere survival, the relationships between people and animals and among animals, and the changes wrought by the coming of civilization are considered with great clarity and an utter lack of nostalgia or pretense. Joseph Smith's *The Wolf* (2008) is similarly accurate.

Timothy; or, Notes of an Abject Reptile (2006) by Verlyn Klinkenborg is a poetic and philosophical consideration of nature and human animal relationships told from the perspective of eighteenth-century naturalist Gilbert White's tortoise.

Elizabeth M. Lauritzen's *Shushma* (1964), Michael Harrington's *Aransas* (1980), Garry Kilworth's *The Foxes of Firstdark* (1990; published in the UK as *Hunter's Moon*), and Asta Bowen's *Hungry for Home* (1997) combine accurate natural history and adventure with philosophical considerations in the tradition of Jack London.

In paleobotanist Charles Pellegrino's scientifically precise cautionary thriller *Dust* (1998), the eradication of fungus gnats creates a huge upsurge in dangerous fungus mites and the near-extinction of pollinating insects. Frenchman Bernard Werber studied ants for fifteen years before writing *Empire of the Ants* (1991, trans. 1997), which describes life from an ant's perspective.

The cetacean world is explored in a realistic manner in *The Last Whales* (1989) by Lloyd Robert Abbey; in *White Whale* (1981), *Whalesong* (1991), and *The Ice at the End of the World* (1994) by Robert Siegel; and in *Sounding* by Hank Searls (1982); and in a more fantastic way in Ian Watson's *The Jonah Trip* (1976), John Varley's *The Ophiuchi Hotline* (1977), and Vonda N. McIntyre's *Star Trek IV* (1986).

Animal adventure books with strong ethical or philosophical components include Barnaby Conrad and Niels Mortensen's *Endangered* (1980), S. L. Stebel's *Spring Thaw* (1989), William Boyd's *Brazzaville Beach* (1990), Alice Hoffman's *Second Nature* (1994), Richard Hoyt's *Bigfoot* (1993), and Stuart Harrison's *The Snow Falcon* (1999). In Jim Dodge's *Fup* (1983), an aging man is given a new lease on life when he cares for a bird with a broken wing that was "all Fup Duck."

Paul Goodman has observed that "in the simple fables of the ancients, the beasts act like men. In the sentimental animal stories of modern times, the beasts act as themselves, but most often in situations related to men and exemplifying passions and virtues interesting in men. . . . There is also a kind of satire in which men act like beasts."[7]

There is a long literary tradition of using anthropomorphized animals to speak to explore and explain that odd species known as *Homo sapiens*. One of the first green efforts of this type was Kenneth Grahame's *The Wind in the Willows* (1908), and the most famous is Richard Adams's *Watership Down* (1972). Other recent examples include Jack Schaefer's *Conversations with a Pocket Gopher* (1978), John Hawkes's *Sweet William: A Memoir of Old Horse* (1993), and George Stone's *A Legend of Wolf Song* (1975). D. H. Melhem provides an interesting twist by making her "animals" foot-tall gnomes growing in irradiated soil in *Blight* (1995). *Firmin: Adventures of a Metropolitan Lowlife* (2006) by Sam Savage considers life, literature, and urban renewal from an anthropomorphized rat's perspective.

Pat Murphy steps beyond anthropomorphizing to actual transformation. *Nadya* (The Wolf Chronicles) (1996) features a rather wild woman who feels bound by the social constraints of nineteenth-century America, so she travels across the continent until she finds a place to be both woman and wolf in the Oregon wilderness. In Murphy's *The Wild Angel* (2000), a young woman raised by wolves is endangered by the man who murdered her parents.

Several authors employ allegory, sometimes via magical realism. The classic is John Gardner's *Grendel* (1971), a retelling of the Beowulf story from the perspective of the "monster." In Melinda Worth Popham's *Skywater* (1990), two elderly settlers and a band of coyotes in the Sonoran Desert struggle to maintain traditional ways in a tale told mostly by the coyotes. Lloyd E. Hill's *The Village of Bom Jesus* (1993) is a fantasy chronicle of life in the Amazon featuring a witch doctor, wild animals, and a very unusual calico cat. Andrzej Zaniewski's *Rat* (1994) provides a rat's-eye view of the world. In Günter Grass's *The Rat* (1987), the author is inspired by a video of the regreening of Germany by the Brothers Grimm and their characters, but conversations with a rat lead him to more apocalyptic conclusions. Anthony Schmitz's *Darkest Desire*

(1998) is an imaginative retelling of the Brothers Grimm from the wolf's perspective.

Similar works have been written by Michael Rothschild (*Rhapsody of a Hermit*, 1973; *Wondermonger*, 1990), Will Bradley (*Ark Liberty*, 1992), Tom La Farge (*The Crimson Bears*, 1993; *Zuntig*, 2001), Ursula K. Le Guin (*Buffalo Gals and Other Animal Presences*, 1987), Ruth Mueller (*The Eye of the Child*, 1985), Michael Peak (*Catamount*, 1992; *Cat House*, 1989), Ray Petersen (*Cowkind*, 1971), Swain Wolfe (*The Woman Who Lives in the Earth*, 1996), and William Wharton (*Birdy*, 1978; *Franky Furbo*, 1989).

In Winifred Elze's *The Changeling Garden* (1995), a boy who can communicate with plants and his mother whose soul transmigrates with animals psychically foil corporate environmental crimes. Elze's *Here, Kitty, Kitty* (1996) is a fantasy about extinct and endangered species wherein a woman crosses into "the other side" ten thousand years ago while searching for her lost cat.

Several stories in T. C. Boyle's *Tooth and Claw* (2005) present Mother Nature as a powerful and sometimes threatening presence. In "Dogology," a young canine researcher abandons humanity to run with the pack. A foolish decision to drive to an alpine lodge during the first snowfall leads not to the literal death of a young couple, just that of their relationship in "The Swift Passage of Animals." Mosquitoes and alligators are among the "neighbors" to be contended with in a new housing development known ironically as "Jubilation." The title story highlights the folly of trying to domesticate a vicious serval cat won in a bar bet.

ECOFEMINIST FICTION

For a definition and discussion of ecofeminism, see chapter 1. Ecofeminist perspectives can be found in the work of a wide variety of creative writers. Several anthologies are available, including *Sisters of the Earth* (Lorraine Anderson, ed., 1991, a superb collection of fiction, poetry, and essays. *Wild Women* (Sue Thomas, ed., 1994), *Westward the Women* (Vicki Piekarski, ed., 1988), *Hear the Silence* (Irene Zahava, ed., 1986), *Spider Woman's Granddaughters* (Paula Gunn Allen, ed., 1989), and *A Gathering of Spirit* (Beth Brant, ed., 1988) are similar. Although there seem to be no similar anthologies published since 1994, ecofeminist novels have proliferated.

Elizabeth Englehardt's *The Tangled Roots of Feminism, Environmentalism, and Appalachian Literature* (2003) is a study of several proto-ecofeminists writing in the late nineteenth and early twentieth centuries, including Susan Warner, Emma Bell Miles, Mary Noailles Murfree (who used the pseudonym Charles Egbert Craddock), Grace MacGowan Cooke, Lucy Furman, Louise R. Baker, Marie Van Vorst, Amélie Rives Troubetzkoy, and Alice MacGowan. Other important precursors of ecofeminist fiction include S. Alice Callahan, Mary Austin, Willa Cather, Charlotte Perkins Gilman, Virginia Woolf, Idah Meacham Strobridge, Mary Webb, Martha Ostenso, and Sarah Orne Jewett. They argued that the land had an inherent value, and should be worked with (as opposed to worked over) as naturally as possible. The landscape is often represented as feminine and sacred. These authors are covered in chapter 2.

Ecofeminist fiction experienced an incredible flowering between 1974 and 1982 as the feminist and environmental movements grew and coalesced. Major novels published during those years, in chronological order, include Margaret Laurence's *The Diviners*, Suzy McKee Charnas's *Walk to the End of the World*, Joanna Russ's *The Female Man*, Lisa Alther's *Kinflicks*, Marge Piercy's *Woman on the Edge of time*, Vonda N. McIntyre's *Dreamsnake*, Charnas's *Motherlines*, Marilynne Robinson's *Housekeeping*, Kate Wilhelm's *JuniperTime*, Alice Hoffman's *Angel Island*, Susan Griffin's *Woman and Nature*, Margaret Atwood's *Surfacing*, and Alice Walker's *The Color Purple*.

Six current multiple literary award-winning ecofeminist novelists deserving particular attention are Andrea Barrett, Ursula K. Le Guin, Barbara Kingsolver, Brenda Peterson, Jane Smiley, and Alice Walker. See chapter 8 for Le Guin.

Andrea Barrett's work concerns itself with family relations and science, often including a historical dimension. *Lucid Stars* (1988) is a drama about a dysfunctional family featuring a variety of female characters whose only commonality is their relationship to an emotionally crippled philandering developer whose arrogant exploitation of the land parallels his relationships with women. In *Secret Harmonies* (1989), a gifted young singer loathes how the medical research animals at her job are mistreated while her retarded sister develops a special affinity with them. When Grace Doerring attends an acid rain conference in China with her older husband in *The Middle Kingdom* (1991), she realizes that her marriage to the cold, imperious man is a failed experiment in the science of love. In *The Forms of Water* (1993) octogenarian Brendan Auberon fools his nephew Henry into helping him abscond from a nursing home so he can visit his boyhood home, now immersed beneath a reservoir. *Ship Fever* (1996) is a collection of seven short stories and a novella, half being set in the present and half in the eighteenth or nineteenth century. The characters tend to be naturalists, ecologists, collectors, scientific illustrators, healers, and their families, friends, and lovers. In *Voyage of the Narwhal* (1998), naturalist Erasmus Darwin Wells joins an Arctic expedition led by his sister Lavinia's ambitious fiancé, Zecharia Voorhees. Scenes of the wonders and horrors of the Arctic expedition alternate with those of Lavinia, brothers Copernicus and Linnaeus, and her friend Alexandra Copeland creating illustrations and paintings, working with sponsors and publishers, and worrying about the fate of their loved ones. Many characters from *Ship Fever* and *Voyage of the Narwhal* reappear in *Servants of the Map* (2002). The novella "The Cure," about how the rest and fresh air cure for tuberculosis was developed by healers and herbalists before physicians even knew its cause, is reminiscent of the work of Sarah Orne Jewett a century earlier.

Barbara Kingsolver's work melds ecofeminism with progressive political activism. Many of the stories included in *Homeland and Other Stories* (1989) concern the challenges to family farms and a traditional rural way of life. Her first novel, *The Bean Trees* (1988), interrelates the issues of adoption, the Central American refugee sanctuary movement, and relations between Anglo and Native Americans as Taylor Greer informally adopts an abandoned Cherokee baby. In the sequel, *Pigs in Heaven* (1993), three years of single parenthood and participation in the sanctuary movement have expanded Taylor's nascent political and environmental consciousness. Codi Noline returns to her tiny hometown of Grace, Arizona, to care for her Alzheimer's afflicted father and teach high school science in *Animal Dreams* (1990). When a mining company announces it will solve a pollution problem by diverting the river away from the town and orchards, Codi and the local women succeed in registering Grace as an official Historic Place, thus forcing the mine to close. The Price family's experience of the Congo in *The Poisonwood Bible* (1998) becomes utterly tragic because evangelical missionary Nathan Price can never see beyond his own righteousness to what is truly right, inadvertently continuing a colonial pattern that despoils the land and impoverishes the people. See chapter 6 for Kingsolver's romance *Prodigal Summer.*

Brenda Peterson offers ecofeminist perspectives on family life and on the unity of all living things. In her first novel, *River of Light* (1978), farmer Lloyd Sloan is not at peace with the land, his abused wife, Nettie, or his traumatized son, Ira. Lloyd's housekeeper and later common-law wife, Jessie Walsh, is an herbalist and spiritual healer, practicing something akin to pagan spiritual possession melded seamlessly to her Christian beliefs. *Duck and Cover* (1991) tells the tale of the damaging psychological effects of the ultimate anti-environmental technology, nuclear weapons, on the nuclear family. See chapter 6 for Peterson's romance *Animal Heart.*

Jane Smiley's stormy personal life is reflected in her fiction, which often focuses upon the dynamics of the modern family. Her first novel, *Barn Blind* (1980), is about the conflicts between a ranch woman and her four sons. *The Greenlanders* (1988) has a very different setting, fourteenth-century Greenland, but also considers family relationships while introducing her second primary concern, the relationship between people and the land. Smiley's Pulitzer Prize-winning *A Thousand Acres* (1991) is a brilliant adaptation of Shakespeare's *King Lear. Moo* (1995), a satire of academic life at a rural university, portrays faculty as a dysfunctional extended family. *The All-True Travels and Adventures of Lidie Newton* (1998) is set in the plains in the 1850s. A "plain" woman and an abolitionist settle in Kansas, where they struggle with the slavery issue, marginal land, primitive conditions, and the worst winter in decades. *Horse Heaven* (2000) is an extended romp through the world of thoroughbred horse racing. It contains a subtle plea for animal welfare and animal rights. Smiley humorously but savagely lambastes the greed of the Reagan years in *Good Faith* (2003), in which a realtor and a former IRS consultant conspire to develop an old rural Pennsylvania estate into a tacky country club and resort, with environmental impacts, taxpayer rip-offs, and anything resembling ethics glossed over.

Alice Walker describes herself as a "womanist" with a deep connection to traditional and contemporary female culture. She is best known for *The Color Purple* (1982, filmed 1985), which has an ecological subtext contrasting love and nature with hatred and social repression. *The Temple of My Familiar* (1989) moves between centuries and continents to explore relations between genders, races, and species. She does not propose that all tribal practices are enlightened and is particularly opposed to female circumcision, the subject of *Possessing the Secret of Joy* (1992), which links oppression of women with that of the earth. *The Way Forward Is with a Broken Heart* (2000) consists of fourteen highly autobiographical short stories, with primary emphasis on social and emotional issues and secondary emphasis on the environment. In *Now Is the Time to Open Your Heart* (2004), Kate Talkingtree journeys down the Colorado and Amazon rivers where she meets the universal grandmother, who is literally a talking tree.

Paganism and Goddess religions have inspired several writers, including Kate Horsley (*Confessions of a Pagan Nun*, 2001; *The Changeling of Finnistauth*, 2003), Francine Prose (*Hunters and Gatherers*, 1995), Elizabeth Cunningham (*The Return of the Goddess*, 1992; *The Wild Mother*, 1993; *How to Spin Gold*, 1997; *Daughter of the Shining Isles*, 2000), Diane DesRochers (*Walker Between the Worlds*, 1995), Ellen Galford (*The Fires of Bride*, 1988), Starhawk (*The Fifth Sacred Thing*, 1993), Mary Mackey (*The Year the Horses Came*, 1993; *The Horses at the Gate*, 1996; *The Fires of Spring*, 1998), and William Sutherland (*News from Fort God*, 1993).

Other significant American and Canadian ecofeminists include Kathleen Alcalá (*Mrs. Vargas and the Dead Naturalist*, 1992; *Spirits of the Ordinary*, 1997; *Flower in the Skull*, 1998; *Treasures in Heaven*, 2000), Katharine Haake (*The Height and Depth of Everything*, 2001; *That Water, Those Rocks*, 2002), Pam Houston (*Cowboys Are My Weakness*, 1988; *Waltzing the Cat*, 1998; *Sight Hound*, 2005), Catherine Bush (*Minus Time*, 1993), Jane Candia Coleman (*Stories from Mesa Country*, 1991; *Borderlands*, 2000), Kiana Davenport (*Shark*

Dialogues, 1994; *Song of the Exile,* 1999), Molly Gloss (*The Jump Off Creek,* 1989; *Dazzle of Day,* 1997; *Wild Life,* 2000), Mary Sojourner (*Sisters of the Dream,* 1989; *Delicate: Stories,* 2004), Susan Lang (*Small Rocks Rising,* 2002), and Susan Vreeland (*The Forest Lover,* 2004).

Important Native American ecofeminists include Louise Erdrich and Leslie Marmon Silko, and significant African Americans include Elaine Perry (*Another Present Era,* 1990) and Gloria Naylor (*The Women of Brewster Place,* 1982; *Mama Day,* 1988; *The Men of Brewster Place,* 1998).

Ecofeminist novelists can be found throughout the world: Nicaraguan Gioconda Belli, Germans Gabriele Wohmann and Christa Wolf; Swede Kerstin Ekman; Australian Thea Astley; Africans Werewere Liking, Buchi Emecheta, Calixthe Beyala, Aminata Sow Fall, and Bessie Head; and Indians Mahasweta Devi and Nina Sibal, among others. See chapter 5.

You don't have to be female to be an ecofeminist. Jack London's *A Daughter of the Snows* and *Smoke Bellew* (1902, 1912), Ken Kesey's *Sometimes a Great Notion* (1964), Ian Watson's *Book of the River* (1984), Frederick Manfred's *Manly-hearted Woman* (1975), William Eastlake's *Dancers in the Scalp House* (1975), Frank Waters's *The Woman at Otowi Crossing* (1988), Ed Moses's *Nine Sisters Dancing* (1996), and Jim Harrison's *Dalva* and *The Road Home* (1988, 1998) feature ecofeminist characters or themes.

Ecofeminists have made major contributions to the genres of science fiction and mystery writing. See chapters 8 and 9.

ENVIRONMENTAL ACTION/ECODEFENSE

The concept of "environmental action" can be applied from the personal to the universal level. It can include living an environmentally sustainable lifestyle, taking simple political action like voting or contacting legislators, and so on, but in this instance I am applying it to a narrower range of actions such as building a mass movement, taking personal responsibility for a problem/issue, ecodefense, and the envisioning and creation of utopias.

Edward Abbey popularized the concept of ecodefense and invented the term "monkey-wrenching." Although some critics tend to equate ecodefense and terrorism, it should be stressed that "monkey-wrenching" is intended only for machines, that violence against individuals is always to be avoided. The point is to stop corporate or government violence against the environment. *The Monkey Wrench Gang* (1975) was praised as a literary masterpiece by some and castigated as a mere comic book by others, but it is neither. It is a compelling adventure story that, like Abbey's subsequent fiction, requires some suspension of disbelief. Vietnam veteran George Washington Hayduke, river guide Seldom Seen Smith, dentist Doc Sarvis, and his assistant Bonnie Abzug team up to remove survey stakes, torch billboards, destroy heavy equipment, and eventually attack a huge open-pit coal mine. Their ultimate target is the hated Glen Canyon Dam. A "Lone Ranger," Jack Burns himself, appears from the shadows at one point to tell Hayduke about similar ecotage throughout the West. When the gang is tracked down, Hayduke seems to die in a hail of gunfire. In the epilogue, Smith, Sarvis, and Abzug settle in a pastoral haven and are visited by Hayduke and Burns. Hayduke explains that it was merely his decoy that was shot and congratulates Smith and Sarvis for destroying a bridge to facilitate his escape. When Sarvis reveals that they didn't do it, they rejoice that others have taken up the cause. Unlike in Abbey's other fiction, virtue is unambiguously triumphant and the valiant are rewarded in the end. *The Monkey Wrench Gang* has sold over a half million copies, generated endless controversy, and inspired countless activists and authors.

The Brave Cowboy's return in *Good News* (1980) appears to be another romantic quest as he and Harvard-educated shaman sidekick Sam ride into early twenty-first century Phoenix to find Jack's longtime missing son, Charley, but it quickly becomes apparent that this is a savage parody of Abbey's earlier work. In a triple irony, the knight-like Burns is apparently killed by a lance, Charley realizes that the old man really is his father after finding an old photo, and Burns's body vanishes. In the preface to *The Fool's Progress* (1988), Abbey lampoons both sides of his personality: shy, scholarly Edward Abbey and Henry Lightcap, a thinly veiled "Cactus Ed" who wishes to enlist the skeptical Abbey's help in publishing his autobiographical novel. Abbey warns readers of *Hayduke Lives!* (1990) that "Anyone who takes this book seriously will be shot. Anybody who does not will be buried by a Mitsubishi bulldozer." The old Monkey Wrench Gang, Burns, Earth First!ers, and other activists organize to oppose a proposed uranium mine near the Grand Canyon. The tone, style, and events are similar to that of *MWG,* but this sequel caricatures the younger activists, particularly ecofeminists and New Age devotees. Typically, Abbey ended his writing career by amusing many while offending friend and foe alike. Nevertheless, the very idea that old ecowarriors would keep on fighting to the end provides inspiration and hope.

Jim Harrison's *A Good Day to Die* (1973) presents a stark contrast to *The Monkey Wrench Gang.* An unnamed man who has opted out of his family and job, a slightly deranged Vietnam War veteran named Tim, and Tim's erstwhile girlfriend blunder into a plan to destroy a dam that the narrator fantasizes is being built in the Grand Canyon. After a frantic cross-country drive, they wind up in Montana intending to blow up a small earth-filled dam that is ruining fish migration. They succeed, but Tim is killed when he tries to save a cow wandering onto the dam.

In Don Metz's *King of the Mountain* (1990), Walker Owen returns to his boyhood home in Vermont and discovers that developers have conspired to destroy the forest to build condos. Walker and a local farmer fail in legal efforts to stop the condos and resort to ecotage.

Ecotage is also featured in novels by William Eastlake, John Nichols, Jim Dodge, Ken Kesey, Peter Matthiessen, Don Metz, Kristine Rosemary, Lawrence R. Smith, Anthony Weller, Lee Wallingford, Thomas King, and D'Arcy McNickle. See chapter 4 for King and McNickle.

Ecotage is just one of many forms of defending the environment, as the following books demonstrate. Approximately half are about land-development conflicts. Other common issues addressed are endangered species or animal rights, nuclear power or weapons, forest or rainforest conservation, dams, pollution, wilderness preservation, and oil spills.

"What a revoltin' development this is!" William Bendix's frequent complaint on the classic radio and television series *Life of Riley* is echoed by many authors, but they are referring specifically to inappropriate land development. When a developer plans a mall on the site of a museum of history and natural history in Ann Arbor, a mother and daughter become involved in efforts to save it in Nancy Willard's *Sister Water* (1993). The Maine woods are the setting for a confrontation between a clear-cutting logger and an activist in Paul Watkins's *Archangel* (1995). In Chris Bohjalian's *Water Witches* (1995), a lawyer representing a proposed ski resort switches sides because of the influence of water dowsers and other environmentalists.

Three critically acclaimed modern western agrarian struggle novels are particularly notable given their strongly developed characters, exciting adventure, and emotional impact. In Dan O'Brien's *In the Center of the Nation* (1991), the policies of banks in favor of developers create hardship and foreclosures of family ranches and farms in South Dakota. The developers are surprised by the gritty and effective resistance of the residents. O'Brien's other books (*Eminent Domain,* 1987; *Spirit of the Hills,* 1988; *Brendan Prairie,* 1996) have similar settings and themes. James Galvin's superb *The Meadow* (1992) and *Fencing the Sky* (1999) are discussed in chapter 7.

Similar books abound. *Leaving the Land* (1984) by Douglas Unger is about a family struggling to keep its farm against economic pressure created by agribusiness price manipulations and other forms of financial pressure. Jane Smiley's *A Thousand Acres* (1991) and Jonis Agee's *Strange Angels* (1993) are *King Lear* adaptations depicting intrafamily land squabbling. In Frank Roderus's *Mustang War* (1991), two ranchers overgraze their own land, then slaughter mustangs on public land to provide more forage for their cattle, but they are caught in the act by two environmental activists. In *Home Is the River* (1989), by the appropriately named M. H. Salmon, a latter-day mountain man reminiscent of Edward Abbey's heroes fights the destruction of a wilderness river. In Oliver Lange's *The Land of the Long Shadow* (1981), a landowner in the remote mountains struggles to keep his land from being bought and turned into a subdivision. Michael Drinkard's multigenerational novel *Disobedience* (1993) begins with Eliza Tibbets starting an orange grove in 1885. A century later, her rebellious great-granddaughter clashes with her upscale husband about the future of the land. *Wish You Well* (2000) by David Baldacci chronicles a Virginia family's attempt to save their farm from mining and logging interests. Joyce Weatherford's *Heart of the Beast* (2001) concerns a woman's efforts to establish both legal and moral justifications to keep an inherited ranch that is also claimed by the Nez Percé Indians. Land struggle goes national in Steve Pieczenik's sagebrush rebellion novel *State of Emergency* (1997), in which the governors of four western states threaten to secede over federal land policies. Poor people unite to oppose the ravages of mountaintop removal mining in Ann Pancake's *Strange as This Weather Has Been* (2007).

Ecoheroes also fight corporate, governmental, and military environmental crimes. This is David Poyer's favorite theme. When Thunder Oil begins secretly dumping toxic waste along Pennsylvania's back roads, a retired oil field worker and a troubled teen team up to stop them in *Winter in the Heart* (1993). Other titles in the series include *The Dead of Winter* (1988), *As the Wolf Loves Winter* (1996), and *Thunder on the Mountain* (1999). Kristine Rosemary's *The War Against Gravity* (1993), a thriller set in the Pacific Northwest, pits the powers of nature and environmental activists against the logging industry, white-collar criminals, corrupt officials, and drug dealers. In Gillian Bradshaw's *Bloodwood* (2007) a PR flunkie facing death from cancer turns against her old firm, reporting their illegal logging of endangered forests and the murders of Malaysian protestors.

In John Cheever's *Oh, What a Paradise It Seems* (1982), the paradise is not so paradisiacal after the mob colludes with local officials to turn a pond into a toxic waste dump, but an older man and a housewife both find their own forms of resistance. An unusual assortment of citizens finally unites in the face of catastrophic chemical pollution in Evan Dara's *The Lost Scrapbook* (1995). Dana Jennings's *Lonesome Standard Time* (1996) is also about resistance to toxic waste production and dumping. *The Burning Ghats* (1996) by Paul Mann is about a lethal chemical spill in the Ganges River. In Bill Hunger's *Clearcut: A Novel of Bio-Consequences* (1996), an herbalist seeks a remedy for a disease that standard medicine cannot cure, but clear-cutting of old-growth forests is decimating hundreds of medicinal species. Thomas Richards's *Zero Tolerance* (1997) finds parallels between the disastrous damming of the Monongahela, Klamath, and Mekong rivers. *Gain* (1998) by Richard Powers links cancer and industrial pollution. Alaskan park ranger Kim Heacox chronicles the controversy over oil drilling in the Arctic National Wildlife Refuge in *Caribou Crossing* (2001).

Sometimes when government and big business are in cahoots, the people strike back. In Matt Ruff's *Sewer, Gas & Electric* (1997), a sweeping conspiracy between government and business is revealed. The philosophy of Ayn Rand is skewered in the persona of an absurd architect who plans to build mile-high skyscrapers. Former Massachusetts Governor William Weld draws from an experience in his youth, the inundation of farmland and wilderness when the Swift River was dammed in 1938, in *Stillwater* (2002). In Anthony Weller's *The Siege of Salt Cove* (2004), a coalition of local residents and outsiders uses passive resistance, the press, imaginative tactics, and finally armed resistance in an attempt to save an old wooden bridge and thereby the character of their rural community. In Bill Smith's *Tanaki on the Shore* (2006), a marine biologist, an environmental lawyer, and Native American activists combine forces to reveal collusion between corporations and Bush administration officials to secretly build a theme park in sensitive Chesapeake Bay.

Annie's Soup Kitchen (2003) by Lawrence R. Smith is a magic realist romp in which a ninety-five-year-old retired nurse realizes that a global plague is caused by pollution and other environmental woes, forms a "Magnificent Seven" alliance of soup kitchen volunteers, and leads them on a monkey-wrenching campaign.

Physician Michael Palmer writes medical thrillers. In *Critical Judgment* (1996), a doctor discovers that a chemical company in "Faustville" has been exposing its employees and the public to carcinogenic cadmium. The deaths of several pregnant women are not actually from *Natural Causes* (1994) but from a dangerous herbal supplement. *Miracle Cure* (1998) is about pharmaceutical companies circumventing safe testing to get their unproven products on the market.

Some green adventure novels take place under water. At least three of Clive Cussler's twenty novels featuring diver Dirk Pitt have an environmental aspect (*Sahara,* 1992; *Shock Wave,* 1995; *Flood Tide,* 1997). In David Poyer's Tiller Galloway series (*Hatteras Blue,* 1989; *Bahamas Blue,* 1992; *Louisiana Blue,* 1994; *Down to a Sunless Sea,* 1996), an intrepid diver takes on corporate marine polluters. Another Galloway, author Les, wrote *The Forty Fathom Bank* (1984), in which fishermen have a feeding frenzy on rare white sharks as a source of vitamin A and a diver discovers related changes in local marine ecology. In V. A. MacAlister's *Mosquito War* (2001), divers and activists attempt to thwart the efforts of a biotech firm and the CIA. James Powlik addresses a life-threatening mass plankton bloom caused by pollution in *Sea Change* (1999).

Other green adventure novels take place on the sea or the coast. Neal Stephenson's *Zodiac: The Eco-Thriller* (1988) is about a New Age Sam Spade and activists fighting the corporate polluters of Boston Harbor. Commercial fisherman Dick Pierce faces the challenges of corporate competition and decreasing catches in John Casey's *Spartina* (1998). In G. F. Michelsen's *Hard Bottom* (2001), a commercial fisherman is driven to action in order to protect land on Cape Cod from being developed into a shopping center. Passages from an imaginary text on the ecology of the Cape are interspersed throughout the story. Cape Cod is also the locale of *Spectacular Happiness* by Peter D. Kramer (2001), in which the Free the Beaches movement blasts mansions off the shoreline.

Biotechnology and human cloning are the subjects of Ken Follett's thriller *The Third Twin* (1996), which spins a dark plot of violence and intrigue around genetic research and human cloning. When the leader of a wine-growing commune in Northern California loses his lease because the government plans to build a dam, he becomes *The Hammer of Eden* (1998), steals a seismic vibrator from an oil company, and threatens a major earthquake if plans for the dam are not shelved.

Nuclear power and weapons, with their horrifying consequences, are frequently the concern of activists. Frank Bergon's *The Temptations of St. Ed & Brother S* (1993) is a fascinating account of nuclear resistance and modern religion set in Nevada. The Green Army Commandos threaten to detonate stolen plutonium to stop the building of a nuclear-powered desalination plant in Norman Spinrad's *Pictures at 11* (1994). In Tracy Daugherty's *What Falls Away* (1996), a Nevada family protests underground nuclear testing despite the consequent ill treatment by their neighbors. The heroes of James Powlik's *Meltdown* (2000) combat rapidly growing environmental problems and potential extinctions in the Arctic caused by radiation. Ann Cummins's

Yellowcake (2007) is a gentler exploration of two families of uranium miners, one white and one Navajo, slowly coming to terms with the health consequences of that activity.

Africa and South America are the sites of many environmental struggles. Sara Cameron's *Natural Enemies* (1993), in which a naturalist, a reporter, and a detective pursue the murderers of the head of the Kenyan Wildlife Service and fight the ivory trade, won the Edward Abbey Award for Ecofiction and the Turner Tomorrow Award. Karin McQuillan's experiences as a Peace Corps volunteer in Africa inform *Deadly Safari* (1990), *Elephant's Graveyard* (1994), and *Cheetah Chase* (1994). Elephant protection is the subject of several books. See "Africa" in chapter 5. In Steven Voien's *Black Leopard* (1997), field biologists themselves become endangered when they discover a government plot to sell protected forests.

Tales from the Jungle (Daniel Katz and Miles Chapin, eds., 1995) is an anthology of fiction and nonfiction about rainforest protection. A German émigré lives deep in the Ecuadorian rain forest as a protector of the native people who are being napalmed and otherwise harassed by an oil company in Marnie Mueller's *Green Fires: Assault on Eden* (1994). Carl A. Posey's *Bushmaster Fall* (1992) is a political potboiler: a British scientist working in the Bolivian rain forest discovers an American radioactive experiment that threatens to poison the entire area. In James Munves's *Andes Rising* (1999), the journal of an atomic scientist turned naturalist who mysteriously disappeared in Colombia reveals that he had refused to participate in the possible extinction of a rare tanager. Two public health volunteers in Peru take action when they realize that the high rate of still births and deformed babies is caused by pollution from the mines in Kate Wheeler's *When Mountains Walked* (2000).

Considering the extent of environmental racism (toxic waste dumps in ghettos, destruction of communities through eminent domain and gentrification, etc.), it is surprising that so little fiction has been written about it. Anita Bunkley's *Balancing Act* (1997) confronts it most directly, but it is also addressed in Gloria Naylor's *The Women of Brewster Place* (1982) and *The Men of Brewster Place* (1992). *Bloodroot* (2001) by Aaron Roy Even is based on the true story of an African-American family that resists being moved from their

Virginia farm so a turpentine plant can be built. For Percival Everett's *Watershed*, see the "Philosophical/Spiritual" section of this chapter.

The Alliance of Magicians and Outlaws, a group of subversives opposed to the prevailing authoritarian, nature-defiling power structure, takes both magical and practical action in Jim Dodge's *Stone Junction: An Alchemical Potboiler* (1990).

Animal welfare and/or rights is the subject of Russell Hoban's *Turtle Diary* (1975), Richard Adams's *The Plague Dogs* (1977), Beat Sterchi's *Cow* (1988), Barbara Ehrenreich's *Kipper's Game* (1993), and the mysteries *Off Season* (1994) by Philip R. Craig, *White Eye* (1994) by Blanche D'Alpuget, *Claw* (1994) by Ken Eulo and Joe Mauck, *Prey* (1992), *Wildfire* (1994), and *Double Blind* (1997) by Kenneth Goddard, *The Quick and the Dead* (2000) by Joy Williams, and the many game warden novels by Gunnard Landers. On a remote island in the Hebrides that is the location of both a wildlife preserve and a biochemical research lab, a hunter wonders why the animals drop dead before he can shoot them in Marshall Pugh's *The Last Place Left* (1969). Peter Clement's *Mutant* (2001) is a chilling thriller about bioengineering and the possibility of cross-species diseases.

Endangered species are protected in *Extinction* (anthology, ed. by Linny Stovall, 1992), *The White Puma* by R. D. Lawrence (1990), *Native Tongue* (1991) by Carl Hiaasen, *The Turquoise Dragon* (1985) and *The Vermillion Parrot* (1991) by David Rains Wallace, *Endangered Species* (1989) by Gene Wolfe, and *Biting the Moon* (1999) by Martha Grimes. *Cry of the Panther: Quest of a Species* (1984) by James P. McMullen is a moving account of a Vietnam veteran hunting the Florida panther in order to help save it and his own soul. In Jake Page's *Cavern* (2000) a spelunker discovers evidence of a previously undiscovered species of bear, leading him to explore the interconnectedness of all living things. In Anastasia Hobbet's *Pleasure of Believing* (1997), a rancher who poisons one of his own cattle and blames it on coyotes finds his perfidy revealed when rare falcons die from eating the poison. This story is based on an incident that led to the Endangered Species Act. Some of Julia Whitty's short stories in *A Tortoise for the Queen of Tonga* (2002) are based on historical incidents. In the title story, a giant tortoise lives until 1966, growing increasingly lonely as other tortoises and whales become extinct. *The Book of Dead Birds* (2003) by Gayle Brandeis features a young woman who loves birds but had frequently accidentally killed her mother's pet birds. She travels to the Salton Sea to help rescue the victims of the worst bird die-off in history. Dave Foreman's *The Lobo Outback Funeral Home* (2000) is an autobiographical novel about the reintroduction of wolves in the Southwest.

The protagonist of Kelpie Wilson's *Primal Tears* (2005) is a human-bonobo hybrid. Wilson deftly explores a variety of issues, including bonobo preservation, animal welfare, human overpopulation, the conflict between fundamentalist Christianity and science, the relationship between human poverty and warfare and species extinction, feminist and environmental politics, and nature-oriented spirituality.

Sometimes the endangered animals act in their own defense. In Margaret St. Clair's *The Dolphins of Altair* (1967), a dolphin reveals how amphibious aliens from planet Altair had interbred with humans while others became dolphins. The dolphins, now threatened by pollution and mistreated by naval scientists, communicate telepathically with a small group of humans to set captive dolphins free. Alarmed by nuclear weapons and nuclear power, the Council of Beasts in Randall Beth Platt's *Out of a Forest Clearing* (1991) gathers an assortment of animals to close a nuclear submarine base. In Dan Simmons's *Fires of Eden* (1994), a talking hog, a shark-mouthed humanoid, Polynesian gods, and a volcano rise up to destroy a massive resort. Zoo animals rebel in Scott Bradfield's *Animal Planet* (1995). In Ken Grimwood's *Into the Deep* (1995), three telepathic children communicate with dolphins. Thirty years later the dolphins contact them again to help save them and humanity from destruction.

T. C. Boyle's position on ecodefense is more complex. By the year 2025 Southern California is a dystopia of global warming, choking pollution, rapid extinction of species, and urban decay, badly in need of *A Friend of the Earth* (2000). Unfortunately, Ty Tierwater believes that one must be an enemy of humanity to be a friend of the earth. Boyle satirizes the excesses of both the radical environmental movement and industry, particularly logging, but manages to convey some compassion for both the earth and humanity.

The Nature Notebooks by Don Mitchell (2004), *The Missing Person* by Alix Ohlin (2005), and *The Tree-Sitter* by Suzanne Matson (2006) are complex considerations of the ethical limitations of ecodefense when the result is unintended violence against individuals.

FOOD AND DRINK

Smoking, eating, and drinking may be hazardous to your health. Christopher Buckley's darkly hilarious satire *Thank You for Smoking* (1994) follows a public relations man as he plans campaigns, appears on talk shows, and is eventually kidnapped by antismoking terrorists who plan to kill him by covering him with nicotine patches. He reveals how the self-named "Merchants of Death" (PR agents for the tobacco and alcohol industries and the NRA) use similar tactics to fool the public. The protagonist of *Tail Tigerswallow and the Great Tobacco War* (1988) by Arthur L. Hoffman resorts to guerilla warfare, including cutting down billboards. *Smokeout* (2000) by S. V. Date features unscrupulous tobacco lobbyists and that rarest of all species, an honest politician in Florida.

Dianne Mott Davidson has written a dozen culinary mysteries, one of which, *Killer Pancake* (1995), includes activists protesting animal testing for cosmetics. Davidson's books include recipes for such delicacies as "chocolate coma cookies."

The Road to Wellville (1993) by T. C. Boyle is a satire of the nascent health food and health resorts movement in the early 1900s. Ruth L. Ozeki's *My Year of Meats* (1998) is an exposé of the beef production and promotion industries. In her *All Over Creation* (2003), Idaho is the setting for a confrontation between organic farming advocates and biotechnologists. The short stories in Janet Kieffer's *Food Chain* (2004) satirize agribusiness, marketing, and the American consumer. In Lawrence G. Townsend's *Secrets of the Wholly Grill: A Satire about Software, Barbecue, and Cravings* (2002), a Silicon Valley firm produces a modem-operated grill and addictive sauces.

Mark Spitzer's *Chum* (2001) is one of the most grotesque, chilling tales in modern literature. The lives of fish cannery workers on an Aleutian island are as debased as the island is devastated, both sacrificed for the production of dog food. Powerful, poetic language and ironic black humor provide comic relief in this otherwise grim tale.

In Irving Warner's *Wagner, Descending: The Wrath of the Salmon Queen* (2004) the obese son of Alaska's Salmon Queen, scion of a corporate fortune, and director of the Northern Institute for Social Reprisal, is a radical who loves "the People," but is more than a bit misanthropic regarding individuals.

There are alternatives. In Paul Theroux's *Millroy the Magician* (1994) a televangelist promotes vegetarianism by promoting the pure foods mentioned in the Bible. Televangelism is also an element in Jon Fink's *Long Pig* (1996), in which a man creates the Humpty Dumpster, a processor capable of turning compost into feed, paper into fuel, waste into fertilizer, and other raw ingredients into sausage.

ECOTOPIAS

The ultimate form of environmental action, though, is creating a new ecologically oriented society. Ernest Callenbach's *Ecotopia* (1975) is but one version.

Some are set on other planets, real or imaginary. Kim Stanley Robinson has explored utopias set in California, Antarctica, Mars, and elsewhere in the universe. Ursula K. Le Guin initially considered the complexities of utopias in *The Dispossessed: An Ambiguous Utopia* (1974), but *Always Coming Home* (1985) focuses more intently on the subject. (See chap. 8 for more on Robinson and Le Guin.) Ian Watson creates an ecofeminist utopia in his Black River trilogy (*The Book of the River*, 1984; *The Book of the Stars*, 1984; *The Book of Being*, 1985), as does Dorothy Bryant in *The Kin of Ata Are Waiting for You* (1971). In *Mirabile* (1991), Janet Kagan depicts genetic engineering, which proves to be somewhat unpredictable, being used to create a utopia on the titular planet. Doris Lessing chronicles millions of years of evolution toward a more ecotopian society in *Canopus in Argos* (1992).

Other ecotopias are set on Earth. In Joel Garreau's *The Nine Nations of North America* (1981), divisions are based on natural bioregional commonalities, not artificial political lines. Starhawk's *Fifth Sacred Thing* (1993) portrays a neopagan society in California. Karen Tei Yamashita sets hers in the jungle in *Brazil-Maru* (1992). Robert Froese's *The Hour of Blue* (1990) combines ecodefense, fantasy, and utopianism: a forest ranger and a marine biologist form a loose conspiracy of trees, dolphins, and psychic children working together to defend nature and live under the principles of Gaia theory. Brad Leithauser has created Freeland, an imaginary island where the people live an existence of gritty Nordic self-sufficiency. *The Friends of Freeland* (1997) fight modernization from the kitchen table to the voting booth. *Curtain Creek Farm* (2000) is the name of Nance Van Winckel's rural commune founded in the 1960s and still thriving and changing, despite many challenges from the outside world. David Margolis's *Change of Partners* (1997) is a fairly evenhanded account of hippie commune life in an only partially realized ecotopia. T. C. Boyle's sixties commune *Drop City* (2003) abandons Northern California but cannot survive the Alaskan winter.

An ecologist who has written practical nonfiction books on building an alternative society, Guy Dauncey might be considered a New Age Ernest Callenbach. *Earthfuture: Stories from a Sustainable World* (1999) consists of forty very short stories intended as the seeds of a more positive future.

Robert Nichols creates an anarcho-syndicalist ecotopian society in Central Asia based on the visions of William Blake, Robert Morris, and Walt Whitman in the series Daily Lives in Nghsi-Alta (*Arrival,* 1977; *Garh City,* 1978; *The Harditts in Sawna,* 1979; *Exile,* 1979). He mixes an imaginative brew of high technology and shamanism in a series that is as delightful as it is thought-provoking.

THE CONTEMPORARY PASTORAL

The traditional pastoral is often a celebration of rural life in bygone times. It may be romantic and sentimental, or gritty and more realistic. Ecodefense novels taking place in the countryside are action oriented, seeking to save or reclaim the land. Occupying the literary ground between them one finds what might be called the "contemporary pastoral." These books are more contemplative in nature, considering the relation between the individual, civilization, and nature, suggesting that some of the old ways may be more appropriate to the modern world than the wasteful, consumption-oriented model now in favor. Wendell Berry's books are a good example of this subgenre, as are

James Galvin's *The Meadow* (1992) and Lesley Choyce's *The Second Season of Jonas MacPherson* (1989). The activist elements in these books are related to a simpler lifestyle and to preserving or restoring the land.

Castle Freeman's *The Bride of Ambrose* (1987) and *My Life and Adventures* (2002) recount rural Vermont in the late 1960s and early 1970s. The serenity didn't last long: *Judgment Hill* (1997) takes place in the same area two decades later, culminating in a tragic confrontation between an old man and a logger.

John DuFresne explores the unique aspects of country life in the bayou country in *The Way That Water Enters Stone* (1991), *Louisiana Power & Light* (1994), and *Deep in the Shade of Paradise* (2002).

The old question, "How you going to keep 'em down on the farm?" is challenged in many novels. Ninety-year-old Reeni Leahy identifies entirely with the land, refusing to leave *The Farm She Was* (1998) by Ann Mohin. The 317 inhabitants of *Travers Corner* (1997), Scott Waldie's fictitious Montana town, are not tempted by modernity in their close-knit community. The joys of a bucolic lifestyle in rural Wyoming are tempered by boredom, infidelity, and loneliness in Jon Billman's *When We Were Wolves* (1999). In Don Kurtz's *South of the Big Four* (1995), a young man returns from the city to work on a traditional farm in Indiana. Christie Hart Lips's *The White Stone* (2000) is a ranch where burned-out city folks seek solace, honest work, and authenticity. Charles Ray returns to Walden Pond in *The Tarheel Connection: An Environmental Romance* (2003).

Anthony Doerr's short stories in *The Shell Collector* (2002) are virtually uncategorizable given their many subjects, and locales ranging from Montana to Scandinavia to Kenya, but all are imbued with a deep appreciation of and complex relation to nature.

The settings of Annie Proulx's fiction vary widely, from Nova Scotia in *The Shipping News* (1993) to Wyoming in *Close Range* (1999) and *Bad Dirt* (2004), but her exploration of the human heart and psyche and their relation to nature is consistent. *That Old Ace in the Hole* (2002), set in Texas, has a more activist tone as Proulx attacks industrial hog farms.

Disaster novels are of two types. Referring back to Gabriel Navarre's distinction between "true" and "false" ecofiction, one might make a similar one between cautionary and dystopian fiction. In the former, disasters may occur and the environmental problems may be steadily worsening, but there is still some hope that utter ruin can be averted. Patrick Murphy identifies two ways that such books fulfill their purpose: by making readers appreciate what is being lost or threatened, and by inspiring people to action.[8] In dystopian fiction, if we are all on the verge of extinction anyway, why should we change our behavior? Cautionary fiction is a warning that we can and must change behavior while we can still save ourselves and promote a rich, sustainable web of life.

Unfortunately, it can be very difficult to distinguish between cautionary and dystopian texts. Consider the work of J. G. Ballard. Ballard has written that his surreal fusion of the external environment and the unconscious provides "redemptive and therapeutic power. To move through these landscapes is a journey of return to one's innermost being."[9] Many of his books are disaster novels, depicting a world ravaged by war, disease, pollution, radiation, global warming, waste, and greed, making life perilous and dehumanizing. These include *The Drowned World* (1962), *The Crystal World* (1966), *Crash* (1973), *Concrete Island* (1974), and *High-Rise* (1975). They seem to be primarily cautionary, but Ballard's sometimes pessimistic tone can ultimately be depressing, leading one to give up hope. His pessimism and anger culminate in *Rushing to Paradise* (1995), a full-fledged dystopia in which a doctor who has lost her medical license founds an albatross sanctuary staffed by an all-female crew. The women mate with men who are disposed of after they have performed their function as inseminators. The morals of this story seem to be that human nature is essentially self-aggrandizing and evil, and that the environmental movement and ecofeminism in particular are not just futile, but dangerous.

With that in mind, and with the caveat that many books could just as easily be categorized in the "Cautionary" or "Environmental Action" sections or

"Green Speculative Fiction" chapter depending on the reader's interpretation and response, let's consider the cautionary fiction of the last three decades. A good place to start is *The Earth Strikes Back: An Anthology of Ecological Horror* (Richard T. Chizmar, ed., 1994). It contains a dozen cautionary tales of things gone wrong, most of which imply appropriate corrective responses to these disasters.

George Turner is a less pessimistic Australian version of Ballard. In *Beloved Son* (1978), a spaceship returns to Earth after forty years only to find a world where most of the population has been exterminated by ecological disasters and the survivors have destroyed most of civilization. The other volumes in Turner's Ethical Culture trilogy are *Vaneglory* (1981) and *Yesterday's Men* (1983). In *Drowning Towers* (aka *The Sea and Summer,* 1987), a boy struggles to deal with a future in a world that is overpopulated, ultra-automated, and being flooded by the rising oceans. By 2069 Earth is so overpopulated and environmentally ravaged that procreation and the treatment of terminal illness are capital crimes in *The Destiny Makers* (1993). In Turner's final novel, *Down There in Darkness* (1999), in the year 2070 the "four horsemen of the greenhouse apocalypse" (overpopulation, pollution, nationalism, unemployment) have made life in Australia almost intolerable, but two men emerging from suspended animation discover that things are even worse one hundred years later.

Some books seem to be primarily horrified descriptions of living in devastated landscapes, whether the cause is radiation, global warming, or something else entirely. These include Neal Bell's *Gone to Be Snakes Now* (1972), Paul Auster's *In the Country of Last Things* (1988), Russell Hoban's *Riddley Walker* (1980), Paul Theroux's *O-Zone* (1986), and Martin Amis's *London Fields* (1989). John Barth's *The Tidewater Tales* (1987) depicts a Chesapeake Bay where you might encounter spies floating in the water, toxic wastes dumped by the Mafia, and espionage stations in a place where nature is fighting a losing battle with an increasingly brutal "civilization." In *Pollen* (1996) by Jeff Noon, plants revolt by releasing deadly pollen.

By 2025 America is an overpopulated, polluted wasteland whose natural resources have been squandered in Whitley Strieber and James W. Kunetka's

Nature's End: The Consequences of the Twentieth Century (1986). This is a chilling portrayal of the potential environmental, political, and personal consequences of humanity's current failure to practice contraception and sustainable lifestyles.

Slowly rebuilding a new society after a major disaster is the primary theme of what many critics consider one of the best science fiction novels of all time, George R. Stewart's *Earth Abides* (1949). Typically the survivors face adversity from a variety of sources, natural and human. Stewart obviously influenced many authors, particularly Octavia Butler. Similar books have been written by Russell Hill (*Cold Creek Cash Store*, 1986, republished as *The Edge of the Earth*, 1992), Gary Knighton (*Isles of Omega*, 1993), James Howard Kunstler (*World Made by Hand*, 2008), Cormac McCarthy (*The Road*, 2006), Pat Murphy (*The City, Not Long After*, 1989), David R. Palmer (*Emergence*, 1990), Michaela Roessner (*Vanishing Point*, 1993), Whitley Strieber and James W. Kunetka (*Warday and the Journey Onward*, 1984), and Susan B. Weston (*Children of the Light*, 1987).

M. K. Wren plays a literary variation on this theme in *A Gift upon the Shore* (1990). After nuclear war and nuclear winter have ravaged the Pacific Northwest, violence and looting proliferate. Mary Hope and Rachel try to preserve civilization by saving the last library, but the fanatical Flock believes all books should be destroyed. Elaine Perry offers another variation. In *Another Present Era* (1990), a young mulatta architect in New York attempts to help people physically and psychically recover from environmentally induced disasters by creating natural, healing designs.

Some disaster novels are also delightful fantasies. In Michael Bishop's *Count Geiger's Blues* (1992), after swimming in a pond contaminated with radioactive waste, snob Xavier Thaxton goes through many changes culminating in his transformation to Count Geiger, the personification of a cartoon superhero he previously scorned. In Bishop's *Unicorn Mountain* (1988), a rancher, an AIDS sufferer, and two Ute Indians have their lives transformed by a band of unicorns, but then must save the magical beasts from a mysterious disease. Neil Gaiman and Terry Pratchett's *Good Omens: The Nice and Accurate Prophecies of Agnes Nutter, Witch* (1990) recounts the tale of a totally reliable witch who has predicted that the environmental Armageddon will occur next Saturday. The Antichrist is an otherwise normal twelve-year-old boy who loves the earth and his dog, who unfortunately happens to be a hellhound. In Gaiman's *American Gods* (2001), ancient gods such as Odin and Thor struggle for survival in a trendy, superficial, culturally and environmentally degraded world against such modern geek "gods" as Media and Internet.

There's a whole lotta shakin' goin' on in Jonathan Franzen's *Strong Motion* (1992). A seismologist discovers that destructive earthquakes were caused by a chemical company's secret dumping of wastes into a deep well. Other earthquake books include Sarah Andrews's mystery *Fault Line* (2002), Ken Follett's *The Hammer of Eden* (1998), James D. Houston's *Continental Drift* (1978), Crawford Kilian's *Ice Quake* (1979), Warren Norwood's *Shudderchild* (1987), and Kate Wheeler's *When Mountains Walked* (2000).

The consequences of nuclear weapons, nuclear power, or the industrial use of radiation are considered in *An Atomic Romance* by Bobbie Ann Mason (2005), *Children of Darkness and Light* by Nicholas Mosley (1997), *Fall-out* by Gudrun Pausewang (1997), *The Prometheus Crisis* by Thomas N. Scortia and Frank M. Robinson (1975), *Gila!* by Les Simons (1981), *Stallion Gate* by Martin Cruz Smith (1986), *A Drink Called Paradise* by Terese Svoboda (1999), *The China Syndrome* by Burton Wohl (1979), and *Tide: A Novel of Catastrophe* by Hugh Zachary (1974).

Political ecofiction, in which conflicts over resources or military adventurism have negative environmental consequences, best describes the work of Richard Moran (*Cold Sea Rising*, 1986; *Dallas Down,* 1987; *The Empire of Ice,* 1994; *Earth Winter,* 1995). Similar books include *Thunder of Erebus* by Payne Harrison (1991), *Operation Malacca* by Joe Poyer (1968), and *Blizzard* by George Stone (1977). In Scott R. Sanders's *Terrarium* (1985), almost all of humanity has escaped ecological disasters by inhabiting a global system of totally enclosed cities and travel tubes. A small group of dissidents returns to the wilderness, where they discover the surprising origins and purpose of the Enclosure. In *Fatal Exposure* (1991) by Michael Tobias, a hole in the ozone layer opens over the Arctic and shifts southward, bringing blinding sun, deadly heat, and murderous swarms of insects.

Arthur Herzog writes about a plethora of problems: earthquakes in *Earth-sound* (1975), global warming in *Heat* (1976), killer bees in *The Swarm* (1974), the only animal besides man who will kill for revenge in *Orca* (1976), pandemic brain viruses in *IQ 83* (1977), and epidemics caused by fad diets and supplements in *The Craving* (1982). Crawford Kilian covers even more ravaged ground than Herzog in just one novel, *Tsunami* (1983). Solar flares, loss of earth's electromagnetic field, ozone depletion, cancer from ultraviolet rays, Antarctic earthquakes, rising sea levels, massive tidal waves, social collapse, and that's just the first fifty pages. Earth strikes back from pollution and other abuse with a variety of meteorological disasters in James Herbert's *Portent* (1996).

Bodies from the Bhopal chemical cloud appear on a Maine beach, a customer receives an electric bill surcharge for dead Nicaraguans, and various other surreal events occur in thirteen stories that make powerful connections between First World consumption and Third World poverty, dehumanization, environmental ruin, and war in Robert Nichols's *In the Air* (1991). In Nichols's *From the Steam Room: A Comic Fiction* (1993), after New York's infrastructure has collapsed, race and class relations have reached an all-time low, the noxious environment becomes a constant threat, and major financiers make a futile attempt to rescue the city.

Beware of corporate greed. In Paul Preuss's *Core* (1993), a shift in the earth's magnetic field produces fatal levels of ozone depletion. A geologist drills a tube to the center of the earth to gain knowledge to prevent further shifting, but a corporation has stolen his new technology for its own gain. The EPA tries to retroactively fine Anthill Chemicals $25 million for dumping toxic waste in L. M. Shakespeare's *Poisoning the Angels* (1993). Anthill uses a forged form to make Lloyd's of London liable; Lloyd's investigates; and a string of double-crosses, blackmailing, beatings, and a murder occur. In Charles Baxter's *Shadow Play* (1993), a bureaucrat who allowed a chemical plant to open in his economically depressed town receives immediate payoff in the Faustian bargain when his cousin contracts terminal cancer working at the plant.

Planned utopias can go very wrong, as in *The Mosquito Coast* by Paul Theroux (1982). An outcast inventor moves his family to Central America to live a more natural life, but his attempts to introduce technology to the natives have disastrous consequences.

One of Don DeLillo's primary themes is the negative and dehumanizing effects of runaway technology on civilization and the individual. The *White Noise* (1986) of radio and television transmissions, microwaves, ultrasonic devices, and the babble of consumerism degrades the quality of life, but most people seem oblivious until an industrial accident releases a chemical cloud. In *Underworld* (1997), the fallout from two "shots heard round the world" on October 3, 1951—Bobby Thompson's classic home run and a Soviet nuclear weapons test—drifts across the physical, psychological, and cultural landscape for fifty years.

In Lewis Gannett's *Magazine Beach* (1996), by 2002 the United States has been attacked by terrorists and is increasingly controlled by the Federal Anti-Terror Bureau (FATBOY), which views environmental activists or any other dissenters as terrorists. One reviewer found the novel absurd at the time, claiming that such events could not happen for sixty years, but the parallels between the fictional FATBOY and the very real Office of Homeland Security and the Patriot Act are truly chilling.

4

Native American and
Canadian Ecofiction

N ative Americans have a rich, ancient oral tradition. Storytelling has been revived in recent decades, there are hundreds of good to outstanding poets, and the number of fine fiction writers continues to grow. Since Indian cosmology includes humanity as part and parcel of nature, it is hardly surprising that much Native fiction is ecofiction. Paula Gunn Allen explains it well: "Essentially, Indians don't think the way non-Indians do: this distinction is partly one of tribal consciousness as opposed to the consciousness of urbanized, industrial cultures, but it is also a distinction between new world and old world thought, between systems based on wholeness and those based on division and separation. One might argue that the distinction is one of inclusiveness and exclusiveness, and in certain ways this is a convenient generalization. One might also suggest that gynarchical systems (systems heavily influenced by the presence of powerful female god-figures and culture-bearers and engenderers) differ in fundamental ways from patriarchal systems."[1] William Brandon has described that difference as being "between a New World god who is hungry and an Old World god who is angry."[2] Please note, however, that there are distinct differences between various Native American cultures, and both commonalities and differences are reflected in the fictional mirror.

Also consider that the post-Columbian history of Native Americans is a continual series of massacres, outrages, deceptions, and economic and environmental exploitation. First, their numbers were decimated by disease and weapons as they were removed from the best lands they had inhabited. Then other land was taken for mining (primarily gold, copper, and coal and, later, uranium) or flooded for electrical power generation. Finally, some of their land became toxic or nuclear waste dumps, as has been the case with some Mexican-American and African-American communities in a phenomenon known as environmental racism. The desecration and potential restoration of native lands and cultures is at the heart of the Native American experience and related literature.

Anthologies of Native American literature typically include a wide variety of literary forms. They include *Spider Woman's Granddaughters* (Paula Gunn Allen, ed., 1989), *A Gathering of Spirit* (Beth Brant, ed., 1988), *Hozho: Walking in Beauty: Native American Stories of Inspiration, Humor, and Life* (Paula Gunn Allen and Carolyn Dunn Anderson, eds., 2001), *All My Relations* (Thomas King, ed., 1992), *Dancing on the Rim of the World* (Andrea Lerner, ed., 1990), *The Sound of Rattles and Clappers* (Greg Sarris, ed., 1994), *Earth Song, Sky Spirit* (Clifford Trafzer, ed., 1993), *The Lightning Within* (Alan Velie, ed., 1991), *Sovereign Bones* (2 vols., Eric Gansworth, ed., 2007), and *Genocide of the Mind* (Marijo Moore, ed., 2003), and *Song of the Turtle* (Paula Gunn Allen, ed., 1996). The selections in *Family of Earth and Sky: Indigenous Tales of Nature from Around the World* (John Elder and Hertha Dawn Wong, eds., 1994) demonstrate that certain themes, images, and values are very common among indigenous peoples, though the details vary greatly.

The first shoots of Native American fiction emerged one hundred and fifty years ago, but the form did not truly flourish until the late 1960s. For a good anthology of early Native American fiction covering the years 1881–1936, see *The Singing Spirit* (Bernd Peyer, ed., 1989). John Rollin Ridge is credited with the first American Indian novel, *The Life and Adventures of Joaquin Murrieta* (1854). S. Alice Callahan wrote the first novel by a Native American woman, *Wynema: A Child of the Forest* (1891), also a proto-ecofeminist novel. Simon Pokagon's *Ogimäwkwe Mitigwäki, Queen of the Woods* was published in 1899.

The slightly fictionalized *Old Indian Legends* of Lakota Zitkala-Sa appeared in 1901, while Mohawk poet and short-story writer E. Pauline Johnson had three volumes of stories published a decade later. Despite the existence of these books, some scholars still mistakenly trace the inception of the Native American novel to Mourning Dove, whose 1927 novel *Cogewea, the Half-Blood* is controversial since it appears to have been heavily revised by her white editor, Lucullus Virgil McWhorter. Mourning Dove's less controversial *Coyote Stories* (1933) preserves existing Okanogan Indian legends while transforming them into poetic prose.

John Joseph Mathews and Luther Standing Bear also started publishing in the late 1920s and 1930s. Mathews, D'Arcy McNickle, John Oskison, and Todd Downing kept the tradition alive for a few decades before a re-emergence of Native identity in the 1960s and early 1970s. *Winter Count* (1967) by Dallas Chief Eagle offered an alternative view of Custer's campaign and the Ghost Dance era.

N. Scott Momaday's Pulitzer Prize-winning *House Made of Dawn* (1968) is widely considered to be the start of a "Native American Renaissance" since its critical and popular success made it "possible that a Native-American writer would be accepted by the literary establishment."[3]

The 1960s was a time of great social and political struggle, comprising the civil rights movement, opposition to the war in Southeast Asia, feminism, multiculturalism, greater interest in Native American culture in both the white and Indian populations, and the American Indian Movement. The takeover of Alcatraz Island in 1971 inspired a wide range of Native writers, musicians, artists, and activists. Nasnaga's only novel, *Indians' Summer* (1975), injects the Alcatraz spirit into a revolutionary alternative bicentennial. Colville Chief George Pierre protests the termination of Indian tribes and Native rights in *Autumn's Bounty* (1972). Native Canadian novelists also began to flourish in the 1970s, beginning with Markoosie's Inuit classic *Harpoon of the Hunter* (1971) and *Bearwalk* (1977) by Lynn Sallot and Tom Peltier.

James Welch, Leslie Marmon Silko, Louise Erdrich, Louis Owens, Dana Stabenow, and Linda Hogan, all winners of multiple major literary awards, have been critically acclaimed as among the finest authors of contemporary American literature. Their work continues to be highly praised and very popular.

Blackfoot James Welch made an immediate mark on contemporary literature with his first novel, *Winter in the Blood* (1974). Welch paints a positive picture of the re-emergence of tribal values on the Fort Belknap Reservation, a sharp contrast to the alcoholism, violence, and hopelessness of Indian life in surrounding towns. *Fools Crow* (1986) is a vivid, but unromanticized depiction of the nomadic life of the Blackfoot people in the nineteenth century. It considers the centrality of the buffalo and other animals to the tribe's physical and spiritual life and includes a lively debate on how to deal with the threat of Manifest Destiny. Welch's *The Indian Lawyer* (1990) and *The Heartsong of Charging Elk* (2000) are also widely critically acclaimed.

Leslie Marmon Silko's first story to appear in a national publication, "The Man to Send Rain Clouds" (1967), addresses the spiritual and practical relations between Laguna and white culture. It became the title story of the groundbreaking collection, *The Man to Send Rain Clouds: Contemporary Stories by American Indians* (1974). Silko is clearly the featured author, with seven stories, including her variation on the Yellow Woman legend. In Silko's first novel, *Ceremony* (1977), a half-breed Laguna named Tayo returns from World War II traumatized and chronically nauseous after his stepbrother Rocky dies in his arms. His elder relatives reconnect him with nature, and he experiences a traditional healing. At first glance, *Storyteller* (1981) appears to be a mere pastiche of poems, stories, legends, anecdotes, and photographs, but Silko weaves these forms together seamlessly to tell the larger story of her family and her people. The sprawling *Almanac of the Dead* (1991) takes place on three continents over five hundred years. The two primary themes are prophecies: the inevitable self-destruction of cultures and technologies centered on death, and the subsequent healing of the land as it is reinhabited by indigenous peoples and others who value it. *Gardens in the Dunes* (1999) is similarly immersed in myth and magic, as many connections are made between Celtic, Roman, and Native American spirituality through gardens, sculptures, dreams, and visions.

Chippewa/German author Louise Erdrich's novels *Love Medicine* (1984, expanded ed. 1993), *The Beet Queen* (1986), *Tracks* (1988), *The Bingo Palace* (1994), *Tales of Burning Love* (1996), *Four Souls* (2004), and *The Painted Drum* (2005) constitute a nonlinear, metafictional, sometimes magic realistic account of the complex relations between three families of German, Cree, Métis (mixed-blood), and Ojibwe heritage. These highly personal histories of cultural, political, spiritual, and environmental change are also extremely entertaining romps, enlivened by eroticism, quirky characters, a full range of emotions, humor, varied dialogue, and Erdrich's poetic narrative voice. *The Last Report on the Miracles at Little No Horse* (2001) is something of a sequel to the *Love Medicine* books, with the same setting and some of the same characters. *The Antelope Wife* (1998) is a more mystical tale of culture clash and accommodation. *A Plague of Doves* (2008), portraying the effect of a massacre over several generations, is of greater social than ecocritical interest. Many of Erdrich's novels, especially *Love Medicine,* have strong erotic and romantic elements. (For romance authors influenced by Native cosmology, see chap. 6.) *The Red Convertible* (2009) is a collection of her short stories.

Erdrich and her then-husband, Michael Dorris, collaborated to produce *The Crown of Columbus* (1991), which utilizes the anniversary of Columbus's "discovery" of America as a device to explore the meaning for and effects of that voyage on people of Native American and European descent then and now. Dorris is best known for *A Yellow Raft in Blue Water* (1987), the story of a mixed-race Native African-American teen.

Louis Owens was a mixed-blood Choctaw-Cherokee-Cajun-Irish author whose characters were sometimes semiautobiographical. *Wolfsong* (1991) is set in a declining logging area in the North Cascades where the road to a proposed open pit mine is being built through a wilderness area. *The Sharpest Sight* (1992) is required to perceive and solve the crises plaguing Cole McCurtain and his murdered brother, Attis. Humans and various animal and spiritual beings interact to shape the story, solve the crime, and finally inter Attis's bones, thus returning the world to its natural balance. Two decades later Cole is a professor at the University of California–Santa Cruz in *Bone Game* (1994). Again, mundane reality, ancient and modern stories, and the dream world intersect as Cole is drawn into the investigation of a series of grisly murders connected to uranium mines and nuclear test sites. When cousins Billy Keene and Will Striker recover nearly a million dollars of drug money from Arturo Cruz, impaled on a juniper, they enter not only a web of earthly crime, but the haunted spiritual realm of *Nightland* (1996). In *Dark River* (1999) Ranger Jake Nashoba (Choctaw for "wolf") receives powerful dreams from elderly relatives. Owens was also notable for his critical and autobiographical work on Native American literature and the mixed-blood experience in such works as *Other Destinies, Mixedblood Messages,* and *I Hear the Train.*

Dana Stabenow's series of thirteen novels featuring Aleut private investigator Kate Shugak are imbued with vivid nature writing, insights into Aleut and Inuit cosmology and life, and impassioned ecodefense. Shugak has "retired" to the backcountry after horrific experiences as an assistant district attorney in Anchorage, but her investigative and wilderness survival skills are constantly in demand. In *A Cold Day for Murder* (1992) Shugak's search for a congressman's son lost in the wilderness also uncovers conflicts between Aleut and white values and pipeline workers desecrating the environment. *Dead in the Water* (1993) finds Shugak seeking two men who mysteriously disappeared from a fishing boat and discovering a deeper appreciation of her own ancestral lore as revealed by two aged basket makers. In *A Cold-Blooded Business* (1994) Kate pursues drug dealers and murderers in oil camps and the wilderness, linking big oil and other industries with social problems such as the drug trade and an increase in both petty and grand criminal activity. Stabenow contrasts the macho blood lust and waste of big game trophy hunting and fishing versus respectfully hunting or fishing for food in *Killing Grounds* (1998), *Hunter's Moon* (1999), and *Midnight Come Again* (2000). Other novels in the series focus on mushroom picking and other traditional native sustenance activities, tribal and local politics, and the environmental excesses of logging, mining, and oil production. *The Singing of the Dead* (2001) seamlessly interweaves the mystery, political, environmental, and historical novel genres.

In addition to Owens and Stabenow, other Native Americans are notable mystery writers. Peter Bowen (who also writes as Coyote Jack) has a Native American protagonist, Gabriel Du Pré, whose work as a cattle brand inspector frequently leads to the scene of a crime. *Wolf, No Wolf* (1996), about a near range war between ranchers and radical environmentalists, and *The Stick Game* (2000), about toxic pollution from a gold mine, are of particular ecocritical interest. Charlie Moon, a Ute reservation policeman, is James D. Doss's protagonist. Moon is assisted by his Aunt Daisy's visions and prophecies. In *The Shaman Sings* (1994), when a grad student makes a breakthrough in superconductivity, she is murdered. In *The Shaman Laughs* (1995) Charlie and Daisy try to find a connection between the mutilation of bulls and the murder of a businessman who had advocated storing nuclear waste in a sacred canyon. (The real mystery is why the first two books in the series combine Ute Indian lore and environmental crime solving so successfully while the following eight are more standard murder mysteries lacking ecological elements.) Wayne Johnson's *The Snake Game* (1990) portrays murder, genocide, and environmental decay on an Ojibwa reservation. His poignant *Don't Think Twice* (1999) concerns Native American lodge owner Paul Two Persons's efforts to preserve his land, marriage, dignity, and sanity against a road project that would cut his land in half. In the sequel, *Six Crooked Highways* (2000), he faces government-tribal-developer duplicity and personal danger when a body appears in the water after he opposes the road and he is named the prime suspect. *The Devil You Know* (2004), a thriller involving canoeing, has been favorably compared to James Dickey's *Deliverance*.[4] In Stan Jones's *White Sky, Black Ice* (1999) Inupiat state trooper Nathan Active discovers that two suspicious "suicides" can be traced to an international copper mining consortium. *The Bird Is Gone: A Manifesto* (2003) by Blackfoot author Stephen Graham Jones combines a murder mystery, wry surreal humor, and the "manifesto" to restore all indigenous plants and animals to the Great Plains, Indians included.

Linda Hogan is a Chickasaw poet, essayist, and the author of superb novels such as the National Book Award-winning *Mean Spirit* (1990), *Solar Storms* (1995), and *Power* (1998). In *Power,* a teenage girl sees a tribal elder kill a panther, which is both a sacred animal to the Taiga people and an endangered species. The elder's arrest creates a deep division in the community and troubles the girl, whose psychic quest leads her to realize that the ailing panther was killed to regenerate the tribe and the spirit of the earth itself.

Three contemporary Native Canadian authors—Jeannette Armstrong, Thomas King, and Joseph Bruchac—have made major contributions, not just as authors, but as critics, editors, interpreters, and promoters of Native Canadian literature, much as Louis Owens did for Native American and mixed-blood fiction.

Armstrong, the grandniece of the legendary Mourning Dove, is the author of two fine juvenile books (*Enwhisteetkwa: Walk on Water*, 1982; *Neekna and Chemai*, 1984) and two excellent novels (*Slash*, 1985; *Whispering in Shadows*, 2000), and is the editor/compiler of a collection of literary criticism, *Looking at the Words of Our People: An Anthology of First Nation Literary Criticism* (1993).

Thomas King is even more significant as a writer and critic. He is a frequent contributor to critical and reference works, and has edited both a collection of criticism (*The Native in Literature: Canadian and Comparative Perspectives*, 1987) and a literary anthology (*All My Relations: An Anthology of Contemporary Canadian Native Fiction*, 1990). His fiction blends magic realism, satire, raucous humor, and nature writing (*Medicine River*, 1990; *Green Grass, Running Water*, 1993; *One Good Story, That One*, 1993; *Coyote Sings to the Moon*, 1998; *Truth & Bright Water*, 1999; *A Short History of Indians in Canada: Stories*, 2006; and, writing as Hartley GoodWeather, *DreadfulWater Shows Up*, 2002; *The Red Power Murders*, 2006). In *Green Grass, Running Water*, four seemingly immortal Indians escape from a mental hospital to recruit modern Indians, Sun Dancers, and Coyote to stop the building of a dam that will flood the grass and to restore harmony to the land.

Joseph Bruchac's work is not as well known as King's, and he is only secondarily a fiction writer, but is a prolific poet, storyteller, critic, promoter, and editor. He has written over eighty books, including several for children and young adults. *Dawn Land* (1993) is an imaginative depiction of life among the Abenaki Indians in Paleolithic times. Young Hunter makes a quest to save his people from a race of huge cannibals and return their world into balance. *Dawn Land* and its sequels *Long River* (1995) and *The Waters Between* (1998) skillfully interweave Abenaki legends with exciting adventure stores, laying their ecological and philosophical messages between the lines.

Other significant Native North American authors include Gerald Vizenor (*Darkness in Saint Louis Bearheart*, 1978); Paula Gunn Allen (*The Woman Who Owned the Shadows*, 1983); Bill Reid and Robert Bringhurst (*Raven Steals the Light*, 1984); Janet Campbell Hale (*The Jailing of Cecilia Capture*, 1985); Ruby Slipperjack (*Honour the Sun*, 1987); Harry Robinson (*Write It on Your Heart*, 1989); Jordan Wheeler (*Brothers in Arms*, 1989); Elizabeth Cook-Lynn (*From the River's Edge*, 1991); Beth Brant (*Food and Spirits*, 1991); Sherman Alexie (*The Lone Ranger and Tonto Fistfight in Heaven*, 1993); Susan Power (*The Grass Dancer*, 1994); Diane Glancy (*Pushing the Bear*, 1996); Naomi Stokes (*The Tree People*, 1995); Eden Robinson (*Traplines*, 1996); Albertine Strong (*Deluge*, 1997); Irwin Morris (*From the Glittering World*, 1997); Greg Sarris (*Watermelon Nights*, 1998); Ray A. Young Bear (*Remnants of First Earth*, 1998); Tomson Highway (*Kiss of the Fur Queen*, 1998); Maurice Kenny (*Tortured Skins*, 1999); Simon J. Ortiz (*Men on the Moon*, 1999); Anita Endrezze (*Throwing Fire at the Sun, Water at the Moon*, 2000); Geary Hobson (*The Last of the Ofos*, 2000); Connie May Fowler (*Remembering Blue*, 2000); William S. Penn (*Killing Time with Strangers*, 2000); William Sanders (*The Ballad of Billy Badass & the Rose of Turkestan*, 2001); and Bernard Assiniwi (*The Beothuk Saga*, 2002). The fact that half of these writers are women demonstrates the important place that women hold in traditional and contemporary Native American life and art, rebutting the offensive "squaw" stereotype. Canadian author Lee Maracle (*Ravensong*, 1993) is an excellent example of a Native ecofeminist. (Only one work per author is mentioned here. See the bibliography for their other fiction.)

Many white writers present stereotypical images and a one-sided view of Manifest Destiny when writing about the Indian experience. Others romanticize the "noble savage." Historically, a small minority—for example, Mary Austin, Frank Waters, William Eastlake, Harvey Fergusson, Oliver LaFarge, Charles Longstreth McNichols, Don Berry, A. B. Guthrie, John G. Neihardt, and Frederick Manfred—paint a more thoughtful picture of both settlers and indigenes. Waters's entire body of work can be viewed as an attempt to reconcile and combine the best of industrial and indigenous cosmology. Anne Cameron (aka Cam Hubert) grew up among many Indians on Vancouver

Island and became fascinated with their culture at an early age. Her *Daughters of Copper Women* (1980) and *Tales of the Cairds* (1989) are fascinating adaptations of legends. In Margaret Craven's *I Heard the Owl Call My Name* (1973), an Episcopal priest sent to British Columbia ends up learning from the people he was supposed to convert.

Good examples of relatively recent books by white authors influenced by Native values include Craig Lesley's *Winterkill* (1984); Will Weaver's *Red Earth, White Earth* (1986); M. T. Kelly's *A Dream Like Mine* (1987); Patrick D. Smith's *Forever Island; and, Allapattah* (1987); Paul West's *The Place in Flowers Where Pollen Rests* (1988); William T. Vollmann's Seven Dreams series (1990— in progress); Ardath Mayhar's *People of the Mesa* (1992); Jack Cady's *Inagehi* (1994); Arnold Krupat's *Woodsmen, or Thoreau and the Indians* (1994); Jesse Browner's *Turnaway* (1996); James A. Houston's *Confessions of an Igloo Dweller* (1995); Colin Kersey's *Soul Catcher* (1995); David London's *Sun Dancer* (1996); Page Lambert's *Shifting Stars* (1997); Don Coldsmith's *Tallgrass* (1997); Pamela Jekel's *River Without End* (1997); Mark T. Sullivan's *Ghost Dance* (1999); Kimberly Kafka's *True North* (2000); and John Hockenberry's *A River Out of Eden* (2001); and David Fuller Cook's *Reservation Nation* (2007). See the bibliography for more works by these authors. For a very different portrayal of Thoreau, see John Pipkin's *Woodsburner* (2009).

5

Ecofiction from All Around the World

Since the earth's current ecological crisis knows no boundaries, it is hardly surprising to find ecofiction being written and read almost everywhere. Before embarking upon this study, I believed that contemporary ecofiction was primarily a product of the American West in the 1970s. I still maintain that that time and place can be considered the golden decade of ecofiction, but having been exposed to such a wide variety of relevant, first-rate work in my armchair travels, I now appreciate just how wide the world of ecofiction truly is and reject my earlier unintentional provincialism.

This chapter is something of a literary expedition traversing a vast body of work, beginning closest geographically and culturally to the United States in Canada and then coming full circle in another similar culture, Australia, with interesting stops all along the way. In some locales, such as eastern Europe, South America, Asia, and the Arab world, it is difficult to know whether the paucity of work I have identified is primarily due to a lack of material or to my own relative ignorance of their languages, literatures, and cultures. There are dozens of excellent green authors from Africa, Asia, and South America whose work has been only partially translated or has not been translated into English at all. This could potentially become a scholarly cottage industry.

For fiction by Native Canadians, see chapter 4.

Ernest Thompson Seton was a naturalist and prolific author/illustrator of animal books appropriate for young adults and adults. He flourished throughout the first half of the twentieth century. Seton expressed lifelong respect for nature and for Native North Americans, because he believed them to have the closest connection with the natural world. For the best introduction to his work, see *Selected Stories of Ernest Thompson Seton* (1977) and *The Best of Ernest Thompson Seton* (1974). The latter was edited by Richard Adams (author of *Watership Down*), who was deeply influenced by Seton.

Martha Ostenso (*Wild Geese*, 1925; *The Waters Under the Earth*, 1930) was an important proto-ecofeminist whose works feature women struggling against patriarchy and environmental ruin.

Some critics consider Sheila Watson's *The Double Hook* (1959) to be the first great modern Canadian novel. After domineering Mrs. Potter is killed by her son, her neighbors see her ghostly image fishing in her favorite stream. Later, when a barren young woman commits suicide by burning down the Potter house, Mrs. Potter's ghost is released to become a spirit of natural rebirth.

The pastoral is a popular form of Canadian fiction. Ernest Buckler wrote two novels about rural Nova Scotia, *The Mountain and the Valley* (1952) and *The Cruelest Month* (1963). Alistair MacLeod celebrates rural Cape Breton in three short-story collections—*The Lost Salt Gift of Blood* (1976), *As Birds Bring Forth the Sun and Other Stories* (1986), and *Island* (2000). New Brunswick writer David Adams Richards's ten novels are part pastoral, but some also depict environmental defense. In *Mercy Among the Children* (2001), one brave man confronts industry and government over carcinogenic herbicides.

Farley Mowat is best known as an author of children's and young adult books and nonfiction, such as *Never Cry Wolf* (1963), but he also wrote *The Snow Walker* (1975), a short-story collection for adults. His most recent book, *The Farfarers Before the Norse* (2000), melds popular history with ecofiction.

Margaret Atwood is widely considered to be Canada's finest author and most significant feminist scholar. She has the highest score in the prestigious

Award Annals list of 415 award-winning authors. Although almost all of her voluminous prose and poetry is from an ecofeminist perspective, the short-story collection *Wilderness Tips* (1991) and four novels are particularly steeped in ecological concerns: *The Edible Woman* (1970), *Surfacing* (1972), *The Hand-maid's Tale* (1985), and *Oryx and Crake* (2003). In *Surfacing,* a young artist and three of her friends who want to "play back to nature" search for her father in the Canadian backwoods, where she experiences a deepening sense of foreboding about her father and her past. The two latter novels explore such issues as abortion, cloning, and genetic engineering.

Martha Ostenso influenced Margaret Laurence, who wrote several novels featuring strong women in rural Canada. *The Diviners* (1974) focuses on an ecophilosophical dowser.

The protagonist of ecofeminist Marian Engel's *Bear* (1976) slowly develops a love relationship with a semidomesticated bear in a fable about women and nature.

In John Keeble's *Yellowfish* (1981), "The mountains, the glaciers, the forests, the deserts and lush orchards and fields of the Northwest, its various winds and its weathers, become as palpable as these fateful people who travel through it" (book jacket). *Broken Ground* (1987) similarly uses the land as a metaphor for the spiritual struggles of its protagonist. The loosely connected short stories in *Nocturnal America* (2006) explore country life in the Pacific Northwest.

Current Canadian ecofiction is highly varied in style and subject matter. M. T. Kelly combines Celtic lyricism, love and concern for the natural world, and respect for Native cultures in books such as *The Ruined Season* (1982), *A Dream Like Mine* (1987), *Breath Dances Between Them: Stories* (1991), and *Out of the Whirlwind* (1995). Sharon Butala's personal experience of moving to the prairies and feeling overwhelmed before slowly integrating herself with the landscape and way of life is reflected in all her novels and short stories, particularly in *Queen of the Headaches* (1985) and *Fever* (1990). Ann Love's *Grizzly Dance* (1994) explores the social and natural environment of the Canadian wilds. Timothy Findley's reframing of the Noah story, *Not Wanted on the Voyage* (1984), excoriates sexism, the failure to create a true conservationist ethic, and the threats of fundamentalism and creationism. Thomas Wharton blends fantasy and historical fiction in *Icefields* (1995) and *The Salamander* (2001). Mary Lawson's family saga *Crow Lake* (2002) is rich in zoological metaphors.

New Jersey transplant Lesley Choyce found fertile personal and literary ground in Nova Scotia, where he has had a unique career as one of Canada's finest fiction authors for children, young adults, and adults; an accomplished poet and nonfiction writer; an environmental activist; and the Canadian surfing champion. His most notable adult ecofiction includes *Downwind* (1984), *Coming Up for Air* (1988), *The Second Season of Jonas MacPherson* (1989), *The Republic of Nothing* (1994), and *Sea of Tranquility* (2003). *The Second Season of Jonas MacPherson* is a moving account of an elderly denizen of coastal Newfoundland as he reminisces about nature, the last Micmac Indians, and the joys and challenges of fishing.

CARIBBEAN

According to Seodial Deena, "Colonial and postcolonial writers have depicted the land and environment in a reverential, personified, and intimate manner. . . . This personification creates a rather complex and interesting mosaic relationship between the peoples and their landscapes."[1] Two of the most important green authors representing the Caribbean, Jean Rhys and Wilson Harris, were born there, migrated to England, but retained a strong sense of Caribbean places and peoples in their work. Rhys's *Wide Sargasso Sea* (1967) and Harris's *Guyana Quartet* (published separately 1960–63, boxed set 1985) achieved widespread critical and popular success. Harris drew upon West Indian/Amerindian culture in his work, as did Edgar Mittleholzer (*Latticed Echoes*, 1960), Michael Gilkes (*Couvade*, 1974), and Michael Anthony (*The Year in San Fernando*, 1965; *Green Days by the River*, 1967). Jamaica Kincaid (*At the Bottom of the River*, 1983; *Lucy*, 1990), who may be the best-known Caribbean writer to American readers, was born in Antigua, but continued to write about her homeland after moving to New York. Her work is steeped in botanic lore and makes a strong connection between people, gardening, and wild places.

Cuban author Mayra Montero's *In the Palm of Darkness* (1995, trans. 1997) takes place in Haiti where an American herpetologist is searching for the nearly extinct blood frog. Voodoo and violence ensue.

CENTRAL AND SOUTH AMERICA

The ecological devastation of the Amazon can be traced in part to escapist romantic literature such as Arthur Conan Doyle's *The Lost World* (1912), in which the wild jungle must be tamed. W. H. Hudson's earlier *Purple Land* (1885) and *Green Mansions* (1904) offer a more sympathetic view of the land and the native culture.

Venezuelan Romulo Gallegos is a transitional figure from these books to later, more environmentally conscious literature. The titular heroine of *Doña Bárbara* (1931) rises from being a river boat helper to becoming a head of an empire of estates. *Cainama* (1935) is a rain forest story pitting civilization against nature. Ecuadorian Jorge Isaacs's *Maria: A South American Romance* (1890) and Peruvian Ventura García Calderón's *The White Llama* (1924) offer appreciative but overly romanticized views of both natives and settlers.

All of these, however, were preceded by Ecuadorian Juan León Mera's *Cumandá* (1879), which is both a romance about a forbidden love between a European and an Indian and a protest of the maltreatment of the Indians by ranchers. A similarly activist, environmentally conscious tone can be found in the works of Argentina's Ricardo Güiraldes, Ecuador's Jorge Icaza, and Colombia's Jose Eustacio Rivera. Güiraldes's *Don Segundo Sombra* (1926) recounts the naturalistic lifestyle of the gauchos and the threats posed to it by fences and railroads. Eustacio Rivera's *The Vortex* (1924) and Icaza's *Huasipango: The Villagers* (1934) are protests against the exploitation of native workers and the destruction of the jungle. Demetrio Aguilera Malta tells a similar story in *Don Goyo* (1933), where he also introduces a very early magic realist element: screaming trees. One of his final novels, *Seven Serpents and Seven Moons* (1970), is full-blown magic realism featuring a talking crucifix and a possible son of the devil battling over an area's natural and cultural resources.

Sounding a contrary voice to those of conquest, resistance to both colonial and postcolonial destruction of the natural environment and indigenous peoples is at the heart of the work of several modern South American magic realist novelists, including Alejo Carpentier (*The Lost Steps,* 1956; *The Harp and the Shadow,* 1979), Gabriel García Márquez (*One Hundred Years of Solitude,* 1970), Marcio Souza (*The Emperor of the Amazon,* 1980; *Mad Maria,* 1985), Jorge Amado (*Tieta, the Goat Girl,* 1977), Mario Vargas Llosa (*The Green House,* 1961; *The Storyteller,* 1989; *Death in the Andes,* 1996), and Isabel Allende (*The House of the Spirits,* 1986; *Eva Luna,* 1989; *City of the Beasts,* 2002). Although written for older teens, *City of the Beasts* is also appropriate for adults. The modern magic realists were preceded by Uruguayan Horacio Quiroga, who published several volumes of short stories between 1917 and 1931, drawing on such diverse inspirations as Kipling and Poe to create gothic tales set in the jungle. The most available English translation in print is *The Decapitated Chicken and Other Stories* (2004).

Uruguayan author and activist Eduardo H. Galeano is best known for the trilogy *Memory of Fire,* which is a hybrid work of very short fiction, poetry, and nonfiction anecdotes. It consists of *Genesis, Faces and Masks,* and *Century of the Wind* (1985–88). His other translated green fiction includes *The Book of Embraces* (1991) and the autobiographical *Voices of Time: A Life in Stories* (2006). Galeano is also the fictional protagonist of David Romtvedt's magic realist novel *Crossing Wyoming* (1992).

Luis Sepúlveda is an environmental and human rights activist who has been both hailed and jailed in his homeland of Chile. In *The Old Man Who Read Love Stories* (1993), an old hunter who lives with the Shuar Indians is forced to join the hunt for an ocelot that has turned man killer after a prospector kills its cubs, in a cautionary tale of nature gone out of balance.

Argentine author Eduardo Sguigla's *Fordlandia* (2000) is based on Henry Ford's failed attempt to produce rubber in the Amazon. Sguigla skillfully uses this as the basis of a fable about the conflict between civilization and nature, development and preservation. At least four American authors have written highly imaginative novels about the Amazon region: Lloyd Hill (*The Village of Bom Jesus,* 1993), Karen Tei Yamashita (*Through the Arc of the Rainforest,* 1990; *Brazil-Maru,* 1992), Karen Heuler (*Journey to Bom Goody,* 2005), and Marie Arana (*Cellophane,* 2006).

Two powerful new Latina ecofeminist voices have emerged recently. In Nicaraguan Gioconda Belli's *The Inhabited Woman* (1994) a young architect becomes "inhabited" by the spirit of a native woman who had fought the Spanish conquest and is now an orange tree. Drinking the juice changes her consciousness and she becomes a revolutionary, rebelling against both political oppression and the destruction of nature. Belli's *Infinity in the Palm of Her Hand* (2009) is an ecofeminist version of Adam and Eve. Costa Rican Anacristina Rossi's *The Madwoman of Gandoca* (2006) is a semiautobiographical novel about efforts to uncover and protest the government's plans to develop a crucial wildlife refuge.

MEXICO

The mysterious B. Traven was probably German anarchist Ret Marut, who moved to Mexico as a young man and set most of his work there.[2] The character named Gerard Gales, who may be an idealized version of Traven himself, is the protagonist of *Das Tottenschiff* (1926; trans. *The Death Ship,* 1934); *Der Wobbly* (1926; trans. *The Cotton Pickers,* 1956); and *Die Brücke im Dschungel* (1929; trans. *The Bridge in the Jungle,* 1938). Although *The Treasure of the Sierra Madre* (1927) is his most famous work, *The Bridge in the Jungle* (1929) and the complex six-novel Jungle Cycle are equally compelling. *The Treasure of the Sierra Madre* contrasts the environmentally rapacious attitudes and behavior of Fred C. Dobbs with fellow miner Old Howard, who loves nature and insists that they restore the damage they have done. Dedicated to all living creatures, *The Bridge in the Jungle* is Traven's most lyrical and moving book and is arguably a precursor of deep ecology. Traven contrasts nature and primitive communalism with economic and cultural imperialism in a more implicit, less didactic fashion than in his later work. *Die Weisse Rose* (1929; *The White Rose,* 1979) details how an American oil company obtained the self-sufficient Hacienda Rosa Blanca through deceit, swindling, and murder.

Traven's next six novels, known collectively as the Jungle Cycle, the Caoba Cycle, the Mahogany Cycle, or the Revolution Cycle, take place during the final years of the Diaz dictatorship and the Mexican Revolution of 1910–11. The cycle consists of *Der Karren* (1930; *The Carreta,* 1935), *Riegerung* (1931;

Government, 1971), *Der Marsch ins Reich der Caoba* (1933; *March to the Monteria,* 1964), *Die Troza* (1936; *Trozas,* 1994), and *Ein General kommt aus dem Dschungel* (1940; *General from the Jungle,* 1954). *General* is the most exciting and amusing of Traven's adventures, as a ragtag band of rebels continually outwit and outfight the army and heavily armed landlords.

Homero Aridjis, one of Mexico's most outstanding poets, is also the author of *Persephone* (1967), a highly poetic and erotic adaptation about the classical goddess of fertility. In *1492: The Life and Times of Juan Cabezón of Castile* (1985) he depicts the horrors of the Inquisition and explores the Spanish mentality that made the devastation of the New World not only possible but inevitable. *La Leyenda de los Soles* (1993), based on a Nahua myth about the elements, has yet to be translated into English.

UNITED KINGDOM

There is a strong pastoral tradition in English literature, but, as with Romanticism, positions on humanity's relation to nature are mixed. Richard Kerridge notes that in the work of Thomas Hardy, for instance, "Nature is the unselfconscious, instinctual drive to pleasure, or it is a Darwinian economy of insensible, competitive struggle, or, drawing on both of these, it is a place of temporary refuge gained only through a deliberate relinquishing of the self-consciousness and wide perception that novelistic narrative cannot forsake for long."[3]

Some other British authors of the late nineteenth century, particularly Kipling, may praise nature, but their work is marred by the nature-culture dichotomy, imperialism, blatant racism, and sometimes a tendency to dominate nature along with people of other races and women. William Morris offered the antidote of a utopian socialist alternative in *News from Nowhere* (1890).

Some critics maintain that modern English ecofiction and green science fiction began in 1896 with the publication of H. G. Wells's *The Island of Dr. Moreau.* When the demented doctor uses vivisection to create half-human animals, they rebel. While several of Wells's later novels are, among other things, polemics against the misapplication of technology, none is primarily ecofictional. *Dr. Moreau* was preceded, however, by *After London, or, Wild England* (1885) by Richard Jefferies, which describes what England would be like if a cataclysm returned it to a wild state. Jefferies was a prolific pastoralist who broke away from the constraints of his typical style to write this unusual disaster novel-jeremiad-pastoral.

Kenneth Grahame melded environmental defense with the British pastoral in *The Wind in the Willows* (1908). On one level it's an engaging animal story for children, but on another it is an angry analysis of the despoiling of the British countryside and rural life through industrialism.

John Cowper Powys incorporated Celtic lore, Romanticism, human romance, the romantic power of nature, and, in the case of *A Glastonbury Romance* (1933), the Grail legend in his pastorals.

D. H. Lawrence was a revolutionary figure in many ways: radical ruralist, blue-collar socialist, bohemian, rebel against sexual and moral codes, and experimental prose stylist. To Lawrence, nature was not something to be quietly contemplated, but a moral touchstone and an integral part of an active life. Many of his novels take place in the English countryside and concern themselves with the issues of male-female relationships and dehumanizing aspects of civilization, and the concept of humans as animals intrinsic to the natural world (*The White Peacock*, 1911; *The Rainbow*, 1915; *Women in Love*, 1921; *Lady Chatterley's Lover*, 1928). *Kangaroo* (1923) found inspiration in Australian Aboriginal cosmology, and *The Plumed Serpent* (1926) in Mexican Indian culture. Lawrence's philosophy clearly influenced several Scottish novelists, primarily his friend and biographer Catherine Carswell (*Open the Door!* 1920), but also Lewis Grassic Gibbon (*A Scots Quair*, 1934), Willa Muir (*Imagined Corners*, 1931), and Nan Shepherd (*The Quarry Wood*, 1928).

A related radical perspective was provided by some of Lawrence's female contemporaries, who made a strong connection between women and nature. Mary Webb (*Gone to Earth*, 1917; *Precious Bane*, 1924), Stella Gibbons (*Cold Comfort Farm*, 1932), and particularly Virginia Woolf (*To the Lighthouse*, 1927; *The Waves*, 1931) can all be considered proto-ecofeminist authors.

A new type of pastoralism arose in Wales. Linden Peach observes that "often where the pastoral approach is reclaimed, it is altered and recontextualized by the impact of industrialization, not only on the landscape, but on the way nature itself is mediated."[4] Such literary reclamation can be found in the work of Rhys Davies (*A Time to Laugh*, 1937), Jack Jones (*Rhondda Roundabout*, 1934), Gwynn Jones (*Times Like These*, 1936) Lewis Jones (*Cwmardy*, 1937; *We Live*, 1939), and Richard Llewellyn (the extremely popular *How Green Was My Valley*, 1939).

Raymond Williams, a Welsh socialist who might be considered George Orwell's literary progeny, transgressed many boundaries, political, personal, and environmental, in a semiautobiographical trilogy: *Border Country*, 1960, *Second Generation*, 1964, and *The Fight for Manod*, 1979. His sweeping alternative history of Wales, *The People of the Black Mountains*, was published in two volumes (1979–80).

Another modern pastoralist, Scots poet George McKay Brown, reclaimed Scotland's natural and mythic past in novels such as *Vinland* (1992) and *Beside the Ocean of Time* (1994). His style and tone contrast sharply with Scottish novelist Muriel Gray, who has written an eco-horror story about Canadian Indians, *The Trickster* (1995).

Rabbits unite when their warren is threatened by developers in Richard Adams's brilliant fable *Watership Down* (1972), and its sequel, *Tales from Watership Down* (1996). *Shardik* (1974) is the name of a giant bear worshipped by the people in a unique novel that is both an ecological allegory and a meditation on spirituality. *The Plague Dogs* (1977) is a protest against animal experimentation and a consideration of ethical relations between humans and animals. Robert E. Lee's horse is the protagonist and narrator of *Traveler* (1998), which contrasts human cruelty and the balance of nature.

Recent British authors provide a very wide range of ethical positions on nature and on environmental action. They include Graham Swift (*Waterland*, 1983; *Ever After*, 1992), Jenny Diski (*Rainforest*, 1987), William Boyd (*Brazzaville Beach*, 1990), Julian Barnes (*A History of the World in 10 1/2 Chapters*, 1989; *England, England*, 1999), Richard Cox (*Eclipse*, 1996), and Nicholas Mosley (*Children of Darkness and Light*, 1997).

Will Self's novel *Great Apes* (1997) and the short stories in *Grey Area* (1995) are dark satires. In *Great Apes* he explores the human psyche and its relation to the rest of the world by transforming the characters into apes.

The work of A. S. Byatt is marked by subtle, complex spirituality and psychology: "these novels approach nature and environmentalism obliquely, with their main concern being to contextualize it, or explore its psychology."[5] The superb *Angels and Insects* (1992) and *Babel Tower* (1996) are perhaps her most overtly environmental work.

Ronald Wright employs H. G. Well's time machine to travel to twenty-sixth-century England, now a depopulated tropical isle in *A Scientific Romance* (1998).

Philip Kerr is best known for *Esau* (1997), a Yeti adventure that is also a consideration of evolution and human-animal relations. *The Grid* (1996) and *The Second Angel* (1999) are techno-thrillers set in a dystopian near future. They protest increasing mechanization and automation and the marginalization of genuine human experience.

Liz Jensen's *Egg Dancing* (1995) and *Ark Baby* (1998) focus on biotechnology and artificial insemination.

Gwen Moffat's many mysteries featuring Miss Melinda Pink (a justice of the peace, mountaineer, and novelist) explore the relationships between people and nature in the Scottish Highlands and the Rockies. *The Stone Hawk* (1989) and *The Raptor Zone* (1990) are recognized by critics as the best books in this series.

Irishman Christopher Nolan's *The Banyan Tree* (2000) is touching tale of a woman's attempts to continue living close to the earth and preserve traditional Celtic culture in changing times.

The legendary seal people known as selkies often swim ashore in Celtic-oriented fiction. *The Selkie* by Charles Sheffield and David Bischoff (1982) is an unusual melding of the horror and romance genres. In *The Nature of Water and Air* (2000), Regina McBride incorporates selkie mythology into family history. *The Selkie* (2003) by Scotswoman Melanie Jackson is part mystery, part romance, and part fantasy. Rosanne Alexander's *Selkie* (1991) combines fantasy, nature lore, and environmental action.

Jean Giono stands head and shoulders above almost all European nature novelists. Montserrat López Mújica considers him "one of the most important French authors of the XX century."[6] Giono's first novel, *Colline* (1929), became part of the Pan Trilogy, fusing Pagan spirituality and the modern pastoral. Although all of his many novels based in Provence are steeped in natural lore and spiritual awe, three stand out as magic realist masterpieces. *The Song of the World* (1934, trans. 1937) is a paean to the unity of all living and spiritual beings. In *Joy of Man's Desiring* (1937, trans. 1940), a simple, Christlike peasant and a seemingly radiant deer sanctify and transform the lives of all they touch. One of his final works, *The Man Who Planted Trees* (1954), is a fascinating pastiche: part biographical novel, part memoir of a man who restored the forests of southern France, and part practical guide to planting trees. This book and the movie adaptation inspired and influenced literally millions of environmentalists of all ages around the world.

Romain Gary was born in Lithuania as Romain Kacew, but he moved to France in his youth. The much acclaimed *The Roots of Heaven* (1956, trans. 1958) begins in a German concentration camp, where a prisoner is inspired by thoughts of elephants running free. Upon his release he learns that they are threatened by ivory hunters and assembles a group of war veterans and former prisoners to stop them. This is a crucial precursor of the contemporary ecodefense novel.

Christian Léourier has written several science fiction novels with ecological themes, but only one has been translated into English to date. In *The Mountains of the Sun* (1971, trans. 1973), colonists from Mars return to Earth where society has devolved to a point where it wages war against nature.

Poet and novelist Gustaf Sobin was born in America but has lived in Provence for over thirty years. In *The Fly-Truffler* (2000), a middle-aged professor unearths truffles that reconnect him with memories of his dead wife. This novel is about preserving love, nature, a rural way of life, and the Provence dialect.

PORTUGAL

Nobel Prize-winner José Saramago has written two wonderful eco-fables. In *The Stone Raft* (1986, trans. 1994), the Iberian Peninsula, with a mind of its own, drifts away from the European mainland. *The Cave* (2002) is a more serious rejection of consumerism in favor of a deeper, simpler, more meaningful way of life.

ITALY

Many of Italo Calvino's dense, complex novels include elements of fables and nature lore. The only two that might be considered ecofiction, though, are *If on a Winter's Night a Traveler* (1979), which presents the concept of infinite evolutions, variations, and mutations in all living things, and *Marcovoldo* (1963). Marcovoldo is the name of an Italian laborer who comes to realize that his estrangement from the natural world is making his life seem artificial.

Codex Seraphinianus (1981, trans. 1983) by Luigi Serafini, a highly surrealistic pastiche of illustrations and prose, is both an "encyclopedia" about an alien world that is a thinly veiled version of our own and an early critique of the information age.

GERMANY

Although celebrated German feminist author Gabriele Wohmann may have satirized environmentalists in *Das Glücksspiel* (1981), the Chernobyl nuclear disaster seems to have changed her tune. It features prominently in her 1987 novel *Der Flötenton* and the short-story collection *Ein russischer Sommer* (1988). None have been translated into English. Chernobyl also inspired Christa Wolf to write *Accident: A Day's News* (1989), in which an East German writer confronts the various effects of modern technology as her brother undergoes brain surgery while radiation from Chernobyl drifts across Europe. A decade later, Olaf Klein's *Aftertime* (*Nachzeit*, 1999) focused on the long-term effects suffered by Chernobyl's victims. Monika Maron's *Flight of Ashes* (1981, trans. 1987), in which a brave reporter sticks to her story that an old power plant is the source of massive pollution, is both an environmental and political protest. It was suppressed in her native East Germany but enthusiastically acclaimed in West Germany.

Gudrun Pausewang has written two young adult novels about the dangers of nuclear power that are also appropriate for adults: *The Last Children* (1982, trans. 1989) and *Fall-out* (1987, trans. 1994). A similar young adult/adult book, Michael Ende's *The Neverending Story* (1979, trans. 1983), was made into a major motion picture. Ende was enraged that the environmental and political guts of the story were, typically, eviscerated, resulting in a nice, safe fantasy. Likewise, Frank Schätzing's best-selling *The Swarm* (2004), a thriller about Mother Nature striking back against climate change and marine pollution was simplified as the basis for the film *The Day After Tomorrow*. Ecofiction rarely fares well in escapist Hollywood.

SWITZERLAND

Beat Sterchi's experience as a butcher and farmer informs *Cow* (1983, trans. 1988). A new dairy worker expecting his job to be a bucolic joy is shocked by the horrors of feedlots and slaughterhouses. His humane treatment of and friendship with the cows, particularly old Blosch—a fascinating character in her own right—make him an outcast.

SCANDINAVIA

Swedish physician P. C. Jersild's *The Animal Doctor* (1973, trans. 1975) examines cruelty to both animals and humans. Her highly imaginative *A Living Soul* (1980, trans. 1988) is a meditation on evolution and the relation between humans and other animals told by a disembodied brain.

Kerstin Ekman is considered by some critics to be Sweden's finest novelist. Although she has demonstrated mastery of a wide range of genres and styles, most of her work contains brilliant evocations of the Swedish countryside and rural life. She is best known in America for *Blackwater* (1993, trans. 1996), an exciting thriller about an environmental crime. The fascinating *The Forest of Hours* (1988, trans. 1998) melds fantasy and magic realism in the figure of Skord, who is neither man nor animal. A tetralogy originally written between 1974 and 1983 considers development from the perspective of working-class women and children (*Witches' Rings*, 1997; *The Spring*, 2001; *Angel House*, 2002; *City of Light*, 2003).

Likewise, Peter Høeg may be Denmark's most honored and popular novelist. *Smilla's Sense of Snow* (1992, trans. 1993) was an international best-seller that was published in seventeen languages. In this unusual thriller, a half-Inuit/half-Danish glaciologist uncovers a conspiracy in Greenland. *Smilla's* is a pro-environmental, feminist, anti-imperialist, pro-native text that is never didactic or a source of easy solutions. In Høeg's fantasy *The Woman and the Ape* (1996), a "trophy wife" rescues a talking ape and initiates a love affair with him.

Although Lise Lunge-Larsen moved to Minnesota from Norway in her twenties, her short-story collections *The Troll with No Heart in His Body, and Other Tales of Trolls from Norway* (1999) and *The Hidden Folk: Stories of Fairies, Dwarves, Selkies, and Other Secret Beings* (2004) are awash in old Norse lore and ecological values. These books are appropriate for readers of all ages.

ROMANIA

The Romanian agrarian novel flourished after World War II. The primary authors were Liviu Rebreanu (*The Uprising*, 1964), Mihail Sadoveanu (*Hanul Acutei*, trans. *Ancuta's Inn*, 1954; *The Hatchet*, 1983), and Marin Preda (*The Morometes*, 1957). The work of more recent authors can be found in the anthology *The Phantom Church and Other Stories from Romania* (Georgiana Fârnoagă, ed., 1996).

In Petru Popescu's *Almost Adam* (1996), a paleontologist discovers a small tribe of proto-humans in Kenya, but when he is threatened by mysterious thugs who may be government agents or the employees of a rival scientist, he must become part of the tribe in order to survive.

RUSSIA

The use, preservation, and spiritual aspects of nature are important themes in Russian literature. "Nature can either be an enemy of the main character or an equal partner, or become itself the main character in a short story or even a novel."[7] Nature and environmental issues permeate many works of classic nineteenth-century novelists such as Aleksandr Pushkin (*The Tales of Ivan Belkin,* 1831), Nikolai Gogol (*Dead Souls,* 1842; *Taras Bulba,* 1835), Fyodor Dostoyevsky (*Poor People,* 1846), and Leo Tolstoy (*War and Peace,* 1866). Ivan Bunin's *The Village* (1910) decried the transformation of traditional rural life and the excesses of the industrial revolution.

Writers during the Soviet period experienced varying degrees of freedom to write works with ecological themes. Leonid Leonov's *The Badgers* (1924) examined the conflicts between rural and urban societies that existed after the Revolution and Civil War. In his *Soviet River* (1932), a group of peasants sabotage a huge, polluting paper mill that represents the past. This fiction seems contrary to the actual mass industrialization and pollution of the Stalinist era. A later nature novel by Leonov, *The Russian Forest* (1966), was popular in both the Soviet Union and the West. In Mikhail Prishvin's novels (*The Lake and the Woods,* 1952; *Shiptimber Grove,* 1954), nature itself seems to be the protagonist and its intrinsic value is celebrated. Konstantin Paustovsky (*Selected Stories,* 1949) treats nature as "a kind of laboratory, where scientists, land-reclamation specialists, and foresters, that is, those who preserve and transform nature, are working."[8] Vladimir Soloukhin (*Honey on Bread,* 1982), Fedor Abramov (*The Swans Flew By,* 1986), Viktor Astaf'ev (*Queen Fish,* 1982), and Vasilii Belov (*Morning Rendezvous,* 1953) might be considered environmental and cultural preservationists.

Siberian author Valentin Rasputin focused on the struggle between rural landscapes and lifestyles and industrialization and urbanization in *Live and Remember* (1978). He crossed the line into active environmental defense and defiance against the Soviet government in *Farewell to Matyora* (1979), in which he depicted hopeless villagers harvesting their last crops before their land and lives are drowned in the deluge of a vast reservoir.

Julia Voznesenskaya blasted the Soviet Union's cover-up of the Chernobyl nuclear disaster in *The Star Chernobyl* (1987, trans. 1989). (Ukranian American Irene Zabytko has also written a Chernobyl novel, *The Sky Unwashed* (2000). See the Germany section of this chapter for other Chernobyl books.) Victor Pelevin has emerged as a leading satirist of the post-Soviet era. In his *The Life of Insects* (1998), visitors to a resort on the Black Sea appear to be insects, their behavior revealing much about insects, but more about humans. The animals in Andrei Bitov's *The Monkey Link* (1995) are sometimes real and sometimes mythical as a traveler in the Russian countryside considers the relationship between people and other animals, civilization and nature, and various artistic and political questions.

SERBIA

Milorad Pavic's experimental novel *Landscape Painted with Tea* (1990) is structured as a crossword puzzle. One of the many threads of the story is about a worker coming to America to produce a carcinogenic defoliant used in the Vietnam War.

TURKEY

Yasar Kemal has written extensively on the marginalization of the rural population of Turkey and the political and environmental problems of development. As a highly political socialist he has endured repression and controversy, but has also won critical and public praise. His Beyond the Mountain trilogy focuses on the struggles of cotton picker Long Ali (*The Wind from the Plain*, 1963; *Iron Earth, Copper Sky*, 1974; *The Undying Grass*, 1977). In *The Sea-Crossed Fisherman* (1985), a dreamy fisherman is shocked into action when the city of Istanbul begins to encroach on his village.

Sait Faik is best known for the untranslated *Mahalle Kahvesi* (1950), but a similar collection of environmentally conscious short stories has been translated as *A Dot on the Map* (1983). Likewise, Fakir Baykurt's *Kaplumbagalar* (1966), an environmental tragedy, is not available in English, but a collection of short stories, *A Report from Kuloba* (2000), is.

The Ownerless Planet (2003) by Akin Tekin is the first volume in a projected five-volume series. Set in the year 5021, an American family finds hope for curtailing environmental destruction in an ancient book.

JAPAN

Takashi Nagatsuka's *The Soil* (1910, trans. 1994) is a lyrical but unsentimental account of the unity of the farmer and the soil. Although Kenji Nakagami's primary themes are social (family, racism, poverty), in some of his novels nature is presented as an uncontrollable force that people must adapt to and dwell within. In *Kisho: Kinokuni nenokuni monogatari* (1978), "the nature of Kisho is supposed to be opposite of the conventional and politically powerful; it is a natural environment where the wild gods dwell, overwhelming human beings."[9] Junzo Shono provides a more contemporary although equally lyrical pastoral in *Evening Clouds* (2000). Michiko Ishimure's *Lake of Heaven* (1997, trans. 2008) is the story of a Japanese city that is about to be inundated by a dam project. This is a parable for the inundation of the natural world and traditional cultures. Yukiko Kato's *Ikebe no Sumika* (2003) an untranslated novel whose English title would be *Living by a Pond*, is about an old woman who becomes aware of her place in the world through bird-watching.

Graphic novels, also known as manga, are very popular in both Japan and America, but the only truly ecological Japanese English-language manga I have found to date is Jiro Taniguchi's *The Ice Wanderer and Other Stories* (2007). Green American graphic novels include Todd Dezago's *Spider-Man and Fantastic Four: The Menace of Monster Isle!* (2006), *In the Small* by Michael Hague (2008), *Ramparts: Unseeing Eyes* (1993) by Turf and Joël Mouclier, and Daniel Quinn's *The Man Who Grew Young* (2001).

KOREA AND CHINA

Korean authors Se-hee Cho, Moon Soon-tae, Suk-young Hwang, and Won-il Kim have written ecofiction challenging pollution and other degradation in their country. None of their work has been translated into English at this time. Sei-hui Cho's *The Dwarf* (1976) is a collection of short stories about the environmental and social problems caused by industrialization.

Taiwan has produced at least four green novelists: Yang Ming-tu, Wang Chia-hsiang, Liu Ke-hsiang, and Chen Fu-yeng, but no English language translations are available.

China's most prominent green novelist may be Wei Zhang. In *The Ancient Ship* (1987) he tells the story of the impoverishment of a town when the overused river begins to dry up. *September's Fable* (1993) is similar. His more recent *Ci Wei Ge* (2007), whose title would translate as *Song of the Hedgehog*, is not

yet available in English, but appears to be a complex consideration of the relation between humanity and nature and elements of folk society that might be
environmentally and personally reinvigorating.

Shen Congwen was a prolific and popular writer whose translated works
include *The Chinese Earth* (1947), *Imperfect Paradise* (1995), *Selected Short Stories* (2003), and *Border Town* (1934). One of his most famous works, identified
in various sources as either *River* or *Long River* (1943), has been only partially
translated by Lillian Chen Ming Chu as part of her doctoral dissertation at
Columbia University.

Rong Jiang's *Wolf Totem* (2007) is a semiautobiographical Chinese epic that
depicts the parallel destruction of the free-ranging, naturalistic Mongol culture and the perfectly balanced ecology of the Mongolian grasslands through
the extinction of wolves.

THAILAND

In *Starship & Haiku* (1981) by Somtow Sucharitkul, Japan is the last outpost
of civilization after an ecological catastrophe. It's up to one woman to save
life on earth. Writing as "S. P. Somtow," he depicts Indians performing lycan-
thropic rituals to drive the white men away and establish a new paradise in
Moon Dance (1989).

INDIA

Indian fiction of the colonial period was dominated by British writers such
as Rudyard Kipling and Jim Corbett, and by Indian authors whose prose
echoed the literary fiction of Great Britain. Although the literary prose tradition continues, political fiction emerged with the Independence movement.
Contemporary Indian ecofiction is largely about one subject: the struggle to
save the forest known as the Chipko movement. This is the subject of Mahasweta Devi's *Imaginary Maps* (1995), Nina Sibal's *Yatra: The Journey* (1987), and
the anthology *Of Women, Outcastes, Peasants, and Rebels: A Selection of Bengali
Short Stories* (Kalpana Bardhan, ed., 1995).

The Chipko authors' angry tone contrasts sharply with the gentler one of
Gerald Durrell, whose humorous fiction (e.g., *The Mockery Bird*, 1982) and

nonfiction (*The Amateur Naturalist*, 1993) has popularized conservation and ecology throughout the English-speaking world, but particularly in Great Britain and India.

David J. Lake wrote several ecologically oriented science fiction novels, most notably *The Right Hand of Dextra* (1977), in which humans disastrously attempt to replace the native people and animals of another planet with their own, and its sequel, *The Wildings of Westron* (1977).

Some important green novelists emerged in the 1960s and 1970s. *Water* (1973, trans. 1993) by Acokamittiran (aka Ashokamitran) describes a devastating drought. *Chemmeen* (*Prawns*, 1956) by Takali Sivasankarapilla (aka Thakazi Sivasankara Pillai) is a tragic love story with a green twist. *Legends of Khasak* (1969, trans. 1994) by O. V. Vijayan is a magic realist tale of land and people.

Seasons of the Palm (2000, trans. 2004) by Perumalmurukan (aka Perumal Murugan) "vividly displays the lives of struggle, magic, and superstition among India's rural poor."[10]

Another major Indian-born author, Amitav Ghosh, primarily an author of social fiction, has recently turned to ecofiction with the publication of *The Hungry Tide* (2005), an account of a marine biologist studying river dolphins and a young, impoverished fisherman who becomes her colleague and lover. The biologist struggles to balance her environmental perspective against her growing awareness of poverty: what she sees as fauna, he sees as food.

SRI LANKA

Romesh Gunesekera was born in Sri Lanka in 1954 and lived there until age fourteen. He currently lives in London, writing primarily about Sri Lanka and the Sri Lankan diaspora. The short-story collection *Monkfish Moon* (1992) opens with the odd epigram, "There are no monkfish in the ocean around Sri Lanka." As we discover through the course of nine stories, there are many other illusions about the island. His first novel, *Reef* (1994), is about the destruction of great coral reefs and piecemeal efforts to restore them. The coral reef, once bounteous but now being attacked from all directions, serves as a metaphor for Sri Lanka itself. *The Sandglass* (1998) is a tale of a bitter personal, political, and commercial rivalry between two families who occupy adjacent land on a former British plantation in the 1950s. *Heaven's Edge* (2002) is Gunesekera's most complex work. A Londoner beguiled by his grandfather's stories about his wondrous home visits Sri Lanka and discovers the violence done to the island and its people by warfare, development, and pollution. He falls in love with a young ecologist who has a wildlife refuge and organic farm secreted deep in the jungle and works hard to make it biologically diverse and self-sustaining. Just as it seems that his Eden is becoming reality, it is discovered by soldiers and its destruction seems assured. Gunesekera seems to be asking a larger question for all of humanity: how do we live after the fall?

AFRICA

Africa has been an economic, political, and environmental victim of colonialism and apartheid. Efforts to overthrow the oppressors and the postcolonial struggles between rival tribal and political forces have killed millions of people and further scarred the land. While the Mau Mau movement and some other revolutionaries have been willing to sacrifice people and the land for freedom, a different attitude is expressed by several novelists. Peter Abrahams's books are primarily political, but in *Mine Boy* (1946) he depicted both labor exploitation and environmental abuses in the diamond mining industry. Author Alan Paton was a true revolutionary: a white South African opposed to both the personal and the environmental devastation caused by apartheid. *Cry, the Beloved Country* (1948) and *Too Late the Phalarope* (1953) have both received strong critical and popular acclaim.

South African Wilbur Smith's many historical and current African adventure stories run the gamut from bodice rippers to more politically and environmentally sensitive books. His first novel, *When the Lion Feeds* (1964), demonstrated his familiarity with the local people, wildlife, and landscapes. *Hungry as the Sea* (1978) depicts a giant oil spill followed by a corporate cover-up. His strongest work of ecofiction is *Elephant Song* (1991). The plight of African elephants has drawn the attention of non-African novelists such as Dalene Matthee (*Circles in a Forest*, 1983), Sara Cameron (*Natural Enemies*, 1993), Barbara Gowdy (*The White Bone*, 1999), Richard Wiley (*Ahmed's*

Revenge, 1998), Nicholas Proffitt (*Edge of Eden,* 1990), Karin McQuillan (*Elephants' Graveyard,* 1993), and Kim Echlin (*Elephant Winter,* 1999). The classic elephant novel, though, is Romain Gary's *The Roots of Heaven* (1956).

Christopher Hope's *Darkest England* (1996) is a brilliant inversion of colonialism in which a contemporary South African Bushman explores the "wilds" of England and its "savage" inhabitants while on a mission to ask Queen Elizabeth to honor the treaty made by Queen Victoria promising to protect his people and their homeland.

South African writer J. M. Coetzee is also best known for political fiction. In *The Lives of Animals* (1999), *Disgrace* (1999), and *Elizabeth Costello* (2003), he considers the ethical and political aspects of cruelty and animal rights. Nadine Gordimer, a longtime opponent of apartheid who has been called the conscience of white South Africa, turns her attention to environmental concerns in *Get a Life* (2005), which links rapid development of the tourism industry with environmental and social devastation.

A progressive view linking environmental and social issues has been advanced by African ecofeminists such as Werewere Liking, Buchi Emecheta, Calixthe Beyala, Aminata Sow Fall, and Bessie Head. Fall's *The Beggars' Strike* (1981) is a particularly incisive analysis of how patriarchy, government corruption, and mismanagement have stifled a true environmental movement. Bessie Head is the only one of these authors well known to American readers. A mixed-race woman forced to flee South Africa, she settled in Botswana and wrote about the struggle between postcolonial modernization and the preservation of African nature and traditional cultures in *When Rain Clouds Gather* (1969), *Maru* (1971), and *A Question of Power* (1973).

Ngugi wa Thiong'o may be Africa's most environmentally oriented novelist. Resisting the Mau Mau call for liberation at any cost, he believed that the land and animals must be preserved and restored to reduce the cost of liberation and to prevent the replacement of one form of oppression and degradation with another. Four of his novels written under the pseudonym James T. Ngugi—*Weep Not, Child* (1964), *The River Between* (1965), *Grain of Wheat* (1967), and *Petals of Blood* (1977)—invoke traditional Kenyan spiritual and ecological values.

Nigerian Tanure Ojaide's *The Activist* (2006) chronicles the efforts of the Nigerian people to overcome the environmental and social devastation caused by the complicity of the oil industry with the corrupt Nigerian government.

South African Zakes Mda's *The Whale Caller* (2005) is a magic realist tale about the relationship between a man and a whale.

ARAB WORLD

Little ecofiction has emerged from the Arab world, partly due to poetry's predominance over fiction in Islamic culture, but also for sociopolitical reasons, as environmentalism is challenged to gain a foothold in such a politically volatile area. But in recent decades some green female voices have emerged. Maysa Abou-Youssef has observed that "for Arab writers, nature has, to a large extent been veiled. . . . In the works of Arab women writers, however, there have been points at which nature has been seen and given voice."[11] Representative examples of this literature can be found in two anthologies, *Opening the Gates: An Anthology of Arab Feminist Writing* (Margot Badran and Miriam Cooke, eds., 1990) and *A Voice of Their Own: Short Stories by Egyptian Women* (Anzhil Butrus Sam'an, ed., 1994).

AUSTRALIA AND OCEANIA

Englishman D. H. Lawrence's *Kangaroo* (1923) provides a fascinating early-twentieth-century view of Australian life. He finds fault with the structured programs of both socialists and fascists compared to what he considers a free and open form of democracy arising from the Aboriginal peoples, the settlers, and even the land itself. Patrick White depicts relations between white and Aboriginal Australians in *Voss* (1957), as does Xavier Herbert in *Capricornia* (1939) and *Poor Fellow, My Country* (1975), one of the longest novels in the English language.

Russell Foreman explains that "my novels show a desire to educate through entertainment."[12] *Long Pig* (1958) and *Sandalwood Island* (1961) are historical fiction written to explain the effect of European entry into the Southwest Pacific with special reference to the Sandalwood wars in the Fiji Islands in 1800. A later novel, *The Ringway Virus* (1977), depicts how human interference with the environment could cause mutations in viruses that could have catastrophic effects for human civilization.

Tim Winton writes both novels for adults and young adult novels that are appropriate for all ages. *Shallows* (1993) is about the decline of an old whaling port; *Blueback* (1997) depicts the emergence of a young abalone diver's environmental consciousness; *That Eye, the Sky* (1987) concerns religion and nature; and *Dirt Music* (2003) has a subplot about fish poaching.

There is a great deal of variety in current Australian ecofiction. James E. Schutte's *The Bunyip Archives* (1992) is satire. Environmental action is portrayed by Thea Astley (*An Item from the Late News*, 1982; *It's Raining in Mango*, 1987), Richard Flanagan (*Death of a River Guide*, 2001; *Gould's Book of Fish: A Novel in Twelve Fish*, 2001), James McQueen's *Hook's Mountain* (1989), Ian Moffitt's *Gilt Edge* (1991), and Colin Thiele (*Fight Against Albatross Two*, 1974; *Shadow Shark*, 1988). Jane Alison's *Natives and Exotics* (2006) is a multigenerational family saga. Peter Carey (*Bliss*, 1996) and Dal Stivens (*A Horse of Air*, 2008) are philosophical, while R. F. Brissenden (*Poor Boy*, 1987; *Wildcat*, 1991) takes a more political approach. Steve Wright's thriller *A Drop in the Ocean* (1991) is about the infiltration of an environmental group by a secret government organization. *Tourmaline* (2002) by Randolph Stow takes place after a nuclear holocaust. Damien Broderick (*The Dreaming Dragons*, 1980; *Transcension*, 2002) and Patricia Wrightson (*The Nargun and the Stars*, 1970; *Moon-Dark*, 1987) write science fiction and fantasy, while magical realism is the realm of Nicholas Jose (*The Rose Crossing*, 1996) and Tom Gilling (*The Sooterkin*, 2000). Thiele and Wrightson write primarily for young adults, but their books are also appropriate for adults. Julie Leigh's *The Hunter* (2000) centers around the search for a mysterious, supposedly extinct wolflike creature known as the Tasmanian tiger. This exploration of wilderness and human wildness won Leigh a place on the *London Times* list of "21 Writers for the 21st Century." Roger McDonald has written several novels with nature themes, most notably *Rough Wallaby* (1989), about an animal trainer; *Water Man* (1993), about a dowser; *Mr. Darwin's Shooter* (1998), about Charles Darwin and the mentality of scientific exploration; and *The Ballad of Desmond Kale* (2005), which explores the early years of the sheep industry. Randolph Stow's *Tourmaline* (2002) is also about a dowser. *Sole Survivor* (1999) by Derek Hansen melds romance and environmental action. *Getting There* (1998), a celebration of life by Michael Roads, tells the tale of an organic farmer and a miraculous spiritual teacher. Gabrielle Lord's *Salt* (1998) is science fiction.

A similar wide variety can be found in fiction being written in and about Australia and Oceania. Much of it is by or about Australian Aborigines and other people indigenous to the region. Their Earth-centered cosmology is somewhat similar to that of Native Americans. Emergence tales, legendary characters, Aboriginal Dreamtime, and other mythical elements are frequently strong elements of fiction from these cultures. The genre known as magical realism takes more specific form as "native realism" in North America and "maban realism" in Australia. (Louis Owens, Leslie Marmon Silko, Thomas King, and Gerald Vizenor are good examples of Native American authors incorporating native realism in their work.) According to Mudrooroo, maban realism arises from the Dreamtime and the indigenous artist's own subconscious mind and spiritual experience. Considering its dislocations of time and space, suspension of objective reality, the text commenting upon itself or breaking down the barrier between reader and writer, and full mythical immersion, some critics might consider native or maban realism to be types of postmodernism. I would argue that these are organic forms of literature arising from ancient cultures, not the intentional rejection of modernism or realism and invention of something new for its own sake sometimes found in postmodernism. Considering the similar experiences of cultural and environmental devastation visited upon Native American and Australian populations over the past few centuries, it is not surprising that both have transformed their ecologically based stories into more modern forms of literature. It should be noted, however, that important differences also exist between and within these cultures, and that all but the most fantastic literature reflects specific historical and cultural contexts.

One theme dominates Aboriginal and Maori fiction: "restoration of degraded ecosystems . . . as an integral element of a broader program of cultural recovery."[13] It would be a mistake, though, to consider this fiction homogenous since there are many variations, subthemes, and related themes. It tends to be complex in both content and style.

Mudrooroo (aka Colin Johnson or Mudrooroo Narogin) wrote the first major published novel by an Aborigine, *Wild Cat Falling*, in 1965. The semi-autobiographical unnamed protagonist is a light-skinned, nineteen-year-old partial Aborigine who while fleeing the police encounters his great uncle, who performs healing ceremonies to reconnect Wildcat with his cultural roots, nature, and the Dreamtime. *Long Live Sandawara* (1979) uses alternating chapters to relate the parallel stories of a group of contemporary youth and the historical rebels who inspired them. Wildcat returns twenty years older as a screenwriter in *Doin' Wildcat: A Novel Koori Script as Constructed by Mudrooroo Narogin* (1988). In an out-of-sequence sequel, he flashes back to another incarnation in *Wildcat Screaming* (1992). *Doctor Wooreddy's Prescription for Enduring the Ending of the World* (1983) is a blend of minor accommodations and passive resistance. Wooreddy is transformed into the more action-oriented Jangamuttuck in *Master of the Ghost Dreaming* (1991). He learns to ride his dreaming animal, a goanna lizard, his wife rides a manta ray, and Wadawaka (a black African sailor born on a slave ship) a leopard to restore the health of the tribe and the sentient island, close the psychic doors that have allowed the white "ghosts" to enter their world, and escape to a new home. Maban reality meets gothic horror in the second volume of the series, *The Undying* (1998). The survivors of the island sail to the Australian mainland to find a new home, reestablish ancient ties with other tribes, and stop the incursion of the "ghosts." The series continues in *Underground* (1999) and *The Promised Land* (2000). When a shady real-estate speculator loses a parliamentary election, he is sent on a "special mission" to a remote island in Mudrooroo's *The Kwinkan* (1993). He becomes a pawn in a game played by the ruling family, a Japanese development corporation, a "neo-Polynesian, self-management" movement, the Australian government, and Aboriginal detective Jackamarra.

B. Wongar was born in Yugoslavia but moved to Australia in his youth, has lived in the outback with his native wife Djumula, and self-identifies as a native. *The Track to Bralgu* (1978) is a collection of somewhat satirical stories about the destruction of the Outback and Aboriginal culture through uranium mining, nuclear testing, and spiritual chicanery. *Babaru* (1982), *Bilma* (1984), and *Marngit* (1992) are similar collections of interconnected stories. *The Last Pack of Dingoes* (1993) is a collection of stories with canine narrators and protagonists. Wongar's Nuclear trilogy is not a series per se, but an exploration of themes that begin on a personal level in *Walg* (1983), move to a national level in *Karan* (1985), and become universalized in *Gabo Djara* (1987). The three novels are unified through the relentless effort to demystify what happened: the discovery of uranium, the horrors of uranium mining and nuclear testing, the slaughter of Aborigines through radiation and medical experimentation, and the massive destruction of the landscape from which they drew their sustenance and their very identity. *Raki* (1994) explores the surprising commonalities of Wongar's dual heritage by presenting parallel Australian and Serbian stories.

Maban realism is also the hallmark of Aboriginal authors Bruce Pascoe (*Fox*, 1988), Archie Weller (*The Day of the Dog,* 1981, and many others), Beverly Farmer (*The Seal Woman,* 1992), and Dorothy Johnston (*Maralinga, My Love,* 1988). New Aboriginal writers are emerging, many of their works appearing in the University of Queensland Press's Black Writers Series. UQP has published two significant anthologies, *Paperbark: A Collection of Black Australian Writing* (Jack Davis, ed., 1990) and *Fresh Cuttings* (Sue Abbey, ed., 2003). *Sweet Water . . . Stolen Land* (1993) by Philip McLaren offers an Aboriginal perspective on the white settlement of Australia. Doris Pilkington's *Follow the Rabbit Proof Fence* (1996), based on a true story from 1931, tells the tale of three Aboriginal girls who escape from an oppressive boarding school and trek hundreds of miles home across the bush. Alexis Wright's *Carpentaria* (2009) is a general consideration of Aboriginal-white relations with an emphasis on the devastating effects of alcoholism on Aborigines. In Wright's *Plains of Promise* (1997), a tribal council turns toward the Dreamtime for help. In Larissa Behrendt's *Home* (2000), a city-bred mixed-blood lawyer investigates her family's history and by extension the relations between whites and Aboriginals. *Unbranded* (1992) by Herb Wharton is the saga of three men's friendship over forty years, in which the white man succeeds as a rancher, an Aborigine helps restore tribal lands, and a (seemingly autobiographical) mixed-blood chronicles their shared experiences.

Fiction by the Maoris of New Zealand reached full fruition in the 1980s. According to C. Christopher Norden, "First novels by three well-known Maori writers, Witi Ihimaera's *Tangi,* Patricia Grace's *Mutuwhenua: The Moon Sleeps,* and Keri Hulme's *The Bone People,* offer variations on a common syntax of alienation, homecoming, and ecosystemic restoration."[14] All three authors continue to write powerful, popular, critically acclaimed ecofiction. Ihimaera's *The Whale Rider* (1987) became a major motion picture. Grace's *Potiki* (1986) depicts the struggle between traditional peoples and resort developers, while *Dogside Story* (2001) contrasts the Maori tradition of *whanau,* or extended family, with the Western notion of tourism.

Samoan Albert Wendt is a significant author, critic, and editor. His major works include *Sons for the Return Home* (1973); *The Birth and Death of the Miracle Men* (1986), a collection of fablelike stories that are also parables about traditional and modern life; and *The Leaves of the Banyan Tree* (1994), a multi-generational novel emphasizing the connection of the Samoan people to the land and sea. *Nuanua: Pacific Writing in English Since 1980* (1995), edited by Wendt, contains a wide variety of short fiction and poetry by dozens of authors located across the Pacific islands.

Solomon Islander Rexford Orotaloa has written two collections of stories about traditional village life: *Two Time Resurrection* (1985) and *Suremada: Faces from a Solomon Island Village* (1989).

Many white Australian novelists, such as Brad Collis (*The Soul Stone,* 1993), Carmel Bird (*The Bluebird Café,* 1991), Janette Turner Hospital (*Oyster,* 1998), Peter Shann Ford (*The Keeper of Dreams,* 2000), Greg Matthews (*The Wisdom of Stones* (1994), and Stuart Fox (*Black Fire,* 1992; *The Back of Beyond,* 1994), employ Aboriginal themes or issues and are sensitive to the subtleties of native culture. Olaf Ruhen's (*Naked Under Capricorn,* 1982) explores the native culture of Australia. The primary themes of such authors' work are a sense of belonging to place, both nature and culture, and a rejection of globalization in favor of a modern adaptation of native values.

English author Jane Rogers's *Promised Lands* (1995) may be the best ecofiction about Australia written by a Caucasian author. The central text in this triptych is a novel about William Dawes, an astronomer on the Botany Bay Expedition of 1788. The author of the text about Dawes is Stephen Beech, whose plans to revolutionize the British school system have failed. His wife Olla has her own project: raising their severely disabled child, Daniel, whom she believes will become a savior. Two variations on the settlement theme include Margaret Simons's *The Ruthless Garden* (1993), which depicts white settlers attempting to tame a wilderness that the natives considered a sacred garden exactly as it was, and Dutch expatriate Lolo Houbein's description of her slow adaptation to the cultures and nature of Australia in *Walk a Barefoot Road* (1990).

Marlo Morgan's *Mutant Message Down Under* (1994) was initially marketed as nonfiction, then as fiction when it was discovered that the story had been fabricated. Whatever else it may be, it is fraudulent, a deceptive act of "New Age" cultural appropriation.

Concern about the traditional cultures and the environment of Hawaii is expressed by many native authors. See *Talk Story: An Anthology of Hawaii's Local Writers* (Eric Chock, ed., 1978) for a representative selection. Native Hawaiian Kiana Davenport's *Shark Dialogues* (1994), *Song of Exile* (1999), and *House of Many Gods* (2006) evoke a Polynesian version of maban realism to make a powerful statement against the commercialization of Hawaii and the marginalization of the native culture. *The Watchers of Waipunu* (1992) by Gary Pak is a collection of eight stories about cultural and environmental preservation and restoration. The subtitle of Dana Naone Hall's collection of stories, poetry, and art, *Malama: Hawaiian Land and Water* (1985), is self-descriptive.

In Pamela Ball's *Lava* (1997), a man places a bounty on sharks after a boy is killed, but a volcano brings retribution. Mark Christensen's *Aloha: A Novel of the Near Future* (1994) is an apocalyptic satire in which a land developer plans to create a new Hawaiian island from a submerged volcano to serve as a haven for smuggling and money laundering. See chapter 9 for James D. Houston's *The Last Paradise* (1998).

6

Ecoromance

W hat could be more natural than sex? Sexual relationships are a common component of ecofiction, typically as a secondary plot integrated into the story, only occasionally as the predominant one. Few ecofictions fit a classic category romance literature formula, in which men are spectacularly handsome but not necessarily deep and can be "tamed" by resourceful but needy women. Other romance novels, though, are not necessarily as restrictive in terms of characterization, plot, subject, or theme. There may be relatively few green standard romances, but love and sex are a very common component of ecofiction. The sex is usually heterosexual, sometimes lesbian, occasionally gay male, and sometimes includes a ménage à trois or even menageries.

Some classic romances do include ecofictional elements, typically involving a couple uniting as a consequence of their activism or one becoming an activist through the influence of the other. Examples include *The Beach House* and *Skyward* by Mary Alice Monroe (saving, respectively, turtles and raptors, 2002, 2003), *Southern Storms* by Marcia Martin (mustangs, 1992), *Carolina Girl* by Patricia Rice (an island off the Carolina coast, 2004), *The Disappearance* by Jasmine Cresswell (the Brazilian rainforest, 1999), *An Atomic Romance* by Bobbie Ann Mason (a nuclear engineer and a biologist saving deformed wildlife, 2005), *Darwin's Wink* by Alison Anderson (two biologists saving endangered birds, 2004), *The Californiad: A Novel of Life, Love, and Protected Species* by Vince Donovan (2006), and Rose Senehi's *Pelican Watch* (2007) and *In the Shadows of Chimney Rock* (2008), both of which are mysteries dealing with habitat destruction and real estate development.

Many traditional Native American legends have a strong erotic component. The most famous is Yellow Woman, or Kochininako, a character who beneficially transcends sexual and other behavioral mores, either being abducted by or seducing various characters, including Buffalo Man, Sun Man, or the K'atsina from the north. In Leslie Marmon Silko's version, a modern woman is abducted by a cattle rustler who may or may not be a K'atsina, but who calls and treats her as Yellow Woman. In the space of a few pages Silko deftly explores the woman's relation to modern society, the past, sexuality, the spirit world, storytelling, the land, and reality itself. *Yellow Woman* was published separately in 1993, with an introduction by Melody Graulich, an interview by Kim Barnes, and eight essays.

The influence of Native American myth can be found in many romance novels. John Straley's *The Woman Who Married a Bear* (1994)is partly based on an Inuit tale. Frederick Manfred's *The Manly-Hearted Woman* (1975) explores Native transexuality when a Dakotah woman poses as a man in order to become a shaman disguised as a woman. His *Scarlet Plume* (1964) is a Romeo and Juliet tale of a Dakotah boy and a white girl, set in 1862. In Brenda Brown Canary's *Home to the Mountain* (1975), when a young white man returns to his Oklahoma home, he meets a Native American woman and a healing bond forms between them and with the land. Florida Native American author Connie May Fowler's *Remembering Blue* (2000) blends romance, animal fantasy, and tragedy. Some of Margaret Coel's books featuring Arapaho lawyer Vicky Holden and Jesuit priest Father John O'Malley have an ecological theme. In *The Dream Stalker* (1997), Holden faces death threats for opposing a nuclear waste dump on Arapaho land. *The Thunder Keeper* (2001) concerns corporate shenanigans in diamond mining, while *Killing Raven* (2003) is about the seamy side of casino operations. Swain Wolfe's *The Lake Dreams the Sky* (1998) is a love story based on the Red Crow Indians' abiding respect for the natural world.

There is a marked contrast between the open eroticism of Native American writing and the moral constraints of Victorian times. One of the most important authors of that period, Sarah Orne Jewett, was more likely to imply sexual relationships than to openly express them. These relationships are frequently between female herbalists and healers, who are inherently conservationists, although there is at least one heterosexual romance that is portrayed in a positive light. Mary Austin was far more open about sex, the erotic aspects of nature, and activism, particularly in *The Ford* (1917), *Starry Adventure* (1931), and *Cactus Thorn* (written 1927, suppressed until 1988). For more on Jewett and Austin, see chapter 2.

The *Winning of Barbara Worth* (1911) by Harold Bell Wright is a mawkish romance set against the development of the California citrus industry and the Salton Sea. His less sentimental novel, *The Shepherd of the Hills* (1907), tells the tale of a man who is recovering from grief over his wife's death. "In all his works, Wright sought to reassure his middle-class audience by emphasizing God and country, home and family, hard work and morality against the panorama of a rapidly changing, industrializing America."[1]

Three early-twentieth-century British authors offer new perspectives on love and sex. D. H. Lawrence was an advocate for a wilder, more authentic, less constrained form of sexuality in many of his books, particularly *The White Peacock* (1911), *The Rainbow* (1915), *Women in Love* (1921), and *Lady Chatterley's Lover* (1928). In Virginia Woolf's fiction, especially *To the Lighthouse* (1927), sex, nature, feminism, and the imagination are potent forces against dehumanization and depression. John Cowper Powys's *A Glastonbury Romance* (1933) evokes the romantic qualities of nature via the Grail.

Ecofiction and romance then seem to go their separate ways until the publication of two fairly revolutionary books in 1969, Ursula K. Le Guin's *The Left Hand of Darkness* and Margaret Atwood's *The Edible Woman*. In *The Left Hand of Darkness* the denizens of the perennially chilly planet named Winter are essentially hermaphrodites who do not know which gender they will be when they enter a monthly estrus period known as "kemmer." Since everyone can become either female or male, misogyny does not exist. For more on Le Guin, see chapter 8.

Critic Marilyn French has observed that Margaret Atwood's work includes "the search for identity . . . a search for a better way to be—for a way of life that both satisfies the passionate, needy self and yet is decent, humane and natural."[2] In *The Edible Woman* a young woman rejects her conventional fiancé and then cannot eat until she feeds him a sponge cake in her shape to satisfy his seeming need to consume her whole life. In *Life Before Man* (1979), none of the characters can truly communicate their feelings, making their lives as dry and sterile as the dinosaur bones at the museum where they work. Unless they break through or move on, they might as well be extinct. In *The Handmaid's Tale* (1985), fundamentalist Christians have taken over the United States. Due to toxic pollution and radiation, few women can still bear children, and those who can are isolated as breeders.

Good examples of contemporary ecofiction with romance as one important narrative strand can be found in the work of Jim Harrison, Barbara Kingsolver, Rick Bass, and Louise Erdrich. Harrison's protagonists tend either to have large appetites for gourmet food and/or wild sex or be in denial of their own nature, hence miserable. *Farmer* (1976) is arguably one of the finest evocations of the changing seasons of nature and the human heart in contemporary literature. By ending his affair with a sexy high school student, a teacher rejuvenates his relationship with a previous lover, love of the land, and joy in life. In Kingsolver's *Prodigal Summer* (2000), four different romances bloom simultaneously, and all of nature seems to be consumed in the glory and fecundity of its own sexuality. Bass's couples are as much in love with the landscape and animals as with each other, particularly Wallis and Mel in *Where the Sea Used to Be* (1998). Erdrich's *Love Medicine* (rev. ed. 1993) works its magic on the people in historic and modern times. For more on Erdrich, see chapter 4.

Some contemporary ecoromances are highly philosophical and/or very complex. Rand D. Johnson's *Arcadia Falls* (2001) is a fable that melds philosophy, psychological fiction, eroticism, and ecodefense. Jim Crace traces the lives and love of two zoologists backward from the moment of their murder in *Being Dead* (1999). In *Robert Crews* (1994), Thomas Berger's imaginative recasting of *Robinson Crusoe,* an alcoholic and a victim of domestic violence experience natural and sexual healing. John Hawkes's *Adventures in the Alaskan Skin Trade* (1985) uses Alaska as a metaphor for inner wildness while exploring nature, human nature, writing, relationships, and eroticism itself. Diana Gabaldon has a master's degree in behavioral ecology. Her environmental values and complex, philosophical writing distinguish the *Outlander* (1991–present) series of historical romances. In Martin Davies's *The Conjuror's Bird* (2005) a modern scientist trying to track down the one specimen of an extinct bird from Captain Cook's expedition of 1774 instead uncovers a romance between naturalist Sir Joseph Banks and a mysterious mistress.

Some novels feature a ménage à trois. Valerie Martin's *The Great Divorce* (1994) may be in a class by itself as a horror fantasy love triangle. Her characters include a veterinarian, her philandering husband, a murderous catwoman, and an emotionally disturbed zoo worker. Claire Davis's *Winter Range* (2000) depicts an equally disturbing set of relationships between a man whose cattle are starving, the sheriff who wants to kill the cattle against the wishes of the locals, and the rancher's wife. In Nicholas Evans's *The Smoke Jumper* (2002), a woman travels to Montana to be with her smoke-jumping husband but falls in love with his partner and best friend, placing them all in emotional and, eventually, physical peril.

A Condor Brings the Sun (1996) by zoologist Jerry McGahan is unique as a postmodern, magic realist, feminist, ecodefense romance. A young Inca woman who embodies twenty-three maternal ancestors partners with a wildlife biologist to fight the environmental and culture depredations of the Shining Path guerrillas and to free a bear being abused in a scientific study.

According to Daniel Barth, Cris Mazza's "favorite subject is the ambiguous nature of reality in relationships between women and men, especially in extreme cases."[3] Her short stories in *Animal Acts* (1988) and the novels *Dog People* (1997) and *Girl Beside Him* (2001) are of particular ecocritical interest. The characters in *Dog People* establish more meaningful relationships with their dogs than they can with other people. In the even more disturbing *Girl Beside Him,* a wildlife biologist must overcome feelings that could drive him to become a rapist and sexual killer.

It can take far less to drive someone over the edge: one thread of Cornelia

Nixon's *Angels Go Naked* (2000) is the conflict between a concert violinist and a marine biologist over consumerism and waste symbolized by a plastic carton of crème fraîche.

Other animals are an important connection to nature, and sometimes people connect with them in unusual ways. In *The Flight of the Osprey* (1996), Ewan Clarkson alternates human and animal perspectives. Alina Reyes's *The Butcher and Other Erotica* (1995) includes the novella "Lucie's Long Voyage," in which a woman mates with a bear and gives birth to a child who is a personification of the mythic eternal feminine principle. In *Bear* (1976), Marian Engel's protagonist also has an intimate relationship with the title creature. In Peter Høeg's fantasy *The Woman and the Ape* (1996), a "trophy wife" rescues a talking ape and initiates a love affair with him, much as the protagonist of Rhoda Lerman's semicomical *Animal Acts* (1994) does.

The contemporary West is the setting for several highly varied romances. David James Duncan's *The River Why* (1983) is a brilliant story about fishing, nature, conservation, spirituality, and sex. James D. Houston's *Love Life* (1985) chronicles a good marriage gone bad because of an affair, then restored when the couple waits out a long rainstorm together. Pam Houston's *Cowboys Are My Weakness* (1988) and *Waltzing the Cat* (1998) are wild outdoor romps, while *Sight Hound* (2005) is a gentler, more philosophical portrayal of the relationships between people, between animals, and between people and animals. One can hardly imagine a more heartfelt love story than Brenda Peterson's *Animal Heart* (2004). It combines thrilling environmental action with more philosophical themes, especially regarding the love between a marine forensic scientist and a man who has vivid memories of life on the savannah and the horrors of a primate research lab after becoming the recipient of a baboon heart. In Rich Shapero's *Wild Animus* (2004), a questing student and his lover leave Berkeley for the wilds of Alaska where Sam is transformed first into the persona "Ransom" and then, perhaps, into an actual ram. Penelope Williamson's *Heart of the West* (1995) is an unusual feminist historical western romance. Nora Roberts has written over one hundred romance novels, at least two of which, *Montana Sky* (1996) and *Heaven and Earth* (2001), have an environmental subtext. Susan Aylworth's Rainbow series (including *A Rain-*

bow in Paradise, 1999) is set in the Southwest, often including environmental aspects and an appreciation of Native American culture. William Kittredge considers the many environmental and social changes in ranch life throughout the twentieth century in his sprawling epic *The Willow Field* (2006), which doubles as a poignant love story.

One common theme in ecofiction is people loving each other, loving the earth, and striving to work for healthier relationships between people and between humanity and the rest of nature. Love is frequently the carrot and indignation the stick as motivations for environmental action. One good early example is Hamlin Garland's *Cavanagh, Forest Ranger*, published in 1910. In Russell Hoban's *Turtle Diary* (1975), a reticent bookstore clerk and a children's book author come out of their own shells to liberate turtles from a zoo. *Swimming in the Volcano* (1993) by Bob Shacochis combines romantic and political intrigue as fishers and divers resist development. In Ann Rivers Siddons's *King's Oak* (1990), a woman recovering from a disastrous first marriage finds love and a meaning to her life with a man committed to wilderness protection. In Siddons's *Low Country* (1998), a woman and her husband clash over his plans to develop an untrammeled Indian settlement into a theme park, she has an affair with a Cuban ecologist, her husband realizes his business and romantic errors, and in the end land, Indians, and the marriage are saved. *Sole Survivor* (1999) by Derek Hansen melds romance and environmental action as three recluses join forces to save their island from a Japanese trawler fleet and cannery. In Jonis Agee's *South of Resurrection* (1997), a woman returns to her hometown, reconnects with an old flame, and fights a massive polluting hog farm. Agee's short stories in *Bend This Heart* (1989) are all love stories, and there is also an element of romance in her *King Lear* adaptation, *Strange Angels* (1993). A career woman falls in love with a farmer named Bear, with whom she rescues animals and establishes a shelter in David Martin's romantic fairy tale *Crazy Love* (2002). In Lauren Wolk's *Those Who Favor Fire* (1998), two people escaping abusive pasts unite to try to prevent the government from buying out the remaining homes in an area affected by underground coal fires.

In Ann Brandt's *Crowfoot Ridge* (1999), a woman leaves her Florida real estate developer husband to return to a simpler way of life and a more fulfill-ing relationship with an old flame in rural North Carolina.

Michelle Chalfoun's *The Width of the Sea* (2001) is a romance with a very unhappy ending. When two New England fishermen undertake a desperate voyage after the fishing has dried up, they not only face disaster but manage to destroy their rocky relationships on land as well.

Marnie Mueller served in the Peace Corps in Ecuador. That experience informs *Green Fires: An Assault on Eden* (1994), in which a honeymooning couple meet a man trying to protect the rain forest and its native inhabitants from being harassed and napalmed into oblivion by an oil company.

Lesbian themes are fairly common. Dorothy Bryant's *The Kin of Ata Are Waiting for You* (1976; orig. title *The Comforter,* 1971) depicts a futuristic les-bian ecotopia, while Ellen Galford's *The Fires of Bride* (1988) creates one in the Celtic era. A New Yorker escapes to the desert where she is nourished by the desert, native healers, and a lesbian lover in Ibis Gómez-Vega's *Send My Roots Rain* (1991). In Sally Miller Gearheart's vituperative *The Wanderground* (1978), women establish a rural, environmentally based society, a sperm bank is set up, and the women encourage the few "good" men to kill the many "bad" men and then commit suicide. Although some critics praised this book, others criticized it for reverse sexism.

Jonathan Strong's *An Untold Tale* (1993) is a consideration of the relation-ship between homophobia and disrespect for nature. In his *A Circle Around Her* (2000), he weaves gay, bisexual, and straight love stories into other plots, including one opposing land development. In William Haywood Hender-son's *Native* (1993), ranch foreman Blue Parker risks abuse by and estrange-ment from his fellow macho ranchers when he falls in love with a young hired hand and meets an Indian who is trying to restore the mystical, androgy-nous berdache tradition. *Sacrament* (1996) by Clive Barker correlates two kinds of extinction: animals from habitat loss and gay men from AIDS. In Annie Proulx's short story "Brokeback Mountain," from *Close Range* (1999), two nature-loving cowboys also develop a forbidden and poignant love for each other. James Conrad's *Making Love to the Minor Poets of Chicago* (2000) contains myriad gay, straight, and bisexual affairs and a conflict between two professors vying to be the cautionary poet for the Yucca Mountain nuclear waste project. *War Boy* (2001) by Kief Hillsbery combines a gay relationship with a plot to bomb a logging company that is destroying the Headwaters redwoods.

Sex is sometimes an important element of science fiction and fantasy. When an android hunter falls in love with an android, he is forced to reconsider the meaning of love, humanity, and life itself in Philip K. Dick's *Do Androids Dream of Electric Sheep?* (1968; movie title *Blade Runner*, 1982). In Marge Piercy's *He, She, and It* (1991), a woman of the mid-twenty-first century escapes from a corporate plundered city to a Jewish free town where she bonds with a man who is both promising and ominous. A seventeenth-century shape-changer's son reincarnates in 1991 to romantically and politically bond with an activist battling water pollution in Jeanette Winterson's *Sexing the Cherry* (1989). Winterson's *The Stone Gods* (2008) is a post-apocalyptic, ecofeminist romance. Chris Foster's *Winds Across the Sky* (1992) is a rather cloying New Age romance about the bond between a reporter, an actress, a humpback whale, and a redwood tree. The sprawling (1228 pages), highly literary *Canopus in Argus: Archives* (1992) by Doris Lessing chronicles five million years of evolution, including projected changes in love relationships and those of humans to the earth. Liz Jensen's *Egg Dancing* (1995) and *Ark Baby* (1998) focus on biotechnology and artificial insemination. Kim Stanley Robinson is never one to throw out the sex with the sexism. His female and male characters alike tend to be strong and athletic yet vulnerable, thoughtful yet action oriented, self-realized yet appreciative of the other, particularly in the Mars series. *A Short, Sharp Shock* (1990) is Robinson's most surrealistic novel, and includes some of the most imaginative, powerful erotic passages I have ever experienced.

7

The Real West

They are the worst of books. They are the best of books.

The worst books about the West tend to be published by eastern publishers and are intended to appeal to and reinforce an eastern or European audience's romantic, simplified notions and biases regarding the West. They tend to be rapidly written, formulaic potboilers: purple prose about the purple sage. Regardless of whether the authors are utter hacks or more accomplished writers like Zane Grey, these are little more than fantasy novels wearing ten-gallon hats. If we regard such books as cultural misdemeanors, then Hollywood could be prosecuted for nearly a century of felonies.

Fortunately, there is also a long established tradition of real westerners writing about the real West. "Western writing" may include the genre known as the western, but is far more expansive in scope. Because perceptions of reality differ over time and space and between individuals, this fiction is generally far more thoughtful and varied than the Manhattan or Hollywood versions of the West. Gerald Haslam notes that "local writers, local editors, and local readers have reintrenched and reexamined regional roots. It is in small presses and little magazines that homogenization has been least evidenced, since they recognize that the universal is most clearly recognizable through the particular."[1]

True western writing is not just about cowboys and Indians or black and white hats. It runs the whole gamut of social, cultural, political, psychological, and environmental concerns. According to Mark Siegel, "western writing has focused sharply on the confrontation of eastern and western cultures, on industrial and 'natural' Americas, in both material and spiritual terms, but it has generally been a bastion of the opposition to changes that meant exploitation. 'Easternization' in this literature has generally meant a loss of individuality, at least in the sense of the individual's one-to-one relationship with the land, a loss of freedom, self-reliance, and the more fulfilling life-styles of the past. Social order, once seen as the contribution of the East, is now either taken for granted or despised as corrupt, vitiating, or emotionally castrating."[2]

Realistic westerns with an environmental aspect begin around the turn of the twentieth century with the work of Mary Austin, Hamlin Garland, Frank Norris, Jack London, and Emerson Hough. Austin was a revolutionary writer, combining feminism, environmentalism, and a pantheistic spirituality inspired by desert landscapes. Garland's early work, set mostly in the Midwest, sought to present a more accurate, less romanticized view of farming than that found in the standard pastoral. His first book, the collected stories of *Main Traveled Roads* (1891), may be his best, since his later novels are less realistic and more romantic. Frank Norris's *The Octopus* (1901), Garland's *Cavanagh, Forest Ranger* (1910), and Austin's *The Ford* (1917) were among the first ecodefense novels. London wrote stirring descriptions of wilderness, and empowered his conservation and political messages by making the reader identify with and care about the land and other animals. Although little known today, Emerson Hough was an important conservationist and influential journalist in his time. He also penned a series of children's conservation books set in Alaska and several novels with the theme of the destruction of the West, most notably *Heart's Desire* (1905).

Willa Cather's *O Pioneers!* (1913) and *My Ántonia* (1918) are agrarian sagas that contrast a natural and a more mechanized approach to farming. *The Professor's House* (1925) also provides a stark contrast, this one between soul-deadening materialism and a deeper mode of existence.

Hollywood almost always portrays cowboys versus Indians, but some Westerners adapted Indian values and practices regarding the land, other animals, and, in some cases, spirituality. Much of Frank Waters's work is an attempt to combine the best aspects of Native American and European cosmology and practices. A. B. Guthrie's trilogy of *The Big Sky* (1947), *The Way West* (1949), and *Fair Land, Fair Land* (1982) offers accounts of the transition of Montana from wilderness to homesteads. The stories feature protagonists who wish to live in harmony with the land and learn from the Native people. Guthrie's *Mountain Medicine* (1960) is a collection of short stories on this theme. Don Berry explores a similar theme in the trilogy of *Trask* (1960), *Moontrap* (1962), and *To Build a Ship* (1963), all set on the Oregon coast around the year 1850.

Some other books reflecting Indian values are *Wolf Song* (1927) by Harvey Fergusson; *When the Tree Flowered* (1952) by John G. Neihardt; and Frederick Manfred's *The Golden Bowl* (1944), *Lord Grizzly* (1954), *Scarlet Plume* (1964), *King of Spades* (1966), *The Manly-Hearted Woman* (1975), and *Of Lizards and Angels* (1992). The *Frederick Manfred Reader* (1996) is a good introduction to his work. Much of Mari Sandoz's Indian-oriented work is written for teens but is also of interest to adults, particularly *The Horsecatcher* (1957) and *The Story Catcher* (1963). Sandoz is the subject of Jane Valentine Barker's fictional biography *Mari* (1997).

Don Coldsmith has been the most prolific writer on the theme of the settlement of the West and encroachment on Indian lands and cultures, covering a time span from 1541 forward, often from the perspective of Native Americans, in his twenty-seven-volume Spanish Bit series (*Trail of the Spanish Bit*, 1980, etc.). Recently he has written even more environmentally oriented fiction on this subject in two excellent novels, *Tallgrass: A Novel of the Great Plains* (1997) and its sequel, *South Wind* (1998).

Conrad Richter examined conflicts between free-ranging cowboys and trappers who wanted to keep New Mexico wild and settlers who wanted to tame it in *The Sea of Grass* (1937). In the Awakening Land trilogy of *The Trees* (1940), *The Fields* (1946), and *The Town* (1950), Richter contrasted the constraints and pressures of urban life with frontier life in the Ohio Valley when it was still an uncharted wilderness of pines. Richter's *The Light in the Forest*

(1953) is a fictional account of a four-year-old white boy who is abducted and raised by the Delaware Indians. When forced to return to his parents at age fifteen, he rebels, preferring life in the forest with his adoptive people. *The Waters of Kronos* (1960) is a thinly veiled autobiographical novel in which an author returns to the site of his boyhood home in Pennsylvania only to discover that it had been inundated when the Kronos River was dammed. Richter also wrote many short stories, the best of which are collected in *The Rawhide Knot* (1978).

Scott R. Sanders provides a more contemporary account in *Wilderness Plots: Tales About the Settlement of the American Land* (1983). Spring Warren's bildungsroman *Turpentine* (2007) takes place not in Ohio, but across the plains.

Walter Van Tilburg Clark's *City of Trembling Leaves* (1945) depicts Reno as a glitzy town where people become neurotic because they are alienated from nature, quite unlike the physically and emotionally healthy backcountry inhabitants living nearby. In his *Track of the Cat* (1949), a rancher wounds himself emotionally by hunting a cougar that local Indians believe to be a symbolic beast that arises when people dishonor the land. Clark is best known for *The Ox-Bow Incident* (1940), which is of great philosophical but not eco-critical interest, and for his oft-anthologized short story "Hook," a delightful and scientifically accurate portrayal of a hawk.

The conflicts between a nature-loving teenage girl and her more macho brother reach a tragic conclusion when he accidentally shoots her while hunting in Jean Stafford's *The Mountain Lion* (1947).

William Eastlake brought postmodernism and magic realism to the western. His four episodic "novels" set in the Southwest explore both a very real landscape and an entirely imaginary country simultaneously. In *Go in Beauty* (1956), a young novelist whose books about "Indian Country" were just becoming successful elopes to Europe with his brother's wife. Alienated from both his brother and *hozho* (a Navajo term for beauty and meaning in all living things), he loses his sense of inspiration and returns to the Southwest to try to find it again. *The Bronc People* (1958) features a would-be bronco rider and his African-American foster brother roaming northern New Mexico.

They learn many lessons from a former missionary who has been converted to Native American values, and from a wide variety of Navajo people. *Portrait of an Artist with Twenty-six Horses* (1963) follows the stream of consciousness of a man sunk up to his neck in quicksand as he ruminates on the meaning of life, nature, Christian and Indian cosmology, and related concepts. Although less acclaimed than Abbey's *The Monkey Wrench Gang* or Nichols's *The Milagro Beanfield War,* Eastlake's *Dancers in the Scalphouse* (1975) is more radical, experimental, lyrical, intellectually challenging, and absurdly comedic. A group of traditional Navajos, a nuclear physicist, and a hippie schoolteacher band together to drive developers from the reservation and restore the land. When the massive Atlas Dam that will inundate their homeland is about to be dedicated, they concoct a nuclear "gift."

Jack Schaefer is famous for his realistic first novel, *Shane* (1949), but his later magic realist work is of greater ecocritical interest. Michael Cleary notes that "the transformation of the frontier that he chronicles is a steadily declining world for which man is responsible."[3] Schaefer utilized anthropomorphized animals in *Mavericks* (1967), *An American Bestiary* (creative nonfiction, 1975), and *Conversations with a Pocket Gopher and Other Outspoken Neighbors* (1978), in which a gopher, shrew, bat, kangaroo rat, jaguar, and puma hilariously chide him for human misuse of the land, dualistic thinking, the arms race, ecological ruin, and the futility of technological quick fixes. *Old Ramon* (1960), the story of an old shepherd and a young boy, is a Newberry Award-winning children's book that also succeeds as an allegory for adults.

Eastlake and his friends Abbey and John Nichols are responsible for some of the first and some of the best ecodefense novels. Western writers played a very crucial role in the great outpouring of ecofiction in the 1970s. See chapter 2.

Louis L'Amour's extremely popular novels offer vivid portraits of the land while implying environmental concerns. In one of his first books, *Hondo* (1953), a father tells his daughter, "We do not own the land, Angie. We hold it in trust for tomorrow. We take our living from it, but we must leave it rich for your son and for all those who will follow."[4]

Dazzling depictions of the Southwest and colorful but fully credible white and Native American characters can be found in all of Tony Hillerman's westerns featuring two Navajo detectives, logical Joe Leaphorn and the more mystical Jim Chee. The only Hillerman novel with a primary ecological theme is *Sacred Clowns* (1993), in which Leaphorn and Chee follow a serpentine trail between many clans seeking the thread that links two murders, a missing teen, and lobbyists for a proposed toxic waste dump.

Earl Murray's *Song of Wovoka* (1992) tells the tale of the Paiute prophet who promised that the Ghost Dance would restore the buffalo and eliminate the white man, which instead ended with the tragic Wounded Knee massacre. His *In the Arms of the Sky* (1998) is based on the exploits of Victorian adventurer Isabella Bird, the author of *A Lady's Life in the Rocky Mountains* (1879). Bird climbs Long's Peak, vowing to protect it for future generations. Rookie forest ranger Ellis Burke finds himself in the middle of a conflict between ranchers who support the new restrictions he is trying to enforce and those who wish to continue depleting resources in Murray's *South of Eden* (2000).

Montana is the home of several fine authors. Norman Maclean's *A River Runs Through It and Other Stories* (1976) is a tough but poignant tale about a father and two sons who were drawn together by their almost mystical love of fly-fishing but torn apart by the recklessness of one son. Maclean influenced Thomas McGuane, whose *Nothing but Blue Skies* (1992) "is a book about land and livestock speculation, about fly-fishing and Montana rivers, about barroom brawls, about male camaraderie, about selling the family ranch—in short, about all forms of western cultural inheritance."[5] Some of McGuane's earlier novels—*The Sporting Club* (1968), *The Bushwhacked Piano* (1971), *Ninety-two in the Shade* (1973), *Keep the Change* (1989), and his more recent *The Cadence of Grass* (2002) and *Gallatin Canyon* (2006)—are also environmentally oriented. Mary Clearman Blew's female heroines ride the new frontier in *Lambing Out* (1977), *Runaway* (1990), and *Sister Coyote* (2000). The multigenerational tale of the McCaskill family is told by Ivan Doig in the trilogy consisting of *English Creek* (1984), *Dancing at the Rascal Fair* (1987), and *Ride with Me, Mariah Montana* (1990), and *Prairie Nocturne* (2003). Doig chronicles the building of the Fort Peck dam in *Bucking the Sun* (1996) and covers environmental journalism in *Mountain Time* (1999). Diane Smith uses an epistolary style very effectively in *Letters from Yellowstone* (1999) and *Pictures from an Expedition* (2002), both accounts of nineteenth-century scientific expeditions. For Montanan Rick Bass, see the "Philosophical/Spiritual" section of chapter 3.

Gerald Haslam has made many contributions as an author, editor, critic, and teacher. Much of his fiction, starting with *Okies* (1973), is set in the San Joaquin Valley, depicting the lives of blue-collar men and women and how they relate to each other and to the land. He chronicles the valley's evolution from wilderness to farms to oil drilling and big agribusiness to suburban sprawl. Two collections of his own stories, *That Constant Coyote: California Stories* (1990) and *Condor Dreams and Other Fictions* (1994), and two anthologies he edited, *California Heartland* (1978) and *Many Californias* (1992), provide a variety of perspectives on life in rural California.

The green-tinged spiritualism that Annie Dillard conveys in *A Tinker at Pilgrim Creek* (1974) and other creative nonfiction is reflected in *The Living* (1992), a novel about settlers and Indians in the Pacific Northwest.

Most fiction written by western Asian American authors tends to be social and political, not ecological. Exceptions include David Mas Masumoto (*Silent Strength,* 1985) and Wakako Yamauchi (*Songs My Mother Taught Me,* 1994), who both depict the California rural experience. Karen Tei Yamashita has written four satiric magical realist novels. *Through the Arc of the Rain Forest* (1990), *Brazil-Maru* (1992), and *Circle K Cycles* (2001) take place in the Amazon. *Tropic of Orange* (1997), set in Los Angeles, is a critique of American greed. Filmmaker Ruth L. Ozeki's *My Year of Meats* (1998) is a satiric exposé of the beef production and promotion industries. In her *All Over Creation* (2003), Idaho is the setting for a confrontation between organic farming advocates and biotechnologists.

Mexican-American authors frequently write about their relation to the land, but their work is predominantly poetry and drama. Significant fiction authors include Tomás Rivera (*The Earth Did Not Part,* 1971, aka *And the Earth Did Not Devour Him*), Lucha Corpi (*Delia's Song,* 1989), Ibis Gómez-

Vega (*Send my Roots Rain,* 1991), Helena Viramontes (*Under the Feet of Jesus,* 1995; *Their Dogs Came with Them,* 2000), and Ana Castillo *So Far from God* (1993).

Rudolfo Anaya is arguably the most significant green Chicano writer. He has edited or contributed to over twenty anthologies, written six plays, five children's books, four works of nonfiction, one epic poem, a short-story collection, and eight novels. His masterpiece is his first novel, *Bless Me, Ultima* (1972), a coming-of-age story that is equally appealing to young adults and adults. An alienated New Mexico teenager seeking the meaning of life and the purpose of his own meets Ultima, a natural healer and mystic who draws her inspiration from nature and the spirit world. Anaya takes us through physical, natural, and philosophic seasons in a quartet of unusual mysteries consisting of *Zia Summer* (1995), *Rio Grande Fall* (1996), *Shaman Winter* (1999), and *Jemez Spring* (2005).

Robert F. Gish is a true multiculturalist, equally at home in Anglo, Chicano, or Indian cultures. In addition to scholarly writing and personal essays, he has written two collections of short stories (*First Horses,* 1993; *Bad Boys and Black Sheep,* 1996) and the wonderful magical realist novella *When Coyote Howls: A Lavaland Fable* (1994). When a modern suburban coyote loses his voice, he embarks on a quest to petroglyphs and pictograms, seeking guidance from other animals on his way. The poetic writing, earthy humor, and inherent wildness of this tale are simply the setting for the gem of the story: that we must find the lost voice and values of the past to survive the present.

Magic realism also looms large in the work of Tom Robbins, whose primary theme is the free-spirited, natural individual versus repressive religious, political, social, and economic institutions. In his debut, *Another Roadside Attraction* (1971), "Robbins' heroine, Amanda, would reconnect mankind with the benign chaos of the natural world, substituting magic for logic, style for substance, and poetry for the analytical measure of authority."[6] In *Even Cowgirls Get the Blues* (1976), Sissy Hankshaw hitchhikes around the West seeking both freedom and connection, finding characters like the reclusive Chink who finds commonalities in Oriental and Native American philosophies. Of

Robbins's remaining novels, *Fierce Invalids Home from Hot Climates* (2000) and *Villa Incognito* (2003) are of greatest ecocritical interest.

Mark Siegel observes that "Robbins has apparently given rise to a number of other hippie-cowboy western writers, most notably Gino Sky and Rob Swigart."[7] Sky establishes a new western mythology based upon the equality and interdependence of all living things in *Appaloosa Rising: The Legend of the Cowboy Buddha* (1980) and its sequel, *Coyote Silk* (1987). Swigart's *Little America* (1977) could be described as a hippie western, but he has also written a New Age fantasy, *Book of Revelations* (1981), which interconnects the consciousness of humans, dolphins, and elephants, and three mysteries. Zen, Taoism, ecofeminism, and hippie pastoralism inform David James Duncan's *The River Why* (1983) and *River Teeth: Stories and Writings* (1995).

The ultimate hippie cowboy, though, is Mike Arans, the hero of James Galvin's *Fencing the Sky* (1999), the fictionalized continuation of *The Meadow* (1982). *The Meadow* was originally written for Galvin's daughter as a record of a disappearing place, time, land ethic, and people. Written in simple but poetic prose, it is postmodern in its nonchronological structure, tone, and in the treatment of the meadow itself and the seasons as actual characters. *Fencing the Sky* is set on the same land a decade later. Much of the land has been subdivided into forty-acre ranchettes by a developer named Snipes, who claims to want "wilderness" (that he has destroyed), and is unwilling to accommodate the needs and rights of the ranchers. A sort of range war develops between Snipes and the cowboys, primarily Mike Arans.

Frank Bergon describes his own work in a *Contemporary Authors* interview: "*Shoshone Mike* (1987) focused on Native Americans. *The Temptations of St. Ed & Brother S* (1993) emphasized contemporary religion. *Wild Game* (1995) concentrated on the environment. In my fourth novel, tentatively titled *Adios, Mexico!* a Basque-American from Nevada discovers all three subjects—Native Americans, environmental issues, and religious concerns—equally interwoven and significant in contemporary Chiapas."[8] In the rollicking *Temptations,* two monks struggle with their own inner demons while protesting the creation of a nuclear waste dump near their abbey in Nevada.

Nancy Lord's nonfiction and fiction are based in Alaska and informed by Inuit culture and outdoor activity. Her three short-story collections (*The Compass Inside Ourselves*, 1984; *Survival*, 1991; *The Man Who Swam with Beavers*, 2001) reflect her philosophy of treating each other and the rest of nature with greater compassion.

Kent Nelson's first green novel was *Cold Wind River* (1981), in which the foreman of a cattle ranch struggles with the murder of a hired hand, abandonment by his wife, the troublesome new ranch manager, and the harshness of the Montana winter. In *All Around Me Peaceful* (1989), Neil Shanks investigates his family's questionable lumber profits. Although this novel offers thrilling suspense, the characters' response to the locale is the central theme. Nelson's *Language in the Blood* (1991) won the Edward Abbey Award for Ecofiction. Ornithologist Scott Talmedge, his ex-wife, current lover, and an old friend smuggle Guatemalan refugees across the Sonoran Desert, where they learn about nature, love, determination, and loyalty. *The Middle of Nowhere* (1991) contains thirteen short stories, approximately half of which have natural settings and themes. There are no real heroes or villains in *Discoveries: Short Stories of the San Juan Mountains* (1998) or *The Touching That Lasts* (2006), just real people working their way through their own emotional and physical landscapes. In *Land That Moves, Land That Stands Still* (2003), a middle-aged South Dakota alfalfa farmer must contend with the death of her husband, the discovery that he was a closeted gay, the comings, goings, and affairs of her daughter, a handywoman, and a runaway Indian boy.

Kent and Dylan Nelson coedited *Birds in the Hand: Fiction and Poetry About Birds* (2004) by Charles Baxter, T. C. Boyle, Jim Harrison, Flannery O'Connor, Pattiann Rogers, Seamus Heaney, Derek Walcott, Ethan Canin, and Jorie Graham.

When a Colorado man discovers Indian cliff dwellings on his ranch in Clyde Edgerton's *Redeye* (1995), he wants to preserve them but foils his own efforts by writing a booklet about them which inevitably leads to tourists, developers, and conflict over the dwellings' future.

The title character of Nicholas Evans's *The Horse Whisperer* (1995) can cure emotionally disturbed horses and their equally damaged owners by quietly talking to them. *The Loop* (1998) is a much grittier novel about conflict over the reintroduction of wolves to Montana, in which Evans attempts to represent all factions, including the wolves themselves, fairly. For Evans's *The Smoke Jumper* (2006), see chapter 6.

Many wilderness adventure and outdoor sports books have an environmental subtext. The smoke jumpers in J. R. Goddard's *The Night Crew* (1970) brave intense natural conditions and their own conflicting emotions to overcome a raging forest fire near Monterey.

Elizabeth Arthur's protagonists are mountain climbers and explorers in Alaska and other icy regions (*Beyond the Mountain*, 1983; *Bad Guys*, 1986; *Binding Spell*, 1988; *Antarctic Navigation*, 1995). Alaska is also the setting for William McCloskey's *Highliners* (1979) and its sequel *Breakers* (2000), in which an independent commercial fisherman struggles to compete against corporate fishing interests. River guide Timothy Hillmer's wilderness experience informs *The Hookman* (1994), an exciting rafting tale set on the Kern River. Pete Fromm's short stories are typically set in the wild, and deal with nature, hunting, fishing, and human relationships (*The Tall Uncut*, 1991; *King of the Mountain*, 1994; *Dry Rain*, 1997; *Blood Knot*, 1998; *Night Swimming*, 1999). In *The Guide and the CEO*, by M. David Detweiler (2001), when the title characters go on a fishing trek together, the former questions the latter's decision to sell a chain of sporting goods stores and strike out for the wild, but in the end tries to set him up with his equally wild daughter.

Place Last Seen (2000) by Charlotte McGuinn Freeman is a compelling account of a search-and-rescue mission for a six-year-old who wanders off in the High Sierra. It provides a firsthand experience of the family's harrowing ordeal.

The ancient and the postmodern are seamlessly melded in Bill Broder's *The Sacred Hoop: A Cycle of Earth Tales* (1992). From a retelling of Genesis to the saga of the Steam God (railroad) in nineteenth-century America, this book depicts the larger chronicle of humankind's changing relationship with the earth, the gods, and the universe. Further into the fields of postmodernism we find Eugene K. Garber and David Romtvedt. In Garber's *The Historian: Six Fantasies of the American Experience* (1993), the historian's intellectual pursuit of his muse, Clio, runs counterpoint to his cousin Simms's outdoor adventures and metamorphoses. Is Simms actually part bear? In Romtvedt's *Crossing Wyoming* (1992), historian Eduardo Galeano time travels around Wyoming and to Uruguay, Buffalo, the Dakotas, England, Guatemala, and various other places between the years 1493 and 2079. The cautionary message of "how the rich and powerful have used their wealth to have their way with others, with nature, with God" (p. v) is couched in hilarious satire.

David Guterson's *Snow Falling on Cedars* (1994) is both a brilliant evocation of the land, water, and weather of the Puget Sound area and a gripping suspense story about conflicts between Japanese-American strawberry growers and fishermen and Anglo fisherman. Guterson's *East of the Mountains* (1999) and *Our Lady of the Forest* (2003) also explore the interconnectedness of physical and moral landscapes. *The Other* (2008) is an account of a young man who becomes a virtually Paleolithic hermit living in a cave.

Over the past quarter century both the traditional western and writing about the West have become more diverse and more deeply environmentally oriented. As Mark Siegel notes, "Serious western literature in its traditional forms will continue to show its distinctive qualities, largely because western fiction reflects its environment more than any other regional literature in the United States. The vastness, aridity, and sublime magnificence of the West that force man to reexamine his relationship to nature will continue to be the hallmark of traditional western writing, and that tradition will necessarily evolve as the face of the West itself changes."[9]

8

Green Speculative Fiction

Speculative fiction is extremely wide ranging and inclusive in presenting a variety of alternatives regarding philosophy and cosmology, political and social organization, applications of technology, environmental thought and practices, the relation between humans and other animals, and the relations between genders, races, and individuals.

The perspective, values, and plots of old-fashioned western "horse operas" and science fiction "space operas" are similar and predictable: nature, whether wilderness or space, is a malevolent force to be conquered by macho men with powerful weaponry for the sake of progress and profit. Red blood once flowed freely over the imaginary purple planets or equally fantastic purple sage, but that's changing. As the negative environmental and social consequences of our current technological age become ever clearer, the simplistic notions that progress and growth are always good, that technology alone can provide the answers to all of the world's problems, and that problems created by technology can be fixed with even more technology are increasingly being called into question. Indeed, the most radical works might be called *anti*-science fiction. Luddite voices are few, however, with most current authors advocating a position that was initially dubbed "appropriate technology" in the 1960s.

The "New Wave" of science fiction that emerged four decades ago and strongly influences current writing pays less attention to technology in and of itself and more to its social, political, psychological, and environmental aspects. The political upheaval of the sixties in the related struggles of the civil rights, anti-war, feminist, and environmental movements influenced "New Wave" and vice versa. Suddenly the specialized scientific subfield known as ecology became a household word, most appropriately since *oikos,* the Greek root of the term "ecology," means "home." "Eco" became a prefix: eco-crisis, eco-responsibility, ecofeminist, and so on. The title of John Stadler's revolutionary 1971 anthology *Eco-fiction* may be the first written use of that particular term.

Future Primitive: The New Ecotopias (1994), edited by Kim Stanley Robinson, is a superb collection of twelve stories and three poems inspired by Ernest Callenbach's *Ecotopia* and by *Dream's Edge: Science Fiction Stories About the Future of Planet Earth* (1980). Gary Snyder, Terry Bisson, Robert Silverberg, Gene Wolfe, Ernest Callenbach, Carol Emshwiller, Ursula K. Le Guin, Robinson Jeffers, and other authors envision a different sort of future on Earth, often combining traditional or even Paleolithic culture with postmodern, nature-friendly technologies. Robinson's introduction, endnotes, and suggested reading list are of particular ecocritical interest. Other relevant anthologies include *Saving Worlds,* edited by Roger Elwood and Virginia Kidd (1973); *Isaac Asimov's Earth,* edited by Gardner Dozois (1992); and *How to Save the World,* edited by Charles Sheffield (1995).

Andre Norton echoed the thoughts of many "New Wave" authors when she observed that "the human race made a bad mistake at the beginning of the Industrial Revolution. We leaped for the mechanics, and threw aside things that were just as important. We made the transition too fast."[1] She specifies that the things left behind were nature, magic, and quality hand craftsmanship.

A commonly accepted distinction between science fiction and fantasy is that the former is based upon what may be scientifically plausible, while the latter is a purely imaginative realm. Since the best contemporary science fiction and fantasy are both genre- and gender-busting, it may be more accurate to use the newer term "speculative fiction" for both. The "what if" nature of speculative fiction provides an excellent vehicle for the consideration of environmental and social issues.

While "space operas," old and new, tend to be penned by men, women hold up half of the sky in ecologically oriented speculative fiction. Many ecofeminist authors have effectively employed fantasy and science fiction to explore the relationship between sexism and the environmental crisis, typically offering positive alternatives to both. If one accepts that a fundamental purpose of speculative fiction is the consideration of alternative modes of thought and behavior, then one might reasonably ask, "What is the particular point of ecofeminist speculative fiction?" Veronica Hollinger has noted that "feminist sf is not simply sf about women; it is sf written in the interests of women—*however diversely those interests are defined by individual writers*. It is a potent tool for feminist imaginative projects that are the necessary first steps in undertaking the cultural and social transformations that are the aims of the feminist political enterprise."[2]

This chapter consists of a long section on general speculative fiction and shorter ones for two special subgenres: green fantasies written primarily for a young adult audience that are also of interest to adult readers, and fantasies about prehistoric times.

GENERAL SPECULATIVE FICTION

In Douglas Adams's *Hitchhiker's Quartet,* Arthur Dent learns that bulldozers are about to level his house for a highway project (*The Hitchhiker's Guide to the Galaxy,* 1979; *The Restaurant at the End of the Universe,* 1980; *Life, the Universe and Everything,* 1982; *So Long, and Thanks for All the Fish,* 1985). His secretly alien neighbor, Ford Prefect, then tells him that Earth is about to be destroyed to build an interstellar highway. Dent and Prefect hitchhike around the galaxy trying to discover where the dolphins went and why Earth was selected for destruction. Adams's Dirk Gently is a philosophical fantasy detective who solves mysteries by considering the interconnectedness of all things in *Dirk Gently's Holistic Detective Agency* (1987) and *The Long Dark Tea-Time of the Soul* (1988).

Brian Aldiss wrote a quartet of popular green novels in the sixties (*Hot-*

house, 1962; *Greybeard*, 1964; *Earthworks*, 1965; *Neanderthal Planet*, 1969). His Hugo Award-winning Helliconia Trilogy (*Helliconia Spring*, 1982; *Helliconia Summer*, 1983; *Helliconia Winter*, 1985; published in one volume, *Helliconia*, 1996) examines life on a planet with a seasonal cycle of 2,500 Earth years that suffers extreme heat in summer; extreme cold, darkness, and barbarism in winter; and plague in both winter and spring. Earthlings monitor Helliconia by satellite, and soon find themselves facing similar challenges as nuclear winter envelops the earth. Aldiss and Roger Penrose penned a book inspired by Kim Stanley Robinson's Mars series, *White Mars; or, The Mind Set Free* (1999), about the establishment of a utopian society on Mars.

Kevin Anderson's debut, *Resurrection, Inc.* (1988), is about a technology that reanimates corpses. Their memories erased, they become virtual slaves to their human masters. He and Doug Beason have cowritten several novels, the most ecologically oriented of which is *Ill Wind* (1995), in which an oil company tries to mitigate the effects of an oil spill with genetically engineered microbes. After the microbes devour the oil spill, they start eating all gasoline, plastics, and all other polycarbons.

Piers Anthony's Battle Circle trilogy (*SOS the Rope*, 1968; *Var the Stick*, 1972; *Neq the Sword*, 1975) is about society rebuilding after a nuclear holocaust, warning against the continuing dangers of overpopulation and centralization. The Omnivore series (*Omnivore*, 1968; *Orn*, 1971; *Ox*, 1976) is pro-vegetarian. In *Being a Green Mother* (1987) a girl's discovery and mastery of "Llano: The Elusive Song of Nature" makes her the Incarnation of Nature. *Hope of Earth* (1997) is a sweeping time-travel book ending with a rousing call for a more environmentally oriented way of life.

Will Baker's *Shadow Hunter* (1993) takes place in the early twenty-second century when the Northern Hemisphere is high-tech and prosperous, but the Southern is an irradiated desert. When the son of an official is attacked by a wild animal and then kidnapped on a hunting trip, a conservative faction arises that seeks to kill the primitive "ginks" and all other disorderly "primitive wildlife."

In Ray Bawarchi's *The Dirt People* (2007), resistance arises to the "corporate Sponsors" who control all aspects of life in domed cities.

Greg Bear primarily writes cautionary tales about misuse of technology. *Blood Music* (1985) examines the creation of a biochip that breeds, spreads, and mutates. In *Eon* (1985), a spaceship from the future warns of an imminent nuclear war, but earthlings fail to act on the warning, so in *Eternity* (1988) they must recover from the war and an alien invasion. *Legacy* (1995) explores life on the planet Lamarckia, which is populated by organisms that sample and share each other's characteristics, incorporating what they find useful. In *The Forge of God* (1987), when the sixth moon of Jupiter mysteriously disappears, a five-hundred-foot cinder cone appears in Death Valley, as does a perfect imitation of Ayers Rock in Australia, and Earth faces disaster from space probes. After Earth has been destroyed by the probes in the sequel, *Anvil of Stars* (1992), surviving earthlings make a pact with benefactor machines to destroy the eco-killing probes before other planets are lost. They create a giant spaceship from the rubble left from Earth to find and destroy the probes. *Darwin's Radio* (1999) and *Darwin's Children* (2003) are considerations of nanotechnology and the possibility of humans being replaced by beings evolved from a retro-virus discovered in recently excavated Neanderthals.

Gregory Benford's *Timescape* (1980) takes place in 1998 when the oceans are being destroyed from pollution, threatening the survival of almost all living things. Scientists send a message to the year 1963, hoping that action will be taken then to save the Earth.

As the title character of Terry Bisson's *Talking Man* (1986), who never actually speaks, travels across the country, change happens faster and more drastically. When he returns home to Kentucky he finds that it has become a rural utopia. *Pirates of the Universe* (1995) is the name of a "utopian" Disney theme park, but the twenty-first-century corporate version of utopia is little more than a Disney-Microsoft monopoly. Bisson's *Bears Discover Fire and Other Stories* (1993) and *In the Upper Room and Other Likely Stories* (2000) are collections of delightful fantasy stories. Following instructions left by Walter M. Miller, author of *A Canticle for Leibowitz,* Bisson completed a sequel awaited for nearly forty years, *Saint Leibowitz and the Wild Horse Woman* (1997). Unfortunately, the result was not up to the standards of either author.

Ben Bova believes that humanity's problems can be partially solved through space colonization, and he examines complex problems that must be overcome, favoring some options over others. In *The Winds of Altair* (1973), earthlings try to solve population problems by terraforming another planet, although doing so would destroy Altair's native species. *Colony* (1978) presents an alternative solution: the creation of a massive space station. In *Empire Builders* (1993), the world has less than ten years before a global warming catastrophe. Its jingoistic prequel, *Privateers* (1985), is little more than an argument in favor of Ronald Reagan's proposed "Star Wars" defense initiative. *Brothers* (1996) is a medical thriller considering such issues as corporate control of science and the ethics of animal experimentation. *Moonrise* (1996) and *Moonwar* (1998) caution against the excesses of corporate greed in colonization efforts. In *The Precipice* (2001), the greenhouse effect is creating economic and environmental crises.

John Boyd is concerned about the inability of human wisdom to keep pace with technology. This concern is expressed in almost all his many books but is the primary theme in *The Pollinators of Eden* (1969), *The Organ Bank Farm* (1970), and *The Doomsday Gene* (1973).

Marion Zimmer Bradley's Darkover series consists of over twenty volumes. The first book (*The Sword of Aldones,* 1962) introduces a long-neglected space colony that is not nearly as bureaucratic or as technologically advanced as the expansionist Terran Empire but possesses a far greater level of freedom and a more ecological approach to life. By creating both a patriarchal elite and groups known as Free Amazons, Bradley reconsiders patriarchy and feminism in depth and attempts to reconcile conflicting ideas in *The Shattered Chain* (1976). Bradley reinvents and reinvigorates Arthurian myth in *The Mists of Avalon* (1983) through a similar method, this time by contrasting pagan and Christian cosmologies.

Gary Braver warns that if you take a miracle elixir to reverse the aging process, you must take it forever or die immediately. *Elixir* (2000) is an exploration of corporate greed and connections to crime syndicates, the ethics of anti-aging drugs, and the consequences of increased human life spans.

Astrophysicist David Brin's two Uplift trilogies consider the ethical aspects of genetic engineering. *Sundiver* (1980) introduces the parallel Progenitors universe, which is teeming with intelligent life. In *Startide Rising* (1983), the Progenitors have uplifted all the other intelligent species in the galaxy. *The Uplift War* (1987) occurs when a small colony of humans and chimps battles the Progenitors over a secret experiment designed to produce the next uplift. In *Brightness Reef* (1995) humans arrive on the banned planet Jijo, illegally searching for other species to uplift and disrupting the planet's delicate ecological web. *Infinity's Shore* (1996) details the disastrous consequences. In *Heaven's Reach* (1998) aliens invade Earth, dolphins flee Jijo on a quest to create universal peace, but their efforts may be futile since the stability of space itself has been compromised. In this series every attempt to circumvent normal evolution, no matter how well intended, has horrifying consequences.

Brin's *The Practice Effect* (1984) is a time-travel fantasy in which tools and other objects actually improve with continued use. *The Postman* (1985) is set in the near future after nuclear war. An itinerant storyteller spreads his message of hope and renewal. In *Earth* (1990), in the mid-twenty-first century, humanity is struggling to reconcile high technology, materialism, resource depletion, and pollution when black holes developing within the planet shift the focus from conservation to a desperate struggle for survival. *Glory Season* (1993) takes place on a world ruled by genetically engineered women. In *Kiln People* (2002) humans use a process called imprinting to temporarily copy their personalities onto clay "dittos." Brin has also published four collections of short stories and several nonfiction works, most notably *Tomorrow Happens* (2003), which includes a story cowritten with Gregory Benford.

John Brunner's *Stand on Zanzibar* (1968) is set in the twenty-first century. Seven billion people experience a ravaged environment, oppression, violence, and the hysteria of extreme crowding stress, but don't realize that they are all slipping into madness in a powerful outcry against violence, overpopulation, drugs, greed, and stupidity. In the sequel, *The Sheep Look Up* (1972), the entire biosphere is threatened with extinction. Humanity must create a solution to restore the damaged environment.

William S. Burroughs's *Ghost of Chance* (1995) is a tale of the rise and fall of Libertatia, an ecologically based community in seventeenth-century Madagascar where humans have deep personal bonds with lemurs. The settlers create a Museum of Lost Species and a Biological Garden of Lost Chances. Burroughs traces the current environmental crisis to Christianity's rise over pantheism.

Octavia Butler's Patternist series chronicles the evolution of a telepathic community over several millennia. (The following books are listed in the order of the events, not by date of publication.) In *Wild Seed* (1980), Doro, a four-thousand-year-old mutant must periodically kill human hosts to continue living. Amoral Doro represents patriarchy, coercion, and destruction, while "wild seed" Anyanwu personifies matriarchy, healing, and creation. Set in the late twentieth century, *Mind of My Mind* (1977) recounts Anyanwu's descendant Mary's creation of a powerful network of telepaths. Destructive climatic, environmental, political, and social trends, religious zealotry, and corporate greed have degraded life on earth in *Clay's Ark* (1984). After Clayark depredations have killed half of humanity, a group of "Missionaries" escapes to colonize another planet in *Survivor* (1978), Butler's only novel not set on Earth. The mentally gifted Patternists struggle against the physically superior Clayarks in *Patternmaster* (1976).

The Xenogenesis trilogy is Butler's most complex consideration of genetic questions and of determinism versus free will. After humanity nearly destroys itself through nuclear warfare, the extraterrestrial Oankali collect the survivors and place them in suspended animation in *Dawn* (1987). *Adulthood Rites* (1988) begins thirty years later, after humans and Oankali have formed a living enclave in the Amazon jungle. A century later, a man named Jodahs develops into what the Oankali fear most: a human-born Ooli with both the Ooli gift for genetic engineering and a dangerous human contradiction that leads to self-destruction in *Imago* (1989).

Butler's *Parable of the Sower* (1993) recounts the creation of a positive alternative to the dystopia of the twenty-first century. Lauren Olamina, an African-American teenager, founds Earthseed, a multiracial, multi-aged group. *Parable of the Talents* (1998) continues Earthseed's story. Denuded of erosion-preventing oaks, the earth itself helps the remaining Earthseed members oust the "Christian" Crusaders with a timely landslide. Eventually people reject right-wing government and corporate domination, Lauren spreads the Earth-seed faith, and in 2090 the first Earthseed colony is sent into space.

Ernest Callenbach's classic *Ecotopia* (1975) presents a vision of an alternative society based on a sustainable economy, de-urbanization, decentralization of political power, solar and alternative energy sources, and feminism: a seamless, stable-state web of living organisms. Although Callenbach's writing is rather prosaic and highly didactic, this is nevertheless an entertaining, inspiring book. *Ecotopia Emerging* (1981) is a prequel, describing the creation, philosophy, and operation of the new society in greater detail. "Chocco," a short story published in *Future Primitive* (1994), might be called "Ecotopia Prevails."

Ember from the Sun (1996) by Mark Canter is the story of a young woman who is the child of a Native American woman who was implanted with the fetus of a frozen Neanderthal. She develops healing and shamanistic powers that prove useful in a search for other Neanderthals who are threatened by a gold-mining operation.

Joy Chant has written a series of three mythopoetic novels. In *Red Moon and Black Mountain* (1970), three children are drawn into a struggle between the hunters and the star warriors. The attitude toward nature is one that rejects the oversimplified pastoral approach in favor of one emphasizing multiplicity, diversity, and complexity. *The Grey Mane of Morning* (1977) features greater emphasis on mythic figures, an even more complex view of the environment, and lush, naturalistic sexuality. *When Voiha Wakes* (1983) is set on a different part of the planet where women are in control while men perform menial labor and crafts.

The war between the sexes is literally a pitched battle for Suzy McKee Charnas, who sometime employs the device that Marlene S. Barr refers to as "exaggerating 'acceptable' sexism . . . [to act as] a microscope in relation to patriarchal myths."[3] In *Walk to the End of the World* (1974), the survivors of a nuclear holocaust form a repressive colony named Holdfast where women have the status of slaves or even domestic animals. In *Motherlines* (1978), an escapee from Holdfast named Alderra finds a tribe of other escaped slaves who are more nature oriented than the men of Holdfast but are equally hier-archical and repressive. Alderra's daughter Sorrel raises an army and invades Holdfast, then rides off with the Riding Women in *The Furies* (1994). In *The Conqueror's Child* (1999), she returns to Holdfast, where the women have reversed sexism and enslaved the men. Sorrell and some of the other women and men are ready to evolve to a more egalitarian society but face many challenges to overcome past prejudices.

David B. Coe's LonTobyn Chronicle (*The Children of Amarid,* 1997; *The Outlanders,* 1998; *Eagle-Sage,* 2000) is set in a land that is initially a fantasy ecotopia rich in magic, but its existence is threatened by Lon-Ser, a nearby land that had rejected magic for technology and become greedy and militaristic.

Elizabeth Cunningham has written two pagan-influenced magical real-ist novels. In *The Return of the Goddess: A Divine Comedy* (1992), developers threaten to fell an ancient grove of mystic trees with reputed healing power, but meet with opposition from four disparate people. A modern Adam ven-tures into the Empty Lands where the immortal descendants of Lillith live in harmony with nature in *The Wild Mother* (1993).

Dennis Danvers's work is similar to Kim Stanley Robinson's. In *Circuit of Heaven* (1998), people have the choice of living physically in a world marked by conflict, religious fundamentalism, poverty, and environmental decay or having their souls uploaded into eternal life without their bodies in "The Bin." This makes things a bit inconvenient when a Bin resident and a mor-tal fall in love. The course of true love runs even less smooth in *Wilderness* (2000), in which a woman who metamorphoses into a wolf once a month and a wolf biologist fall in love. In *End of Days* (1999), the sequel to *Circuit of Heaven,* some Bin residents attempt to return to a more authentic life, but the potential confrontation with fundamentalists threatens not just them but the survival of the universe itself.

Todd Dezago and Shane Davis team up in the graphic novel *Spider-Man and Fantastic Four in The Menace of Monster Isle!* (2006), sending the super-heroes out to save the environment.

Philip K. Dick poses the provocative question: *Do Androids Dream of Elec-tric Sheep?* (1968). After nuclear war and subsequent radiation have destroyed much of the biosphere, artificial animals become status symbols and highly humanized androids escape back to Earth. A vicious android bounty hunter falls in love with a female android. The movie *Blade Runner* is an adaptation of *Androids*. The original book is much deeper than the film, questioning what constitutes humanity and offering a cautionary note about nuclear war and environmental degradation. Dick's Hugo Award-winning alternative history *The Man in the High Castle* (1964) is considered by many critics to be one of the finest in that genre. Many of his other novels are considerations of the relationship between humanity and technology or explorations of human consciousness.

In Carole Nelson Douglas's *Cup of Clay* (1991), reporter Alison Carver makes a quest to find a magical cup in the "otherworld" of Veil. Darker forces emerge after she heals some ruined farmland, forcing her and former rival Rowan to seek the Heart of the Earth to heal the planet. In *Seed upon the Wind* (1992), when Carver returns the magical cup to Earth she learns that blight is occurring in Veil, so she and Rowan make another quest.

L. Warren Douglas has written three novels about the dangers of genetic engineering: *Plague of Change* (1992), *Stepwater* (1995), and *Glaice* (1996). *The Sacred Pool* (2001) and its sequel, *The Veil of Years* (2001), are time-travel books portraying pagan societies.

Communication is the key for linguist Suzette Haden Elgin in her Native Tongue series: *Native Tongue* (1984), *The Judas Rose* (1987), and *Earthsong* (1994). After extraterrestrials leave Earth, economic and environmental collapse ensues. A female linguist presents a startling plan for the survival of the human race and the restoration of environmental quality.

Although Philip José Farmer's Riverworld series has a definite ecological undercurrent, *The Lavalite World* (1977) is his greenest novel. When Anana and the trickster Kickaha arrive in Los Angeles, the overpopulation and pollution make them wish they were back on their own planet. The living mountains, man-eating trees, and other unusual characters make for exciting reading.

After a devastating comet strike and subsequent meteorological madness, engineers save the world in engineer Samuel C. Florman's *The Aftermath: A*

Novel of Survival (2001). In an inversion of the theme of the misapplication technology leading to disaster, nature here is the perpetrator and technology the cure.

Exit to Reality (1997) by Edith Forbes is set in the year 3000. With the population stabilized, crime and poverty have been eradicated. When an information analyst meets a rare unemployed person, she discovers that he is actually a shape-shifter, causing her to question morality, mortality, bioengineering, sexuality, and the nature of reality itself.

Kathleen Ann Goonan has written a trilogy on the dangers of nanotechnology: *Queen City Jazz* (1994), *Mississippi Blues* (1997), and *Crescent City Rhapsody* (2000).

Wildside (1996) by Steven Gould tells the tale of two teens trying to explore and protect a parallel Earth where humans never existed and the now-extinct species of Earth still flourish.

In Richard Grant's *Rumors of Spring* (1987), Earth's final forest starts growing uncontrollably and the First Biotic Crusade begins.

In the Small (2008) by Michael Hague is a graphic novel in which human beings are shrunk to six inches tall, greatly changing the ecological balance by turning humans from predator to prey.

Harry Harrison's *Make Room! Make Room!* (1966) is set in the early twenty-first century when overpopulation and resource depletion are so advanced that there are few natural sources of food. The movie *Soylent Green* was adapted from this novel. In *West of Eden* (1984), *Winter in Eden* (1986), and *Return to Eden* (1988), a new ice age emerges. Most of the stories in Harrison's short-story collection *One Step from Earth* (1980) also have environmental subjects.

Into the Forest (1996) by Jean Alma Hegland takes place in the redwood forests in the near future when civilization has collapsed from environmental and social problems and warfare. Two teenage sisters lose their parents, eat the remaining food in their crumbling house, and then go semi-feral.

Davie Henderson's *Tomorrow's World* (2008) is a science-fiction mystery about genetic engineering and government-corporate control.

Frank Herbert wrote over thirty books, approximately half of which have ecological themes. His debut, *The Dragon in the Sea* (1956), takes place in a nuclear sub that is stealing oil from underwater wells after sixteen years of war have depleted the world's resources. In Herbert's *Soul Catcher* (1972), a Native American inspired by his totem becomes the avenging balancer of heaven and Earth and kidnaps the son of a politician who he hopes will help him restore the balance.

Developed over the course of six books in twenty years, Herbert's desert planet Arrakis may be the most complex, multidimensional, fully realized alternative world in modern literature (*Dune*, 1965; *Dune Messiah*, 1970; *Children of Dune*, 1976; *God Emperor of Dune*, 1981; *Heretics of Dune*, 1984; *Chapter House: Dune*, 1985). Herbert's consistent message is that humanity hangs in the balance between its self-destructive and self-sustaining instincts, and that the behavioral and social changes needed for survival are only possible through a wise and compassionate evolution of consciousness.

Herbert and Bill Ransom cowrote a series set on another desert planet, Pandora. In *The Jesus Incident* (1979), adaptation to the harsh environment involves mating a human being and sentient kelp to produce a hybrid female. The themes of survival, adaptation, and genetic engineering are interwoven in *The Lazarus Effect* (1983). In Herbert's swan song, *The Ascension Factor* (1988), as the desert becomes engulfed by the sea, the remaining humans attempt to restore land and build settlements.

Man of Two Worlds (1986) was cowritten with his son Brian. It satirizes both the Dune books and science fiction in general through the inversion of presenting human beings as the product of alien imaginations. Brian Herbert and Kevin J. Anderson have continued the Dune Chronicles, now at twelve volumes. Brian Herbert edited *The Notebooks of Dune* (1988) and *Songs of Muad'dib: Poems and Songs from Frank Herbert's Dune Series and His Other Writings* (1992) and wrote *Dune Concordance* and *Dreamer of Dune* (2003), a biography of Frank Herbert.

Brian Herbert's own novels are distinguished from his father's work by their edgy black humor. In *Sidney's Comet* (1983), the gods return a massive wad of garbage dumped in space. He followed it with the sequel, *The Garbage Chronicles* (1985), and *The Race for God* (1990), in which religious intolerance is deemed responsible for oppression, warfare, and environmental ruin.

James Herbert's *Portent* (1996) depicts a world undergoing earthquakes, wind storms, and other catastrophes accompanied by bright lights that may signal the end of the world. A climatologist discovers psychic, healing Romanian twin children who may hold the key to survival.

In Stan Kahn's *Y3K* (2007), a group of thirtieth-century hippie commune members consider interwoven social and ecological crises.

Philip K. Dick Award winner Kay Kenyon is perhaps the most promising author of green science fiction to emerge in the last decade. With Earth on the verge of environmental collapse and species extinction, in 2019 a woman is sent through time to find regenerative seeds in *The Seeds of Time* (1997). In *Leap Point* (1998), a woman trying to discover the truth of her son's suicide discovers an alien conspiracy and an addictive game known as Nir, short for Nirvana. After the terraforming of the planet Lithia fails, a resident wants to return it to its natural state, but soon discovers the potential disaster of a deep geologic *Rift* (1999). *Tropic of Creation* (2000) is about the dangers of rapid climatic changes. In *Maximum Ice* (2002), the crew of a starship returns from a 250-year mission to find resources to replenish Earth only to discover that it has become an ice world whose meager human population consists of warring tribes. In *Ice*'s sequel, *The Braided World* (2003), a mission to find genetic material to repopulate Earth leads to a species that appears to be humanoid but whose lack of ethics threatens rather than enhances humanity's prospects. Kenyon's impressive new Empire and the Rose series currently consists of *Bright of the Sky* (2007) and *A World Too Near* (2008).

In T. J. Kirby's *Dangerous Nature* (1993), a disabled scientist seems to be on the verge of a breakthrough on limb regeneration when animal activists break into his lab, release the animals, and steal the serum. What will happen if the experimental drug is released into the environment?

Why Do Birds: A Comic Novel of the Destruction of the Human Race (1992) by Damon Knight is the story of a man who claims he's been in suspended animation since the 1930s when he was kidnapped by aliens. The aliens return to Earth to convince its leaders to build a massive vault to place the entire human population in suspended animation to survive the planet's impending crisis.

In Michael P. Kube-McDowell's *The Quiet Pools* (1990), the rapidly deteriorating environment of twenty-first-century Earth accelerates the effort to colonize other planets. One subplot features environmental activists using computers and other high-tech devices in their struggle against corporate polluters.

All the Gods of Eisernon (1973) by Simon Lang is the tale of an ecologically based world that is attacked by another planet but saved by a mission from Earth led by a brash commander and his dispassionate half-human science officer who resemble Kirk and Spock of *Star Trek* fame.

Based on the quality, quantity, and complexity of her work and her popular and critical acclaim, Ursula K. Le Guin is arguably the most significant green speculative fiction author. Her work varies between forms, often melding "hard" science fiction, fantasy, and mainstream fiction. She is also a fine poet and essayist. Her work will be considered by theme and form here rather than chronologically, beginning with the Hain cycle.

In *Rocannon's World* (1966), *Planet of Exile* (1966), and *City of Illusions* (1967), a highly intelligent race from the planet Hain has colonized planets throughout the universe, pursuing universal peace through a League of All Worlds later named the "Ekumen." They attempt to strike a balance between preservation of nature and technological development, with not all technologies being considered beneficial. Although the two primary issues addressed in *The Left Hand of Darkness* (1969) are trust/betrayal and gender, how people adjust to a frigid, hostile environment is an important subtext. *The Lathe of Heaven* (1971) opens with the image of a jellyfish floating harmoniously in the ocean until it is expelled upon the shore, a good symbol for a planet threatened by overpopulation, pollution, and radiation. In *The Word for World Is Forest* (1972), the Athshe is being clear-cut after Earth's forests have been destroyed. This book is an implicit condemnation of the Vietnam War's massive environmental destruction and the dehumanization of the Vietnamese. The subtitle of *The Dispossessed: An Ambiguous Utopia* (1974) is particularly revealing: anarchists have traded the class divisions, sexism, social control, warfare, and wastefulness of a lush planet for a hardscrabble existence on a desert planet, but their freedom is not as absolute as they believe. *The Telling*

(2000) is the name of a Taoist-like religion on the planet Aka whose suppression has upset Aka's social and environmental balance. *The Birthday of the World* (2002) consists of seven previously published Hain stories and a new novella, *Paradises Lost*.

The first three of the Earthsea books (*A Wizard of Earthsea*, 1968; *The Tombs of Atuan*, 1970; *The Farthest Shore*, 1972) formed an exciting series for young adults featuring the young wizard Ged and his friend Tenar. It emphasizes maintaining balance in the natural world, the social sphere, and, most importantly, the self. *Tehanu: The Last Book of Earthsea* (1990) is somewhat darker. The now aged Ged has lost most of his power, but Tenar, two witches, and the fire-disfigured girl Therru all display various aspects of feminine Earth-power. *Tales from Earthsea* (2001) contains five stories in which all sacred or magical power is inherent to the earth and only lent to humans. Personal and planetary issues of life, death, immortality, and reincarnation dominate *The Other Wind* (2001).

In *The Eye of the Heron* (1983), a Terran prison planet contains two settlements: prisoners in the city and a smaller group of exiled pacifists in bucolic Shantih. The Shantih people adapt themselves to a new environment while the city dwellers struggle unsuccessfully to master it.

After our current society is destroyed by toxic wastes, radioactivity, pollution, and earthquakes in *Always Coming Home* (1985), civilization slowly reestablishes itself. To the Kesh, all animals are "people," no distinction is made between human and natural history, and social organization is based upon natural cycles. The Condors form a hierarchical, militaristic, sexist, monotheistic society. Their expansionism threatens the Kesh, but the Condors eventually self-destruct under the burdens of maintaining their military and of factionalism resulting from a lack of democracy.

Le Guin's stories appear frequently in both mainstream and science-fiction magazines and anthologies. *The Wind's Twelve Quarters* (1975) was her first collection, containing "Vaster Than Empires and More Slow," about an exploratory mission to a planet that is actually a sentient being, and "Direction of the Road," a wry commentary on technologies that separate humans from the rest of nature told from the perspective of a roadside oak. Several stories in *The Compass Rose* (1982) reflect environmental concerns. "The Author of the Acacia Seeds" is simultaneously a consideration of animal and plant communication and a clever satire of academic writing. In "The New Atlantis," an island rises along with the world's oceans while the United States becomes a corporate police state. The protagonist of "Mazes" is human, but she is treated like a laboratory rat. *Buffalo Gals and Other Animal Presences* (1987) is an anthology of stories and poems about the consciousness of animals, plants, and even rocks. *Searoad: Chronicles of Klatsand* (1991) tells the tales of several generations of women living in close connection with the earth and each other on the Oregon coast between 1906 and 1986. Le Guin focuses on time-space theories in *A Fisherman of the Inland Sea* (1994). In "Newton's Sleep" a group of travelers escapes the degradation on Earth in favor of a sterile space station, but mysterious Earth-like features and human wildness mysteriously reappear onboard. *Unlocking the Air* (1996) is strongly nature-oriented throughout. In "Limberlost," a middle-aged novelist can't quite connect with nature, her inner wildness, or her past. How does one cope when the water turns bad "In the Drought"? The people in "Olders" live a life based on deep ecology, surviving as trees after their human demise. In *Changing Planes* (2003), Sita Dulip is traveling astrally to a variety of what may be different planets or different planes of experience.

Stanislaw Lem, one of the world's most popular science fiction authors, is also an important philosopher of science. In *Solaris* (1970), when Kris Kelvin arrives on the planet Solaris he discovers that the ocean itself is a vast living intelligence whose only means of communicating with humans is to create replicas of their memories. Lem's concept thus foreshadows the Gaia principle. *The Futurological Congress: From the Memoirs of Ijon Tichy* (1974) is the account of a conference on overpopulation that is attacked by revolutionaries. *Invincible* (1973) and *Fiasco* (1987) also have green themes.

In *Girl in Landscape* (1998) by Jonathan Lethem, a family leaves post-apocalyptic New York to settle on another planet where they hope to live harmoniously with the gentle inhabitants. A racist antihero based on John Wayne's character in *The Searchers* opposes their plans.

Ian MacLeod's *The Great Wheel* (1997) is set in North Africa in 2170. The whole world is blanketed by a foul cloud produced by global warming, which was exacerbated by attempted climate control. In *The Light Ages* (2003), society has been organized around the mining and production of a drug known as the Aether, but poverty, sweatshop conditions, and the creation of changelings from Aether consumption bring about sufficient unrest to create a revolution.

George R. Martin's *Tuf Voyaging* (1986) is a critique of overpopulation, reliance on science to solve social problems, and the inherent dangers of meddling with ecological balance.

In Julian May's *Intervention: A Root Tale to the Galactic Milieu and a Vinculum Between It and the Saga of Pliocene Exile* (1987), human evolution seems to be reaching the next step when some people in various parts of the world are born with tremendous psychic powers. Although the "metapsychics" are humankind's best hope against nuclear and environmental annihilation, the "normals" consider them a threat.

Anne McCaffrey is known as the Dragon Lady for her many novels set on the planet Pern, where humans and dragons have a close symbiotic link protecting the planet from ecological destruction by space spores. The Dragonriders series, which begins with *Dragonflight* (1968), currently runs to twenty volumes. McCaffrey and Elizabeth Ann Scarborough have produced a trilogy beginning with *Powers That Be* (1993), in which the sentient planet of Petaybee heals a miner. When the miner learns that the mining company plans to evacuate all humans from Petaybee so they can pillage its mineral resources, she is forced to choose between Earth and her longtime employer or her new planet and its life forms. In *Power Lines* (1994) and *Power Play* (1995), Petaybee faces a variety of external threats. The series incorporates Druidic and Inuit myth, including a woman who mates with a selkie.

In *Dreamsnake* (1978) by Vonda N. McIntyre, a healer undertakes a perilous journey to replace her Dreamsnake, an animal used for insight and healing. *The Moon and the Sun* (1997), which takes place in the plush court of Louis XIV, is reminiscent of the work of Rikki Ducornet. McIntyre contrasts an exploitative relationship with a more loving, sustainable way of encountering beings and things previously unknown.

McIntyre also wrote the books adapted from the second through fourth *Star Trek* movies, which were released simultaneously with the films. In the critically acclaimed *Star Trek IV: The Voyage Home* (1986), the starship *Enterprise* returns to the twentieth century to recover a pair of humpback whales in order to save Earth from environmental ruin in the twenty-third. *Star Trek* has become a literary cottage industry, with dozens of authors writing over one hundred books and several spin-off television series. *Star Trek* is intrinsically green and optimistic, with its subtext of respect for all environments, races, and cultures, but *Star Trek IV* has the most overtly ecological message.

Sean McMullen's works generally take place in a low-tech, post-apocalyptic future. *Voices in the Light* (1994) depicts a futuristic nonelectric Australia that uses all manner of appropriate technologies and retains a vast library of now incomprehensible knowledge staffed by militant librarians. The *Mirrorsun Rising* (1995) involves a satellite that blocks solar radiation and automatically destroys advanced technologies on Earth. Humans are tormented by the mysterious telepathic "Call," which lures them to walk into the sea and drown. In *Souls in the Great Machine* (1999), scientists construct a massive "Calculor" consisting of two thousand people working abacuses to generate knowledge to prevent an ice age. The scene shifts to the former United States in *The Miocene Arrow* (2000), where humanity faces extinction from an alien race that is immune to the Call. In *Eyes of the Calculor* (2001), the Call has been silenced, but the Calculor must be rebuilt to face new challenges, including conflict with Americans who wish to eradicate a species of bird people in Australia, as they had already done on their home turf.

Towing Jehovah (1994) by James Morrow tells the tale of an oil tanker captain, guilt-ridden by an earlier spill, who accepts an assignment by the Angel Raphael to tow God's decaying two-mile-long body from the tropical Atlantic to an Arctic ice cave. Along the way he encounters militant atheists who want to destroy the body, crew members who want to eat it, and various adventures.

In David Morse's brilliant alternative history *The Iron Bridge* (1998), Ecosophian scientists from the environmentally ravaged future (2043) send an agent back to the eighteenth century to derail the industrial revolution and its consequent pollution, warfare, and commercial brainwashing. Naturally, all sorts of unintended results ensue. The author's seamless weave of science fiction, fantasy, and social and historical fiction will appeal to readers of all these genres.

In Edward Myers's *The Mountain Made of Light* (1992), anthropologist Jesse O'Keefe discovers a secret race descended from the Incas who fled conquest to save their mystical, Earth-centered culture. Jesse's retreat to the mountain triggers the action that might begin the end of civilization in *Fire and Ice* (1992). In *Summit* (1994), survivors of the civil war make the perilous ascent to the summit of the Mountain Made of Light to save the Mountain-Drawn people from annihilation.

Larry Niven's *Rainbow Mars* (1999) is a collection of six linked stories about a time traveler in the year 2300 searching the past for extinct species to return to the present.

In Rebecca Ore's *Gaia's Toys* (1995), a young woman involved in ecodefense is manipulated by ecoterrorists into setting off a "baby nuke." This novel probes the ethics of various levels of ecodefense and the countervailing threats of overpopulation and uncontrolled technology.

Barbara Paul's *Under the Canopy* (1980) is set on the jungle planet Gaia, where a colonial administrator threatens the planet's perfect ecological and social balance.

Operation Elbow Room: An Interplanetary Ecofiction (1995) by Joseph J. Phillips takes place in a militarily supported biosphere on Mars. When "The Tribe," a Martian mineral life form, appears, a clairvoyant naturalist learns of their plan to return the human mind to childlike innocence and wonder, thus creating a new Eden.

Marge Piercy's *Woman on the Edge of Time* (1976) is a classic work of ecofiction, linking patriarchy, militarism, mental illness, and environmental problems. After Consuelo Ramos is subjected to neurological experiments in a mental hospital, she foresees two possible futures: a hierarchical, militaristic one in which both human freedom and the environment are degraded, or an androgynous, nature-loving society using appropriate technology. According to the author, "My first intent was to create an image of a good society, one that was not sexist, racist, or imperialist: one that was cooperative, respectful of all living beings, gentle, responsible, loving, and playful. The result of a full feminist revolution."[4] In the mid-twenty-first century, mega-corporations have plundered Earth's resources, ravaged the environment, and sharply curtailed human freedoms in Piercy's *He, She, and It* (1991).

In Frederik Pohl's *Midas World* (1983), fusion power is so cheap that robots do all the work, flooding a massive new leisure class with luxurious goods, but in so doing they squander all the natural resources. *The Years of the City* (1984) portrays myriad social problems arising from placing New York in a dome, totally separating it from the natural world. *Chernobyl: A Novel* (1987) is based closely on the actual events of that disaster. At the end of their long careers, Pohl and Isaac Asimov wrote *Our Angry Earth* (1991), a nonfiction clarion call to environmental action.

An earlier book, Christopher Priest's *Inverted World* (1974), is similar to *Years of the City.* "A hero lives in 'The City' which is completely isolated from the outside. He is allowed to go outside and there he . . . finds that the city is constantly on the move in an environment which is degrading."[5]

Jonah (2000) by Dana Redfield is a visionary New Age fantasy about the attempted restoration of the union between the female world Gaia (Earth) and its male counterpart Geshlama.

Kim Stanley Robinson's short fiction has been published in many magazines and anthologies, and republished in two collections. The stories in *The Planet on the Table* (1986) include "Venice Drowned," which portrays a society thrust back into primitivism as a result of global warming. The mountains themselves are sentient beings in "Ridge Running." Several stories in *Remaking History* (1991) are alternative histories, including "Muir on Shasta," in which the legendary conservationist experiences an epiphany that inspires him to greater activism. (The stories making up two additional collections, *A Sensitive Dependence on Initial Conditions* and *Vinland the Dream,* also appear in the revised *Remaking History and Other Stories,* 1994.)

The Three Californias trilogy presents alternative histories set in Orange County. *The Wild Shore* (1984) depicts life in the year 2047 after America has apparently been devastated by a nuclear war and is being quarantined by Japanese overseers. While Scavengers pillage wreckage and collude with the Japanese, Newtowners rebuild their communities from scratch, subsisting through communal fishing and farming. *The Gold Coast* (1988) is a dystopia created by materialism: a polluted, overcrowded "autotopia" of freeways and malls, relying on the military-industrial complex for ever-expanding growth. *Pacific Edge* (1990) depicts a positive alternative to nuclear war or materialism in the year 2065: a sustainable society based on renewable energy sources, population control, and appropriate technology, emphasizing direct democracy and living in harmony with the earth.

The four linked novellas in *Escape from Kathmandu* (1989) are hilarious tall tales featuring two hippie adventurers, George and Freds. In the title novella, they save the Yeti by concealing it from expeditions, tourists, poachers, and collectors for zoos. George and Freds preserve another mystery in "Mother Goddess of the World" by hiding the remains of Mallory's body on Everest. "The True Nature of Shangri-La" (aka Shambhala) is that it serves as a center for refugees from Tibet and is in danger of being discovered by the outside world if a World Bank road project is completed. "The Underground Kingdom" of thousands of miles of tunnels and vaults centered in Shambhala is essential to the survival of Tibetan/Nepalese Buddhist culture, but its existence is threatened by a much-needed sewage system for Kathmandu.

A Short, Sharp Shock (1990) is Robinson's most surrealistic, erotic long fiction. A man washed ashore on a beach of a water planet whose only continent is a thin, globe-spanning peninsula and a "woman" known as "The Swimmer" encounter various beings who seem to be both natural outgrowths and defenders of the planet, such as fisher folk made of kelp, people with small trees growing from their shoulders, and a sandman who guides them across a difficult passage.

In *Red Mars* (1993), in 2026 one hundred scientists establish a colony on the red planet. Although the UN treaty forbids terraforming and some of the scientists are "Reds" who would keep Mars as a wilderness, the "Greens" are pro-terraforming, arguing that what they learn can help solve global warming on Earth. The transition to *Green Mars* (1994) is accelerated through mass terraforming. Various factions of the underground overcome their differences to draft principles for an independent, evolutionary Martian society. Just as another crackdown from Earth seems inevitable, a volcano under the Antarctic ice shelf erupts and sea levels rise rapidly, forcing earthlings to focus on survival. This provides the opportunity to forge a free Mars in *Blue Mars* (1996), interdependent with Earth but *not* a colony. The Martians manage to create new cities and biomes, becoming an alternative model for Earth with a fairer society and a syncretic reintegration of postmodern and Paleolithic elements. *The Martians* (1999) isn't a sequel to the Mars trilogy but variations on its stories and themes. The novella "Green Mars," originally published in 1985 in *Asimov's Magazine* and republished here, is not to be confused with the novel from the trilogy.

Antarctica (1998) also addresses such issues as the appropriate role of science and technology, international ecopolitics, and permaculture. During a massive blizzard, ecoteurs disrupt all communication and destroy the oil stations. A deal is brokered to renew the treaty to keep Antarctica demilitarized, allow sustainable resource extraction, maintain it as a site of special scientific interest and as a sacred ritual space, and establish zero-impact lifestyles.

The Years of Rice and Salt (2002) is an alternative history of the years AD 622–2002 based on the premise that the Black Death eradicated almost all Europeans. China, India, Dar al-Islam, and eventually the Hodenosaunee, a Native American confederation, struggle for political, economic, scientific, and religious precedence. Environmental issues are not explored to the same extent as in Robinson's other alternative histories, but Travancore (India) and the Hodenosaunee develop strong ecotopian and democratic tendencies.

Forty Signs of Rain (2004) is the first volume in a trilogy about global warming set in the very near future. Some of the characters, organizations, and issues from *Antarctica* reappear. Although the crisis shakes the National Science Foundation from its bureaucratic doldrums with the realization that scientists need to become political activists, the corporate agenda of both major political parties is a major obstruction. In *Fifty Degrees Below* (2005), global warming continues, the Gulf Stream stalls, and the world is plunged into a new ice age. The NSF, with strong international cooperation, attempts to reverse the situation by dumping millions of tons of salt into the Gulf

Stream to reinvigorate it and warm the ocean and air. *Sixty Days and Counting* (2007) recounts the relative, but still uncertain, success of these efforts and the election of an environmentalist president resembling Al Gore.

Joanna Russ's *The Female Man* (1975) deals primarily with feminism and secondarily with the environment. Four genetically identical women from different planets have been acculturated into four very different personalities, reflecting the values of the divergent societies. In *Picnic on Paradise* (1979), a woman from ancient Greece visits the future and rescues hapless vacationers whose overreliance on technology has destroyed their ability to survive in the wilderness.

Robert Silverberg's *The World Inside* (1971) portrays life in the year 2381 when seventy-five billion people inhabit enclosed high rises, living a hedonistic lifestyle of sex, drugs, and rock and roll. The cost is meaninglessness, neurosis, and a lack of freedom. Pollution, industrial espionage, ruthless megacorporations, genetic engineering, and orbital habitats all come into play in Silverberg's ecothriller *Hot Sky at Midnight* (1994).

Joan Slonczewski's fiction reflects both her Quaker faith and a PhD in molecular biophysics. In her debut, *Still Forms on Foxfield* (1980), a Quaker settlement on a distant planet is visited by earthlings with Internet-like communication devices instantly linking them with all other humans. The earthlings contend with native plants with a group mind, a hostile environment, an end to their isolation, and threats to continuing their simple lifestyle. *A Door into Ocean* (1986) depicts the oceanic world of Shora, where a clan of nature-oriented, pacifist women known as the Sharers have accepted the ways of the Elysians, a high-tech society of seemingly ageless beings. When the Windclans settle in Shora in *Daughter of Elysium* (1993), they find it difficult to adapt to the Elysians. A greedy interstellar corporation plans to terraform and mine the planet Prokaryon, threatening both the native species and, allegorically, a colony of orphans on *The Children Star* (1998). *The Wall Around Eden* (1989) has an earthly setting. Nuclear winter has exterminated most of the biosphere, but one small town was saved by an alien force field. The residents overcome their fear of the aliens and struggle to support themselves in a primitive lifestyle, farming a small patch of ground.

Other Nature (1995) by Stephanie Smith takes place in rural Oregon in the early twenty-first century, a time of ecological collapse and pandemics. Mutated children may be the next step in humanity's evolution.

Naomi Stokes's *The Tree People* (1995) is a fantasy mystery about a logger who decides to preserve an ancient tree on the Quinault Indian Reservation that the evil shaman Xulk was buried alive beneath. When a descendent of Xulk's lover chops the tree down, his spirit is released, leading to all sorts of consequences.

Sheri S. Tepper is outraged by all forms of oppression and intolerance. She sometimes employs inversions, putting the high-heeled shoe on the male foot as it were, or uses parallel story lines to examine stories from different perspectives. In *The Gate to Women's Country* (1988), she portrays a future society where men and women have been separated into two colonies, the former a military camp, the latter a center of government, commerce, law, and culture. In *Grass* (1989), a husband-wife-ambassadorial team sent to the title planet wonder if the residents are immune to a plague as the result of a strange symbiosis of the human settlers and the planet's native races. In *The Family Tree* (1997), police officer Dona Hensley develops a special relationship with trees that have become sentient and are starting to fight back by springing through streets. *Singer from the Sea* (1999) is set on the low-tech planet Haven, where a young noblewoman has been mystically chosen to restore the natural balance of life and death and save Haven from both invasion from the war planet Ares and ecological doom. The two interweaving strands in *The Visitor* (2002) are an extremely repressive government-corporate Regime of the distant future that trades with demons for profitable technologies and an account of the time of "The Happening" when both magic and true science were eradicated.

In Harry Turtledove's *The Case of the Toxic Spell Dump* (1993), an Environmental Perfection Agency employee is forced to find new resources within himself when he discovers an ancient Aztec god of death in the physical and spiritual murk of the Toxic Spell Dump.

In Jack Vance's *Araminta Station* (1988) a scientific outpost with a limited population studies and preserves the wilderness world of Cadwal. Police cadet Glawen Clattuo is drawn into a conflict with humanoid settlers known as Yips. In *Ecce and Old Earth* (1991), when the Conservationist Charter of Cadwal disappears, Clattuo suspects the despoiling Yips. As the Yips prepare to invade Araminta Station and take over Cadwal in *Throy* (1992), Clattuo and Eustace Chilke search several planets for an interstellar engineer in league with the Yips.

John Varley's Gaean trilogy (*Titan,* 1979; *Wizard,* 1980; *Demon,* 1984) is about a living, sentient, planet-size being orbiting Saturn. She is filled with a variety of species, including humans, and can take on any of their shapes. In *The Ophiuchi Hotline* (1977), first-order-intelligence space invaders land on Earth to save the second-order whales and dolphins from destructive third-order humans. Humans living on the Moon and other planets receive transmissions from the star Opiuchi, and learn bioengineering, cloning, and sex-change techniques to transform their existence. Ninety-ninth-century Earth is dying from the accumulated poisons of war and industrialism in *Millennium* (1983). In *Steel Beach* (1992), humans have been relegated to the Moon, where they live a life of ease, perfect physical health, and ease in gender changing, but their lives are controlled by the sentient Central Computer. Lacking true self-determination, they become prone to serious depression. *Mammoth* (2005) is about cloning.

Two clones, the good Moon Dawntreader and the manipulative Queen Arienhod, battle for control in Joan Vinge's Snow Queen series (*The Snow Queen,* 1980; *World's End,* 1984; *The Summer Queen,* 1991). Arienhod tries to coerce Moon to prevent the change of the seasons, thus destroying life as we know it.

Elisabeth Vonarburg's work contrasts freedom and personal power against the domineering forces of government, business, and religion. When the Outside is ravaged by war, the people closed away in *The Silent City* (1988) genetically engineer a girl, Elisa, with powers of transformation and rejuvenation. Elisa eventually must choose between saving the City that created her or the entire Outside. *In the Mothers' Land* (aka *The Maerlande Chronicles,* 1992), after man creates the Decline through toxic waste and pollution, Elli, the creator, radically limits the number of males who may survive the Malady. The semiautobiographical *Reluctant Voyagers* (1995) is about a writer who explores alternative universes and modes of consciousness through her work. *Slow Engines of Time* (2000) contains short stories set in an outward world of rising oceans, radiation, and dwindling resources, and an inner world of unrooted boundlessness and ontological anxiety.

In Sage Walker's *Whiteout* (1996), the only safe source of food and water is Antarctica. The Tanaka Corporation hires virtual-reality media manipulation experts, theoretically to extend limitations on krill fishing, but inter- and intra-corporation rivalries create crime and conflict. Walker's message seems to be that technology and virtual reality should serve humanity, not vice versa.

Ian Watson considers humanity's metaphysical and ecological relationship with the universe in the Black River/Yaleen trilogy (*The Book of the River*, 1984; *The Book of the Stars*, 1984; *The Book of Being*, 1985; published in one volume as *Yaleen*, 2004). In Yaleen's world, men and women live on opposite sides of the river, only women can sail on the black current at all, and nobody can cross it or know what may lie on the other side. When the current mysteriously recedes, all manner of other divisions also disappear. The Book of Mana epic (*Lucky's Harvest*, 1993; *The Fallen Moon*, 1994) is an adaptation of a Finnish folk legend about a man who can talk to the stones, in this case a sentient asteroid that responds to storytelling.

Most of the energy in the twenty-first century is generated by oceanic geothermal waters in Peter Watts's *Starfish* (1999). The genetically modified "rifters" who work in the deep pay a serious psychic toll as a result of isolation, pressure, and claustrophobia. In the sequel, *Maelstrom* (2001), a massive tidal wave created by a marine geothermal station also creates invasive soil microbes dubbed Behemoth that could eradicate other species.

One of Kate Wilhelm's primary themes is how individuals and society survive through and evolve beyond our current cataclysmic era. In the Hugo Award-winning novel, *Where Late the Sweet Birds Sang* (1976), after Earth is ravaged by nuclear warfare, radiation, and pestilence, a family tries to survive through bioengineering and cloning. When they discover they can replicate their own bodies, but not their humanity, they must decide whether to take their chances in what remains of the natural world. In *Juniper Time* (1979), after drought devastates the West, the government resettles people in concentration camps. *Children of the Wind* (1989) is a collection of five novellas in which nature may be frightening at times, but if experienced rather than resisted it is sustaining and magical.

Liz Williams's *The Ghost Sister* (2001) depicts the planet of Monde D'Isle where colonists who were supposed to terraform the planet instead went feral as part of a collective unconscious known as the Bloodmind. The Bloodmind makes them incredibly aware of the environment, even to the point of sensing underground wells and minerals, but it can also turn them into a primitive pack whose prey may include other humans.

Gene Wolfe's *Endangered Species* (1989) contains thirty-seven short stories on a variety of subjects, including nature, philosophy, and relations between men and women.

A variety of extinct species, including Neanderthals, are genetically engineered and domesticated on the moon Anee in Dave Wolverton's *Serpent Catch* (1991). The isolation of the different species causes an ecological crisis until Tull, a Neanderthal-human half-breed, returns serpents to the sea to restore the balance. In the sequel, *Path of the Hero* (1993), Tull leads the slaves in rebellion against the ironically named "Creators," which are actually machines designed to destroy all living things.

The End of the Dream (1972) by Philip Wylie is set in the year 2030 when ecological disasters have reduced the world's population to only four million people living in bubbles. They look back to see where things went wrong and how people could have lived differently to avoid the catastrophe.

Sarah Zettel writes action-packed yet philosophical novels about intergalactic encounters and complex cautionary tales about intolerance, environmental responsibility, and the limits of technology. In *Playing God* (1998), the war-ravaged planet Dedelphi employs the Terran corporation Bioverse to save them from environmental collapse via nanotechnology. Humans living in a floating colony and the inhabitants of a planet whose environment is dying both have plans for Venus in *The Quiet Invasion* (2000). In *Kingdom of Cages* (2001), ecocrises and pandemics are sweeping all human space colonies. The only hope may exist on Pandora, where people have been forbidden to interact with local species or make changes to the environment. However, for humanity to continue, some changes must be made, and the fanatical Pandorans employ biochemical weapons in their defense.

FANTASY FOR CHILDREN OF ALL AGES

Some fantasy books written for young adults can also provide entertainment, education, and enlightenment for adult readers. When you explore your inner wildness, don't be surprised to find your inner child running around.

T. A. Barron employs a nature-loving mystical teenager as the protagonist of the Adventures of Kate series. In *Heartlight* (1990), Kate and her grandfather use one of his inventions to travel faster than the speed of light on a mission to save the sun from a premature death. While helping her Great Aunt Melanie protect an Oregon redwood forest from loggers, thirteen-year-old Kate goes back five centuries through a time tunnel to face an evil creature bent on destroying the same forest in *The Ancient One* (1992). In *The Merlin Effect* (1994), Kate and a marine biologist discover that some strange ecological events on the ocean floor are being caused by an evil enchantress.

Cat lovers will take delight in Clare Bell's Ratha series. Twenty-five million years ago, a society of intelligent wild cats pushed close to extinction meets an enemy band of raiding predatory cats in a decisive battle that will determine the future for both in *Ratha's Creature* (1983). In *Clan Ground* (1984), the stranger Orange-Eyes, recognizing that the one who controls fire can become absolute ruler, challenges Ratha's authority over the clan. *Ratha and Thistle-Chaser* (1990) is about a solitary cat physically crippled and tortured by paralyzing nightmares who finds a new life for herself with the strange tusked creatures of the seashore. In *Ratha's Challenge* (1994), the clan plans to domesticate the tusked creatures for food production, but must first meet the challenge of another intelligent breed of cats that act and think as a pack under telepathic control of their leader.

Bell has written several other books, at least three of which have ecological themes. In *Tomorrow's Sphinx* (1986), two unusual black cheetahs share a mental link, one cat coming from the past to reveal scenes from his life with the young pharaoh Tutankhamen, and one struggling to survive in a future world ravaged by ecological disaster. Two centuries after the *People of the Sky* (1989) have emigrated to Oneway, a planet of plateaus and canyons like their native Southwest, the Pueblo Indians have evolved their own high-tech society, but in Barranca Canyon the old ways persist, and people live in symbiotic harmony with the Aronans, a species of intelligent flying beasts.

An Aztec slave girl with shape-changing and other powers known as *The Jaguar Princess* (1993) is sought by the nature-loving king of Tezcotzinco to prevent the onslaught of the imperialistic Tenochtitlan.

Terrill Miles Burke's Dolphin Magic books (*The First Encounter*, 1992; *Adepts vs. Inepts*, 1993; *Ancient Knowledge*, 1994; *The Unexpected Stranger*, 1995; *Unobstructed Universe*, 1996) is a New Age fantasy about human-dolphin relationships, telepathy within and between the species, and the fall of the ancient civilization of Lemuria.

Abandoned by both her parents, a nine-year-old girl goes to live with Juniper, who has become a Wiccan priestess and begins to train the girl in the ways of herbs and magic in Monica Furlong's *Wise Child* (1987). In the prequel, *Juniper* (1991), a young girl apprenticed to a witch struggles to save her family from the machinations of her power-hungry aunt.

In Louise Lawrence's *The Warriors of Taan* (1988), Prince Khian and the Stonewraiths must drive the despotic earthling Outworlders from their home planet before the Outworlders completely plunder their planet. Lawrence comes back to Earth in *The Patchwork People* (1994), in which people walk a socioeconomic treadmill in a dystopic Britain threatened by rising sea levels.

Madeleine L'Engle is best known for her Time Fantasy series, but she has also written several young adult novels with a greener hue. *The Arm of the Starfish* (1965) is about a marine biology student on the island of Gaea who finds himself in the middle of a power struggle over a project with huge ecological and sociopolitical ramifications. If starfish can regenerate new arms and if humans and starfish were originally in the same phylum, can humans regenerate destroyed or diseased tissue? In *Dragons in the Waters* (1976), a boy who wishes to stay with a tribe in Venezuela is warned that he will revert to "savagery," but he counters that the tribe lives in harmony with nature while "civilization" is destroying it. *A Ring of Endless Light* (1980) is about a girl finding comfort and perspective from her grandfather's suffering and imminent death through her work with dolphins. In *An Acceptable Time* (1989), Polly's visit to her grandparents becomes an extraordinary experience as she travels through time to play a crucial role in a prehistoric confrontation between the Earth-centered People of the Wind and the rapacious People across the Lake.

The Mer-Child: A Legend for Children and Other Adults (1991) by Robin Morgan relates the friendship between a girl whose legs are paralyzed and a boy whose mother is a mermaid and whose father is human. Morgan conveys an implicit moral about the importance of friendship and accepting all people regardless of race, gender, age, or physical abilities.

A boy takes the oath of magic, is transformed into an animal, and is transported back into a world described in Indian legends in Andre Norton's *Fur Magic* (1968). In *Breed to Come* (1972), when pollution drives all humans from Earth they leave an experimental virus behind that increases the intelligence in successive generations of the remaining animals. A group of cats realizes that human beings will be returning to Earth soon and must decide how to deal with the new threat.

Neo-Paganists Diana L. Paxson and Adrienne Martine-Barnes based the Fionn MacCumhal series on Celtic myth (*Master of Earth and Water*, 1993; *The Shield Between the Worlds*, 1994; *Swords of Fire and Shadow*, 1995). Young Demry learns the secrets of trees, stars, and water in order to battle beasts, monsters, and human enemies.

Meredith Ann Pierce adapts the Native American myth of an animal casting off its skin to take human form in *The Woman Who Loved Reindeer* (1985). This is an allegory about people overcoming adversity, escaping destruction, and adopting a more natural way of life. In *Birth of the Firebringer* (1985), Aljan, the headstrong son of the prince of the unicorns becomes a warrior and discovers his destiny in his people's struggle against the hideous wyrms usurping their land. Jan, the prince of the unicorns, pursues his destiny to save his kind from their enemies by seeking fire in a distant land of two-footed creatures in *Dark Moon* (1992). The quests are concluded in *The Son of Summer Stars* (1996).

In nature writer Scott R. Sanders's *Bad Man Ballad* (1986), a seventeen-year-old boy helps a lawyer find a murderer who just might be a Sasquatch. Thirteen-year-old Mooch runs afoul of the authorities controlling her floating domed city by helping an old engineer build realistic robot animals and by seeking her spiritual roots with the wild animals left on the outside in *The Engineer of Beasts* (1988).

A different beast is the narrator of Whitley Strieber's *Wolf of Shadows* (1985). In the terrible aftermath of a nuclear holocaust, a wolf and a woman form a mysterious bond that brings each closer to the spirits of the shattered earth.

In Paul J. Willis's *No Clock in the Forest* (1991), a mountaineer and two teenage hikers finds themselves in a parallel world when they disappear into thin air on a mountaintop. They are called upon to help save the wilderness from an evil princess and commercial development. In *The Stolen River: An Alpine Tale* (1992), a research assistant encounters strange animals, a flowering ice ax, and other mysteries in the Three Queens Wilderness.

PREHISTORY

Some authors turn to the distant past to find social and environmental lessons for the present and future. The writers featured in this section speculate upon prehistoric life to show not just where we're from, but which values from those times might be reintroduced into a troubled modern world. The first modern novelist to do so was probably J.-H. Rosny. In Rosny's *La Guerre du Feu* (*The Quest for Fire: A Novel of Prehistoric Times,* 1920, trans. 1980), an ancient tribe considers the best ways to use fire and to inhabit the land. (Please note that the book is more ecological in its orientation than the movie based on it.)

Four ecofeminist authors are responsible for much of the finest contemporary prehistory: Jean Auel, Sue Harrison, Linda Lay Shuler, and Joan Wolf. All evoke a world featuring greater harmony between women, men, and animals. Hardship and conflict certainly exist, but can be overcome. Although their work tends to be categorized as fantasy, Mary Mackey's term "visionary fiction" may be a better description. Most of their work was written in the 1980s and 1990s.

The books in Jean M. Auel's Earth's Children series are all international best-sellers and critically acclaimed (*Clan of the Cave Bear*, 1980; *The Valley of Horses*, 1982; *The Mammoth Hunters*, 1985; *The Plains of Passage*, 1990; *The Shelters of Stone*, 2002). Ayla and her mate Jondalar invent the bow and arrow, dream of domesticating the horse, face conflicts from a ferocious tribe, and learn to speak to animals. The implied moral of the series is that the Cro-Magnon will survive because of their adaptability to a changing natural and social environment while the change-resistant Neanderthal will not.

Sue Harrison has written a trilogy about a Native American tribe's migra-tion from the Aleutian Islands to Michigan. *Mother Earth, Father Sky* (1990) is the story of one tribe member's spiritual journey and quest for survival against the elements and enemies, an account of life in the ice age, and a love story. *My Sister the Moon* (1992) is based on the Aleut sea otter incest leg-end, moon myths, and the Raven-trickster legends. The saga concludes with *Brother Wind* (1994). Her Storyteller Trilogy (*Cry of the Wind*, 1995; *Song of the River*, 1997; *Call Down the Stars*, 2001) is set in ancient Alaska, employing Inuit storytellers as narrators.

Linda Lay Shuler's Time Circle trilogy is about ancient Native Americans. In *She Who Remembers* (1988), Kwami is banished from her tribe, wanders the ancient Southwest with the Toltec trader Kokopeli, and becomes the keeper and teller of ancient Earth secrets that only women can know. Kwami uses her understanding of nature and consequent spiritual powers to protect the Ana-sazi people from marauding tribes in *Voice of the Eagle* (1992). *Let the Drum Speak: A Novel of Ancient America* (1996) is the tale of Kwami's daughter, who learns the terrible secret of her tribe's eventual conquest by the Spanish.

Joan Wolf writes feminist historical romances, some of them set in the Pyrenees during Cro-Magnon times. *Daughter of the Red Deer* (1991) begins when all the women in one tribe are poisoned by foul water and the men raid another tribe for women. *The Horsemasters* (1993) takes place a few generations later when an outcast domesticates wild horses just in time to meet an invasion by mounted aggressors. They face an even greater threat in *The Reindeer Hunters* (1994): global warming decimating the reindeer herds they rely on for survival.

A variety of other writers have also contributed to this subgenre.

In *Mundane's World* by Judy Grahn (1988), plants, animals, and humans all have a voice and what matters most is their interrelationships.

Mary Mackey's Earthsong Trilogy, set in ancient Europe, is based upon the archaeological work of Marija Gimbutas. In *The Year the Horses Came* (1993), the peaceful life of the Motherpeople in Goddess-worshiping Neolithic Brittany is threatened by an incursion of "beastmen" from the steppes. With *The Horses at the Gate* (1996), the Motherpeople face the challenge of learning to fight and kill without becoming like their vicious enemies. *The Fires of Spring* (1998) follows the conflict into the next generation. Mackey foreshadowed this series in an earlier, similar novel, *The Last Warrior Queen* (1983).

The Last Patriarch (2000) by Sharman Apt Russell depicts the end of the Pleistocene era and, with it, the mystical connections between humans and other animals, particularly mammoths.

In anthropologist Elizabeth Marshall Thomas's *Reindeer Moon* (1987), prehistoric life is viewed through the eyes of a gifted rebel. It depicts a world where animals and humans are physically and spiritually interdependent. In *The Animal Wife* (1990), when a young hunter abducts a naked woman from a pond he learns more about women, life, and nature than he bargained for. For her Christmas parable *Certain Poor Shepherds,* see the "Philosophical/ Spiritual" section of chapter 3.

Under the pseudonym Margaret Allen, Quentin Thomas has written a trilogy that resembles Jean Auel's work. *The Mammoth Stone* (1993) tells the tale of the followers of the mammoth herds during the last ice age. An outcast learns the secrets of a talisman called the Mammoth Stone and leads her people to a new way of life. *Keeper of the Stone* (1994) and *The Last Mammoth* (1995) continue the story. An interesting inversion here is that women have often written under male names for their books to be published or their accomplishments accepted, but Thomas adopted a female moniker writing for a market where most of the authors and readers are women. (John R. Dann's debut novel *Song of the Axe* [2001] seems like a better reprise of Auel's work. Are these indicators of ecofeminist social evolution or just authors cashing in on a trend?)

Also see Joseph Bruchac's Dawn Land series in chapter 4; Jim Crace's *A Gift of Stones* in the "Philosophical/Spiritual" section of chapter 3, and Dave Wolverton's and Meredith Ann Pierce's work referred to earlier in this chapter.

9

Mysteries

Development deals, high-tech secrecy, corporate-political corruption, endangered species, and animal rights controversies are all inherently controversial and loaded with subterfuge: perfect mystery material.

The most significant current trend in mystery writing is the prevalence of female authors and protagonists, with over half of these books featuring one or both. Many have an ecofeminist subtext: working Mother Nature's beat can be confusing and dangerous, the perfect job for a smart and sensitive but tough and decisive woman. Unlike their drawing-room predecessors, the new female detectives are not content to rely on gossip and the assistance of helpful male policemen to solve crimes. Kimberly Dilley notes that "detective fiction of the 1980s and 1990s critiques stereotypic assumptions of gender and expands the vitality of the everyday. The characters use wit and humor as they deal with social issues. The women heroes are resourceful, strong, independent."[1] Women may hold up half the snub-nose .38s, but are much less likely to use them, preferring to outsmart their opponents.

According to Marion Shaw, "Our Feminist Gumshoe must be young and extremely active . . . live alone for the most part, and have . . . an occasional sexual relationship, usually of an unsatisfactory nature, which must not seriously interfere with her investigation. She will probably own a beat up old car. . . . She will also eat badly, snatching pizza and doughnuts as she goes, sleep irregularly, drink a lot of coffee and a fair number of stiff martinis and single malts, and she may smoke, sometimes marijuana. She will use bad language . . . (and) will speak in a wise-cracking sardonic way."[2] Shaw also notes that "Dick Tracy has become a woman."[3] That may be a cute line, but in their values, methods, and personalities one cannot imagine a greater contrast between today's ecosleuths and a simplistic, sexist cartoon character. They more closely resemble Sheila O'Donnell: an actual fifty-year-old private investigator who specializes in right-wing attacks on environmentalists. Her nickname is "Dickless Tracy."[4]

The books in this section tend to have protagonists who are private investigators, game wardens, or police officers. Reasonable readers may disagree whether a particular book is a mystery, a thriller, or a suspense novel. Basically, the former emphasizes a murder investigation, though many thrillers also include murders. See the "Environmental Action/Ecodefense" section of the chapter 3 for thrillers by Karin McQuillan, Kenneth Goddard, David Poyer, Neal Stephenson, Ken Follett, Clive Cussler, Kim Heacox, and others. See chapter 4 for works by Native American mystery writers such as Louis Owens, Dana Stabenow, James D. Doss, Peter Bowen, Wayne Johnson, Stan Jones, and Stephen Graham Jones.

It should also be noted that many mystery writers are highly prolific and sometimes formulaic, churning out books at an incredible pace. (The most formulaic of mystery subgenres, the "police procedural," is rarely employed by green mystery writers who generally prefer a less restrictive form.) Some authors, such as Sarah Andrews, Richard Hoyt, Skye Kathleen Moody, and Randy Wayne White always focus on environmental issues, but many other mystery authors include ecofiction among a wider variety of work. This chapter can hope to survey only a representative sample of it. Hence not every title by every author is noted here, or included in the biliography.

Susan Wittig Albert's protagonist China Bayles is a former lawyer who has opened an herb shop but keeps getting involved in intrigues, some of which have an environmental aspect. In *Thyme of Death* (1992), an apparent overdose victim may have been murdered by the developer of an airport she opposed.

When a controversial biology professor is murdered, an animal rights activist is the prime suspect, but Bayles tracks the real culprit in *Hangman's Root* (1994). The series had grown to sixteen titles as of 2006. A delightful new series features a variety of human and animal characters, including Beatrix Potter as an amateur environmental sleuth in *The Tale of Hill Top Farm* (2004), *The Tale of Holly How* (2005), *The Tale of Cuckoo Brow Wood* (2006), and *The Tale of Hawthorn House* (2007).

The three novels by Christine Andreae set in Montana featuring English professor turned camp cook Lee Squires are all immersed with wilderness lore. *Grizzly* (1994), with its theme of bear preservation, drew particularly strong critical acclaim.

Sarah Andrews's experience as a forensic geologist informs her ten Em Hansen novels, in which crimes committed against the earth can often be solved by clues derived from it. In *Mother Nature* (1997), the discovery of the body of a geologist who was attempting to remove polluting underground gasoline tanks leads to the unraveling of a conspiracy. Conflicts between evolutionists and creationists and rivalries within the two communities are examined in *Bone Hunter* (1999). Andrews explores both the environmental and moral issues raised by mining in *An Eye for Gold* (2000). Earthquakes in Salt Lake City expose both a physical and a regulatory *Fault Line* (2002) of shady building inspectors endangering citizens.

Tony Lowell, the creation of E. C. Ayres, is a long-haired Vietnam veteran who loves Florida's natural environment and hates violence, but can't seem to avoid it. In *Eye of the Gator* (1995) he discovers a suspicious phosphate plant while investigating the death of an EPA employee. A game warden zealously protecting a nature preserve becomes a murder victim in *Night of the Panther* (1997).

Nevada Barr debuted with the Anthony and Agatha Award-winning *Track of the Cat* (1993) set in Big Bend National Park, Texas. When a park ranger is apparently killed by a normally reclusive mountain lion, several other lions are killed, supposedly for protection of visitors, but really in retaliation. Barr's seemingly semiautobiographical protagonist, ranger Anna Pigeon, follows her instincts that the real predatory killers were actually human. Pigeon goes underwater in Lake Superior in *A Superior Death* (1994). In *Ill Wind* (1995) she uncovers mysteries about the ancient Anasazi culture and crooked, environmentally unfriendly construction practices. *Firestorm* (1996) is an incredibly vivid and dramatic account of firefighting in Lassen Volcanic National Park. Loggerhead turtles are the primary *Endangered Species* (1997) at Cumberland National Seashore. Anna must overcome claustrophobia to perform a harrowing rescue of a spelunker friend trapped in Carlsbad Caverns in *Blind Descent* (1998). *Liberty Falling* (1999), *Deep South* (2000), *Hunting Season* (2002), *Flashback* (2003), and *Hard Truth* (2005) don't have a strong environmental component, although *Deep South* and *Hunting Season* contain some excellent descriptions of the lush environment of Natchez Trace, Mississippi. Set in Glacier National Park, *Blood Lure* (2001) is Barr's gristliest, grizzliest, most troubling work. Neither humans nor nature are to be trusted in this case. Anna Pigeon returns to the *High Country* (2004) of Yosemite National Park when four seasonal employees mysteriously disappear. In *Winter Study* (2008), Pigeon investigates unusual wolf activity, but the most dangerous creature turns out to be a Homeland Security officer shadowing the case.

John Billheimer's Owen Allison series is set in West Virginia. In *Highway Robbery* (2000) Allison discovers both the long ago murder of someone supposedly killed in a dam collapse and current government corruption involving the widening of a highway. *Dismal Mountain* (2001) also involves the struggle between economic development and environmental protection. Corruption and greed lead to the collapse of another dam in *Drybone Hollow* (2003).

Cara Black's *Murder on the Île Saint-Louis* (2007) includes a subplot about environmental activists' opposition to a proposed oil agreement.

In Jennifer Blake's *Shameless* (1994), a "nearly divorced" woman has an affair with a man who has returned to Louisiana to take over his late father's lumber mill. He wants to sell to a British firm that will infuse new money into the depressed economy while speeding environmental degradation.

While investigating the death of a poacher, Wyoming game warden Joe Pickett uncovers chicanery by an oil company and threats to endangered species in C. J. Box's *Open Season* (2001). In *Savage Run* (2002), Pickett tries to track down the murderers of several radical environmentalists. He faces a confrontation with right-wing survivalists in *Winterkill* (2003), while animal mutilations are the subject of *Trophy Hunt* (2004).

In Louis Charbonneau's *The Ice* (1991), a joint American/Soviet research team discovers dying, oil-soaked birds in a part of Antarctica where there was no reported drilling. They must race against both the encroaching winter and a corporate "scientific" expedition that is concealing its true activity. A marine biologist confronts an ivory-poaching operation in Alaska in *White Harvest* (1994). *The Magnificent Siberian* (1995) is about poaching endangered Siberian tigers.

Lincoln Child and Douglas Preston write thrillers with a science-fiction twist, a few of which have an environmental theme. *Mount Dragon* (1996) is about genetic engineering, *Still Life with Crows* (2003) includes a subplot about genetically engineered crops. (These are listed under Preston's name in the bibliography.) Child's solo effort *Terminal Freeze* (2009) is about global warming.

April Christofferson is a biotechnology attorney and author of biomedical mysteries. *The Protocol* (1999) is a tale of illegal organ procurement and human cloning. In *Clinical Trial* (2000), well-intentioned attempts to develop a vaccine to protect Blackfeet Indians from the hanta virus are foiled when a Russian scientist contaminates it with smallpox. When buffalo are slaughtered to prevent the spread of the brucellosis, controversy erupts in *Buffalo Medicine* (2004). She departs from biotechnology issues in *Edgewater* (1998), in which Coeur d'Alene Indians are cheated out of their land and a right-wing militia group tried to develop a massive lakeside condo. For another thriller involving biotechnology, see Marvin L. Zimmerman's *The Ovum Factor* (2008).

Ann Cleeves has written a series starring ornithologist/investigator George Palmer-Jones. In *Come Death and High Water* (1987), the owner of a nature reserve is shot after he announces his plans to sell it. A seller of endangered birds of prey becomes the prey herself in *A Prey to Murder* (1989). Palmer-Jones investigates the supposed suicide of a renowned conservationist in *The*

Mill on the Shore (1994) and the murder of a birder raising funds for a sham environmental group in *High Island Blues* (1996).

Off Season (1994) by Philip R. Craig is about a conflict between hunters and animal rights activists, leading to the death of a recluse who was mysteriously killed by his own bow and arrow. Fisherman/gourmet chef J. W. Jackson's investigations turn up connections to politicians and to organized crime, not to mention some delicious scallops. Craig and William G. Tapply cowrote *First Light* (2001), in which developers and conservationists clash over whether unspoiled land should be a vast golf course or a wildlife preserve.

The shooting of an endangered species of grouse on federally protected land leads to a series of incidents in Bill Crider's *The Prairie Chicken Kill* (1996).

Considering the pelican mutilations, water pollution, and sabotage on the Monterey Peninsula, one should heed Janet Dawson's advice: *Don't Turn Your Back on the Ocean* (1994).

Nelson DeMille's *Plum Island* (1997) is the site of a buried pirate treasure, a biological warfare lab disguised as an animal research facility, secret vaccines, and much intrigue.

The leader of Oregon's Earth Everlasting forest defenders is murdered by a bomb in Jerome Doolittle's *Half Nelson* (1994).

Greed-driven agricultural researchers employing animal testing and extreme animal rights activists both come under fire in *Fatlands* (1995) by Sarah Dunant.

A Native American artist's work that uses sacred objects to protest exploitation of Indian land and culture arouses so much ire that he is murdered in *The Death of a Blue Mountain Cat* (1996) by Michael Dymmoch.

Cindy Dyson's *And She Was* (2005) melds romance, ecofeminism, mystery, and Aleut culture.

In G. M. Ford's *Who the Hell Is Wanda Fuca?* (1995), a wisecracking private investigator becomes the prime suspect after a friend of a young environmental activist he is protecting at the request of her mobster grandfather is murdered.

A detective discovers that the death of a world-class fly-fisher was no accident in Bartholomew Gill's *Death on a Cold, Wild River* (1993). But who killed her: the fly-fishing cowboy, the poacher she reported, a professional rival, or someone yet to be discovered?

In Linda Grant's *Lethal Genes* (1996), several employees of a plant genetics lab die of mysterious diseases that may be linked to a biotech entrepreneur.

James W. Hall's work is similar to Carl Hiaasen's, but the humor is darker and less frequent, and in most of his books the ecological themes are implied. In *Bones of Coral* (1993), a paramedic realizes his father's death was murder, not suicide, leading him to the operator of a trash incinerator that was also surreptitiously disposing of carcinogenic wastes from the U.S. Navy. After the mysterious underwater death of his girlfriend, a prickly fishing-lure maker and guide named Thorn becomes caught up in a deadly web of violence, obsession, and ecological vengeance in *Mean High Tide* (1994). In Hall's John D. MacDonald Award-winning *Gone Wild* (1995), Thorn travels to Malaysia when a friend's daughter is murdered by poachers of orangutans and other endangered species. Hall sometimes depicts the horrors of the endangered species trade from the perspectives of the tortured animals. Thorn returns in *Red Sky at Night* (1997), in which he links the decapitation of dolphins to harvest their endorphins with experiments being conducted on human guinea pigs in VA hospitals. In *Under Cover of Daylight* (2001), Thorn uncovers a shady development scheme. *Blackwater Sound* (2002) is a thriller about high-tech military technology in which Thorn laments that as a fishing guide he had "aided and abetted men . . . much less capable of beauty and grace than the animals they killed" (260).

Patricia Hall's *The Poison Pool* (1993) is set in a Yorkshire town choked by grit and coal dust, a failing economy, moral corruption, and steadily worsening environmental and social conditions. The polluters set up a brain-damaged teenager as their fall guy. In *Dead of Winter* (1997), both a real estate agent and an activist protesting a development are murdered.

Jamie Harrison, the daughter of acclaimed author Jim Harrison and a fine author in her own right, has set four mysteries in the small town of Blue Deer, Montana, the greenest of which is *Going Local* (1996). When a lawyer representing Dragonfly, an eco-friendly resort and nature preserve, is murdered, suspicion turns to his ex-wife, but when she is murdered, the trail leads to a group of developers in rivalry with Dragonfly.

When three of four friends are killed by a crossbow in J. F. Healy's *Foursome* (1993), a detective is called on to prove the innocence of the fourth. Because the victims were considered intruders who built ostentatious homes and disturbed wildlife, there is no shortage of suspects, including Shotgun Ma Judson, a double-amputee environmental activist, and various relatives of the Boston foursome.

The suspect being sought in Joseph Heywood's unusual quasi-mystery *The Snowfly* (2000) is a fly that may or may not actually exist. His more conventional mystery series, Woods Cop, is set in the Upper Peninsula of Michigan and features Conservation Officer Grady Service. In *Ice Hunter* (2001), while investigating poaching and fires, Service uncovers a plot that would hasten development of a wilderness area. *Chasing a Blond Moon* (2003) centers on the illegal hunting of a rare species of bear. Conflicts over commercial, native, and sports fishing are covered in *Running Dark* (2005). In *Blue Wolf in Green Fire* (2005), Service searches for both arsonists and a rare wolf that escaped during the fire.

Like his primary influence, John D. MacDonald, Carl Hiaasen's theme is the environmental and social degradation of Florida. Can Florida stop the onslaught of *Tourist Season* (1986) by killing tourists? In his first solo novel, Hiaasen establishes an effective formula: a courageous journalist or investigator, a mix of good and bad cops and officials, corporations employing the technology of plunder, bizarre criminals, one or two resourceful female characters (often a friend/lover/ex-wife), and even some animals, in this case a rare crocodile. Bass fishing has become a real *Double Whammy* (1987): a competitive sport and growth industry, replete with cheating, beatings, and even murder. The despoilers are opposed by the fearsome "Skink," the nickname of Clinton Tyree, a former war hero and progressive governor of Florida gone feral in the swamps as an occasional fishing guide and environmental avenger. Although *Skin Tight* (1989) is chiefly about plastic surgery scams, there is an environmental subplot involving collusion between a crooked board of county commissioners and developers. The misadventures and plans of Francis X. Kingsbury, the owner of the massive Amazing Kingdom amusement park, start to unravel when the world's final two "blue tongue mango voles" are killed by burglars working for the Mothers of Wilderness in *Native Tongue* (1991). An unusually wholesome exotic dancer struggling to regain custody of her daughter becomes enmeshed in skullduggery involving a corrupt congressman working for the sugar industry in *Strip Tease* (1993). Shoddy contractors, crooked building contractors and politicians, and a variety of insurance scam artists and looters run amuck in south Florida after some very severe *Stormy Weather* (1995). When veterinary assistant JoLayne Lucks wins fourteen million dollars in the Florida Lottery (*Lucky You*, 1997), she has the opportunity to purchase forty-four acres of wilderness known as Simmons Wood before it becomes a shopping mall. Lobbyist Palmer Stoat's litterbug behavior makes him a target for ecoterrorist Twilly Spree in *Sick Puppy* (2000). *Basket Case* (2002) is about the seamier sides of pop music and of journalism, but also contains some interesting environmental content. When young Roy Eberhardt moves from Montana to Florida, he is disgusted by the artificiality of Disney World and strip malls, but he quickly learns to give a *Hoot* (2002) about endangered burrowing owls whose habitat is threatened by a planned pancake house. *Hoot* was written for young adults, and Hiaasen also addresses the issues of domestic violence, dealing with bullies, and trying to fit in to a new school. In Hiaasen's second young adult book, *Flush* (2005), a brother and sister discover that a floating casino has been dumping bilge in the Florida Keys, while his third, *Scat* (2009), involves a mysterious disappearance, a fire, an oil company, and an endangered panther and her cubs. *Skinny Dip* (2004) revolves around a scam in which corrupt marine biologist Chaz Perrone aids and abets the destruction of the Everglades by filing fraudulent reports on the extent of pollution by an agribusiness operation. Telemarketers and real estate developers meet their match in Honey Santana in *Nature Girl* (2006).

Thirteen Florida novelists, including Hiaasen, Elmore Leonard, James W. Hall, and Carolina Hospital collaborated to produce *Naked Came the Manatee* (1996), a hilarious satire of ecothrillers and of the bestselling romance *Naked Came the Stranger.*

Corson Hirschfeld's *Aloha, Mr. Lucky* (2000) reads like a Hiaasen caper novel transplanted to Hawaii. When a free-spirited journalist places a personal ad to gain background for a story, he encounters quirky characters, bizarre situations, and a conflict between conservationists and golf resort developers.

Versatile author James D. Houston tries his hand at mystery writing in *The Last Paradise* (1998), a sequel to the mainstream *Continental Drift* (1978). It seamlessly blends ecodefense, native resistance, mystery, romance, and magic realism.

Richard Hoyt's series featuring investigator John Denson are animal-oriented mysteries. In *Fish Story* (1985), Denson protects a Cowlitz Indian who is threatened by a variety of people opposed to the Cowlitz regaining their traditional fishing grounds. *Whoo?* (1991) is the question Denson considers as he investigates logging and spotted owl controversies. Will Denson find a real Sasquatch or just a corporate scam in *Bigfoot* (1993)? Denson and his Indian sidekick Wayne Pretty Bird are hired by an anti-environmental lawyer when a rancher's cattle develop hoof and mouth disease and he blames environmental activists for intentionally poisoning them in *Snake Eyes* (1995). Denson's interviews of humans and Pretty Bird's hallucinogenic contacts with "the animal people" lead them to other suspects. One novel in his series featuring former CIA operative James Burlane, *Tyger! Tyger!* (1996), has an ecological theme: the poaching of endangered tigers.

When journalist Lydia Miller investigates the disappearance of animals and volunteers at an animal shelter in Eleanor Hyde's *Animal Instincts* (1996), she discovers many abuses inflicted upon animals by the cosmetics industry, and their extensive public relations effort to cover it up.

Poet Maxine Kumin's *Quit Monks or Die!* (1999) is an unusually intimate, lyrical, witty mystery about animal testing and animal liberation.

Special agent Reed Erickson of the U.S. Fish and Wildlife Service is the nemesis of poachers, habitat destroyers, and other assorted forest villains in Gunnard Landers's *The Hunting Shack* (1979), *Rite of Passage* (1980), *The Deer Killers* (1990), *The Violators* (1991), and *Eskimo Money* (1999).

Jane Langton finds someone other than *God in Concord* (1992). On the land around Walden Pond, preservationists, ex-cop Homer Kelly, and the elderly residents of a trailer park who are dying at an inexplicably fast rate are pitted against developers and a corrupt planning commission.

Death in a Strange Country (1993) by Donna Leon is a detective story set in Italy featuring the Mafia, political corruption, military cover-ups, and illegal hazardous waste disposal.

The first major modern mystery with an environmental theme was written by an acknowledged master of the genre, John D. MacDonald. He wrote three major novels about the sleazy side of land development. In *A Flash of Green* (1962), the Palmland Development Company takes over the mythical town of Palm City on Florida's Gulf Coast. Bribery, nonenforcement of zoning and building codes, blackmail, and raising public fears about alligators, snakes, and mosquitoes are Palmland's modi operandi. Golden Sands is a vast, shoddily built, high-rise *Condominium* (1977) on the Gulf Coast. Retirees are fooled into condos more expensive than advertised, small investors into bad deals, and voters by politicians, but it's not nice to fool Mother Nature. A hurricane blows it all away, making the developers murderers by default. *Barrier Island* (1986), a small, unspoiled island off the Mississippi coast, becomes a pawn in a game between a developer who fraudulently acquired it with the help of crooked judges, politicians, and businessmen and the inept government agencies who want to include it in a proposed wilderness area. MacDonald's popular twenty-one volume Travis McGee series consists mostly of pop fiction potboilers, with McGee frequently cracking wise, philosophically or angrily about the negative effects of overdevelopment and corruption. MacDonald was very influential, and by the time of his demise a wide variety of writers were transforming the traditional whodunit to the subgenre of "whodunit to the environment?"

In Sheila MacGill-Callahan's *Forty Whacks* (1994), a modern Lizzy Borden, an endangered species veterinarian, is accused of the ax murder of a philanthropist, but was someone else trying to abscond with the institute's endowment funds?

When Tori Miracle visits Amish country to judge an apple butter contest in Valerie Malmont's *Death, Lies, and Apple Pies* (1997), she encounters protests over a proposed nuclear waste dump and murders most foul.

During a fishing trip off the North Carolina coast, Judge Deborah Knott discovers the body of an old angler who had opposed a land development scheme in Margaret Maron's *Shooting at Loons* (1994).

Imagine supercharging William Faulkner's dense Yoknapatawpha County novels with the moral ambiguities and foreboding tone of Conrad's *Heart of Darkness* and you might begin to comprehend Peter Matthiessen's sprawling Watson trilogy. *Killing Mister Watson* (1990) is based on the true story of Edgar Watson, a Kurtz-like plantation owner and entrepreneur who was one of the early settlers of the Everglades and south Florida Coast in 1892. He was initially regarded as a leader who would bring development and wealth to the area, but as he abuses both his employees and the land, dead bodies start showing up mysteriously, and as rumors about his bloody past emerge, his neighbors fear they may be next and ventilate his body with thirty-one bullets. Fifty years later, Watson's troubled historian son Lucius attempts to solve the puzzle in *Lost Man's River* (1997). Lucius's investigations of the historical record and interviews of the few remaining witnesses lead to the discovery of even more tragic and environmentally devastating deeds by his family and other settlers. Watson himself is the narrator of *Bone by Bone* (1999), a far more straightforward account of his childhood poverty and trauma in the Civil War, failure as a farmer, previous murders and flights from the law, reinventions of himself, and emergence as a powerful plantation owner. Matthiessen thus provides insights into Watson's motivations and dark complexity without condoning his actions, presenting him as a tragic figure: the product of racism, poverty, and the frontier mentality, who inflicts further tragedy upon the land and people. Matthiessen combined these three volumes, compressing, rewriting, and expanding, to create *Shadow Country* (2008).

Occam's Razor by Archer Mayor (1999) centers on an abandoned truck used to transport toxic wastes. Brattleboro policeman Joe Gunther follows a trail of related murders that eventually leads to the Vermont state legislature.

In Peter McCabe's *Wasteland* (1994), a contractor/bribery artist who is working on a waste dump for a corrupt land developer, assaults a geologist for making a pass at his wife. He becomes the prime suspect in the geologist's murder the next day, but was he set up?

Ranchers and environmentalists in the Jackson Hole Wyoming area come into conflict when a wolf is shot in Lise McClendon's *Blue Wolf* (2001).

Sharyn McCrumb likens her fiction to patchwork quilts, combining seemingly disparate elements to create a colorful picture of Appalachia. One of the swatches in *The Hangman's Beautiful Daughter* (1992) is a polluted river causing cancer and stillbirths. *The Rosewood Casket* (1996) includes one plot line of a real estate developer trying to evict poor farmers from land that had been taken from the Cherokee generations ago.

The books in Michael McGarrity's Kevin Kerney series set in New Mexico are more like tattered pistol targets than patchwork quilts. In *Mexican Hat* (1997), Kerney finds a connection between current cougar poaching operations and anti-environmental militia groups and cattle rustling and land grabbing in the thirties. *Hermit's Peak* (1999) is partly about illegal logging operations. It looks like a win-win situation for both Kerney and Mother Nature when he agrees to sell his land to a nature conservancy group, but he can hardly enjoy his newfound wealth when a string of murders occurs in *The Judas Judge* (2000).

Fish and Wildlife agent Venus Diamond is Skye Kathleen Moody's motorcycle-riding, no-nonsense heroine. In *Rain Dance* (1996), she returns to Seattle from busting international bear poachers in Bangkok only to become embroiled in the murder of a timber baron, odd behavior by pelicans and the environmentalists protecting them, and a drug ring. She finds connections between endangered butterflies, illegal cutting of wildflowers on protected land, and the death of a model for a perfume company in *Blue Poppy* (1997). In *Wildcrafters* (1998), she weaves her tale from the strands of Americans' fear of aging, the kidnapping of a Native American baby (perhaps by Bigfoot or a mysterious elk), elk poaching, romantic interruptions and interrupted romances, and native herbal lore. When a brilliant embryologist who was controversial for using genetic engineering to protect endangered species is murdered in *Habitat* (1999), Venus is surprised to learn that the will stipulates that she has been selected to protect "Hannah's Ark" of embryos and accompany them aboard a space shuttle for safekeeping. Then the ark disappears and Venus herself becomes endangered when she uncovers a different genetic engineering scheme that may involve the Russian mafia. When bombs destroy dams on the Columbia River, Venus goes undercover as a "demolitions expert" in *K Falls* (2001). *Medusa* (2003) includes subplots about trafficking in endangered species to produce Chinese naturopathic drugs and the development of an illegal toxin for biological warfare. In *The Good Diamond* (2004), someone steals a huge diamond from a Canadian mine, leading Venus on a trail to a white supremacist group. *The Good Diamond* demonstrates not only that African "blood diamonds" have a horrific cost in African lives and limbs, but that the greed to mine "good diamonds" also has serious environmental and social costs.

In Barbara Moore's *The Wolf Whispered Death* (1986), a New Mexico rancher is killed, but are the tracks around his body those of a feral dog, wolf, or the white werewolf of Indian lore?

Marcia Muller, who created hard-boiled super sleuth Sharon McCone of the All Souls Legal Cooperative in 1978, and who has won virtually every mystery writing award, is considered by some to be the foremost contemporary female mystery writer. Many of her books include subplots or commentary on such subjects as the bitter fruits of land development, the destruction of natural habitats, and the social consequences of urban sprawl and the suburbs, but a few deserve special ecocritical attention. McCone investigates shady land deals and the proposed reopening of a gold mine that threatens not only the delicate alpine environment of Mono County, California, but the lives of environmentalists who oppose the mine in *Where Echoes Live* (1991). This novel introduces McCone's boyfriend and sometimes partner in crime solving, a wealthy environmental activist named Hy Ripinsky. McCone crosses international and legal boundaries trying to find Ripinsky after he disappears with a two million dollar ransom to free a CEO whose firm planned to develop a cancer drug from dolphin cartilage in *Wolf in the Shadows* (1993). In *A Walk Through the Fire* (1999), a series of "accidents" on the set of a film about Hawaiian legends leads her to discover the ill will many native Hawaiians feel toward the settlers and tourists who have degraded their natural and cultural environments.

Sara Paretsky's V. I. Warshawski mysteries are always concerned with social justice issues. In *Blood Shot* (1988), she adds environmental concerns when a search for a friend's missing father reveals complicity between an energy company dumping pollution illegally and the Chicago mob, which provides protection for them.

When investigator Lauren Maxwell of the Wild America Society investigates the death of a biologist in Elizabeth Quinn's *Murder Most Grizzly* (1993), she discovers that he may not have been mauled by the suspected bear after all. Set on an Alaska wildlife refuge, *A Wolf in Lamb's Clothing* (1995) is about conflict between preservationists and corporate interests. In *Lamb to the Slaughter* (1996), she is set up as the murderer of a distinguished Russian biologist and must find the real killer quickly. *Killer Whale* (1997) finds her back in Alaska preventing the capture of wild orcas.

One Foot in Eden (2002) by Ron Rash is a murder mystery told over time by five characters. A man murders his wife's lover, but when the valley is flooded for a dam, the murder is revealed. Rash skillfully depicts the negative social impacts of uprooting farmers and rural communities.

In Bob Reiss's *Purgatory Road* (1996), the agreement to preserve Antarctica from commercial exploitation is threatened by a forthcoming diplomatic summit about oil and mineral rights.

Ann Ripley and Rebecca Rothenberg are the mavens of mossy mysteries. Ripley's Louise Eldridge is an organic gardener with a show on PBS who just keeps digging up corpses in *Mulch* (1994), *Death of a Garden Pest* (1995), *Death of a Political Plant* (1998), *The Garden Tour Affair* (1999), *The Perennial Killer* (2000), and *Death at the Spring Plant Sale* (2003). Rothenberg's less genteel protagonist, plant pathologist Claire Sharples, protects endangered species, opposes herbicide use and clear-cutting, reveals the abuse of migrant workers, and investigates a variety of murders in *The Dandelion Murders* (1994), *The Bulrush Murders* (1991), *The Shy Tulip Murders* (1996), and *The Tumbleweed Murders* (2001).

In Alan Russell's *The Forest Prime Evil* (1992), when the "Green Man" protesting the logging of the redwoods is murdered, an investigator must find the real culprit among loggers, a fundamentalist preacher, pot growers, and a rival environmental group.

At least two of Sheila Simonson's mysteries featuring independent bookstore owner Lark Dodge have an ecological theme. In *Mudlark* (1993), a "California carpetbagger" who has moved to coastal Washington receives a bag of dead seagulls on her doorstep, the promoter of a proposed resort in an environmentally sensitive area is found dead, and the murder suspect's house is firebombed. Long-standing disagreements among former commune members lead to the murder of the organizer of a writer's conference on environmental issues in *Meadowlark* (1996).

Jessica Speart's protagonist, Rachel Porter, is a Fish and Wildlife ranger specializing in protecting endangered species in *Gator Aide* (1997), *Tortoise Soup* (1998), *Bird Brained* (1999), *Border Prey* (2000), *Black Delta Night* (2001), *A Killing Season* (2002), *Coastal Disturbance* (2003), *Blue Twilight* (2004), *Restless Waters* (2005), and *Unsafe Harbor* (2006).

For Dana Stabenow's Native American-oriented mysteries, see chapter 4.

Les Standiford's debut *Spill* (1991) is about a conspiracy between the federal government and the PetroDyne Corporation that allows PetroDyne to ship biological weapons disguised as nontoxic chemicals across the country. After a truck overturns in Yellowstone Park, the cover-up involving a secret team of government assassins is even more terrifying than the crime. Standiford then wrote several nonenvironmental mysteries before *Black Mountain* (2000), which is about a group of New Yorkers trying to reach civilization after their plane crashes in the Absaroka Wilderness.

The Cecil Younger mysteries written by actual investigator John Straley are set in Alaska. All provide luminous wilderness depictions, glimpses into Tlingit and Inuit life, and a few have distinctly environmental themes. While investigating the "closed" murder of an Indian hunting guide, Younger is hunted by someone protecting the killer in *The Woman Who Married a Bear* (1992). In *The Curious Eat Themselves* (1993), when Younger investigates the sexual assault of a cook at a remote mining site, he discovers that she was preparing to blow the whistle on the mine's environmental hazards. *The Angels*

Will Not Care (1998), which is about serial killings on a cruise ship for senior citizens, includes a chapter in which Cecil and his marine biologist girlfriend are forced ashore on an island of bears where she saves them by cooking a gourmet meal out of sea slugs and seaweed while talking the hungry bears out of their appetite for fresh human meat. *Cold Water Burning* (2001) is about the arson of a fishing boat.

In Whitley Strieber's *The Wolfen* (1978), a murderer with unusual strength and speed, incredible vision, and the apparent ability to transform or disappear at will is loose in New York City. This thriller was adapted into an award-winning motion picture in 1982.

Rob Swigart's Kaui-based mysteries feature wisecracking Lieutenant Cobb Takamura and molecular biologist/martial arts instructor Chazz Koenig. *Vector* (1986) is about the creation of a secret deadly virus. In *Toxin* (1989), a wealthy developer is shot and a satellite releases the toxin when it crashes. A ship carrying seven activists returning from an antinuclear protest drifts ashore with all aboard poisoned in *Venom* (1991).

A private investigator retreats to a remote cabin to recover from chronic fatigue syndrome, but gets little rest in Elizabeth Atwood Taylor's *The Northwest Murders* (1992). When two backpackers are attacked and scalped, she is employed to find evidence to defend the accused Karuk Indian and to determine the motives that will lead to the real murderer.

Environmental lawyer/investigator Neil Hamel is a spiritualistic ecofeminist Perry Mason in a series of mysteries by Judith Van Gieson set in New Mexico. Called upon to investigate threatening notes sent to her ex-lover after he adopts a Mexican baby, Hamel must deal with smuggling rings, sleazy political machinations, and an attempt to make a windfall profit by turning an old gold mine into a nuclear waste dump in *North of the Border* (1988). In *Raptor* (1990), when a poacher of the rare arctic falcon is killed, Hamel defends the conservationist charged with the murder. Alone in a rugged wilderness, Neil herself becomes the target of human predators. This thriller is her best book to date. When the death of a vocal opponent of the proposed "world's tallest, largest, ugliest building" is ruled a suicide, Hamel decides to sniff out the real rats in *The Other Side of Death* (1991). *The Wolf Path* (1992) is about the reintroduction of wolves to the New Mexico. When a federal official is murdered, a radical environmentalist becomes the fall guy whom Neil must defend. In *The Lies That Bind* (1993), Hamel gets involved in a case involving racism, the drug trade, international assassinations, and devastating development around Albuquerque and Phoenix. When a rare indigo macaw and the wife of the man it was stolen from both go missing, Neil searches for a notorious parrot smuggler in *Parrot Blues* (1995). *Hotshots* (1996) questions whether firefighters' lives should be sacrificed to save homes inappropriately located in wild areas. *Ditch Rider* (1998), primarily an examination of teen gangs in Albuquerque, also explores the relationship between the natural and human landscapes of New Mexico. Van Gieson's second series featuring rare books librarian Claire Reynier is similarly fascinating, but not particularly ecological in its themes or subjects.

David Rains Wallace's multiple-award-winning *The Klamath Knot: Explorations of Myth and Evolution* (1983) is an excellent work of creative nonfiction, combining ecology, geology, anthropology, and myth. He has also written two mysteries steeped in nature lore. In *The Turquoise Dragon* (1985), forester George Kilgore learns that a murdered biologist had discovered the breeding grounds of one of the world's rarest animals. Kilgore finds himself plunged into a wilderness intrigue involving strange detectives, cocaine smugglers, and self-described "redneck loggers." In *The Vermilion Parrot* (1991), Kilgore becomes the manager of a land preserve where he discovers that rare California condors are being removed from the area so it can be logged.

When national forest cop Frank Carver and ranger Ginny Trask investigate the murder of an illegal alien working on a Christmas tree plantation, they also discover a suspicious "suicide," blackmail, and other unsavory activities in Lee Wallingford's *Cold Tracks* (1991). In the sequel, *Clear-Cut Murder* (1993), Carver and Trask are back on the case when a confrontation between a logging company and radical environmentalists results in the murder of a would-be peacemaker.

The popular Joseph Wambaugh has written one green mystery, *Finnegan's Week* (1993), in which a San Diego police detective joins forces with two female cops to chase a killer with a fifty-five-gallon drum of toxic chemicals.

Randy Wayne White created Doc Ford, a former CIA agent turned wildlife biologist in Florida. Doc's peaceful life in *Sanibel Flats* (1990) is disturbed when he is called to investigate an abduction in Central America that he eventually connects to the destruction of the Florida coast. In *The Heat Islands* (1992), when a despised marina owner is found dead, an environmentalist friend of Doc's is accused of murder, but Doc traces the death to a development scheme. In *The Man Who Invented Florida* (1993), aging Tucker Gatrell claims he has found the fountain of youth in a sulfur spring on land he once owned, but when Doc discovers that it made Tucker's horse grow new genitals and revitalized Tucker's best friend, he suspects it part of a scheme by Tucker to get his land back from developers. *Captiva* (1996) tells the tale of hostility between sports and commercial fishermen resulting in murder when a net-fishing ban is imposed to protect marine habitats. *North of Havana* (1997), *The Mangrove Coast* (1998), *Shark River* (2001), *Twelve Mile Limit* (2002), and *Tampa Burn* (2004) are thrillers with kidnapping, drug running, smuggling, and political chicanery, and whose ecological content consists of Doc's frequent commentaries on nature and conservation and a fascinatingly detailed description of collecting marine specimens. In *Ten Thousand Islands* (2000), a search for a Calusa Indian medallion with reputed mysterious powers that was poached from a girl's grave leads Doc to a developer whose son is about to enter politics. This was based on a true story. In *Everglades* (2003), the glades are imperiled by a scheme between a phony guru and a former Mossad agent to build a "theme park ashram," including a series of explosions intended to mimic earthquakes prophesized by Chief Tecumseh in 1811. *Dark Light* (2006) and *Hunter's Moon* (2007) are less environmentally oriented than the earlier Doc Ford books.

Robin White's experience living in the Siberian oil fields informs *Siberian Light* (1997), a thriller that contains multiple murders, dirty deals by a shady and environmentally ruinous American oil company, false murder accusations made against an ecologist trying to save the Siberian tiger, and the duplicity of the Russian mob.

Walter Jon Williams strayed from his usual cyberpunk style to write *Days of Atonement* (1991). A copper mine closes in early twenty-first-century Atocha,

New Mexico, and unemployed people accept the arrival of the super-secret Advanced Technologies Labs. When strange events start taking place and a man drops dead in the police chief's office, he is forced to deal with the hazardous activity at ATL.

There's a little murder, a lot of ecodefense, and a whole lot of quirky black humor in Lana Witt's *Slow Dancing on Dinosaur Bones* (1996), in which the denizens of Pick, Kentucky, sort of unite to try to close down a coal company.

In M. K. Wren's *Wake Up, Darlin' Corey* (1984), when a family double-crosses an environmental group by selling their unspoiled Oregon coast property to a resort developer, their environmentalist daughter dies in a mysterious car accident. A bookstore owner/private investigator searches for her missing diary, which he believes will reveal the killer.

Mad Season (1996) by Nancy Means Wright is based on the true story of developers and bankers going to any length, including arson and murder, to frighten an old couple in Vermont enough to sell their farm. In *Poison Apples* (2000), a picker in Moira and Stan Earthrowl's orchard dies when pesticide is overused. *A Gift upon the Shore* (1990), while not exactly a sequel, is similar.

Professor of pharmacology Duncan H. Haynes writes medical murder mysteries under the name of Dirk Wyle. The titles of *Pharmacology Is Murder* (1998), *Biotechnology Is Murder* (2000), and *Medical School Is Murder* (2001) are self-explanatory. *Amazon Gold* (2003) might be titled *A Dual Career Couple is Murder.* Dr. Ben Candidi stays at home working on a process to discover new drugs while Dr. Rebecca Levis delivers medicine to the Yanomama Indians, but when she doesn't return with the expedition, Ben flies to the Amazon, hoping she is still alive.

In *Hardrock Stiff* (1997) by Thomas Zigal, "hippie sheriff" Kurt Muller of Aspen, Colorado, investigates the death of an old man in a silver mine. Since the unpopular miner had made enemies among both the eco defenders known as the Green Briars and the militant right-wing Free West Rebellion, Muller must try to penetrate the rival groups.

APPENDIX: 100 BEST BOOKS

Listed are the author name, book title, and subject category. The top ten books appear in **boldface**.

Adams, Richard. *Watership Down.* England.
⟳**Abbey, Edward. *The Monkey Wrench Gang.* Environmental Action/ Ecodefense.**
Allende, Isabel. *City of the Beasts.* South America.
Amado, Jorge, *Tieta, the Goat Girl.* South America.
Anaya, Rudolfo. *Bless Me, Ultima.* West.
Atwood, Margaret. *Surfacing.* Canada.
Austin, Mary. *Lost Borders.* History.

Barrett, Andrea. *Voyage of the Narwahl.* Ecofeminist.
Barton, Emily. *The Testament of Yves Gundron.* Philosophical.
⟳**Bass, Rick. *Where the Sea Used To Be.* Philosophical.**
Bergon, Frank. *The Temptations of St. Ed & Brother S.* West.
Berry, Wendell. *Jayber Crow.* Pastoral.
Brautigan, Richard. *Trout Fishing in America.* West.
Brin, David. *Earth.* Speculative.
Bruchac, Joseph. *Dawn Land.* Native.
Brunner, John. *Stand on Zanzibar.* Speculative.
Butler, Octavia. *Parable of the Sower.* Speculative.

Callenbach, Ernest. *Ecotopia* History.
Cameron, Sarah. *Natural Enemies.* Environmental Action/Ecodefense.
Carpentier, Alejo. *The Lost Steps.* South America.
Choyce, Lesley. *The Second Season of Jonas MacPherson.* Canada.

Clark, Walter Van Tilburg. *The Track of the Cat.* West.
Crace, Jim. *Continent.* Philosophical.

Davenport, Kiana. *Shark Dialogues.* Native.
DeLillo, Don. *White Noise.* Cautionary.
Dick, Philip W. *Do Androids Dream of Electric Sheep?* Speculative.
Dillard, Annie. *The Living.* West.
Dodge, Jim. *Fup.* Animals. ·
Duncan, David James. *The River Why.* Romance.

Eastlake, William. *Dancers in the Scalp House.* West.
Ekman, Kerstin. *Blackwater.* Scandinavia.
ᵒ **Erdrich, Louise. *Tracks.* Native.**
Fall, Amanita Sow. *The Beggar's Strike.* Africa.
Faulkner, William. *The Bear.* History.

◊ **Galvin, James. *The Meadow.* West**
Gary, Romain. *The Roots of Heaven.* France.
Giono, Jean. *The Man Who Planted Trees.* France.
Gish, Robert. *When Coyote Howls.* West.
Grahame, Kenneth. *The Wind in the Willows.* England.
Guthrie, A. B. *The Big Sky.* West. ·

Hall, James W. *Gone Wild.* Mystery.
Harrison, Jim. *The Road Home.* Philosophical.
Head, Bessie. *When Rain Clouds Gather.* Caribbean.
Herbert, Frank. *Dune.* Speculative.
Hill, Lloyd. *The Village of Bom Jesus.* Animals.
Høeg, Peter. *Smilla's Sense of Snow.* Scandinavia.
Hogan, Linda. *Power.* Native.
Hope, Christopher. *Darkest England.* Africa.
Houston, James D. *The Last Paradise.* Mystery.

Jersild, P. C. *A Living Soul.* Scandinavia.
Jewett, Sara Orne. *The Country of the Pointed Firs.* History.

King, Thomas. *Green Grass, Running Water.* Native.
ᵔ **Kingsolver, Barbara.** ***Animal Dreams.*** **Ecofeminist.**

ᵔ**Le Guin, Ursula K.** ***Always Coming Home.*** **Speculative.**
Lem, Stanislaw. *Solaris.* Speculative.
London, Jack. *The Call of the Wild.* History.
Lopez, Barry. *Winter Count.* Animals.

MacDonald, John D. *A Flash of Green.* Mystery.
Maron, Monica. *Flight of Ashes.* Germany.
○ **Matthiessen, Peter.** ***At Play in the Fields of the Lord.*** **History.**
Melville, Herman. Polynesian trilogy (*Typee, Omoo, Mardi*). History.
Momaday, Scott. *House Made of Dawn.* Native.
Montero, Mayra. *In the Palm of Darkness.* Cuba.
Morse, David. *The Iron Bridge.* Speculative.
Mudrooroo. *Master of the Ghost Dreaming.* Native.
Mueller, Marnie. *Green Fires.* Environmental Action/Ecodefense

Ngugi, James T. *A Grain of Wheat.* Africa.

O'Brien, Dan. *In the Center of the Nation.* Environmental Action/Ecodefense
Owens, Louis. *Lost River.* Mystery.

Paton, Alan. *Cry, the Beloved Country.* Africa.
Peterson, Brenda. *Animal Heart.* Romance.
Piercy, Marge. *Woman on the Edge of Time.* Speculative.
Popham, Melinda. *Skywater.* Animals.

✓ Quinn, Daniel. *Ishmael.* Philosophical.

Robinson, Kim Stanley. Mars trilogy. Speculative.

Robinson, Marilynne. *Housekeeping.* Ecofeminist.

Rogers, Jane. *Promised Lands.* Australia.

Schaefer, Jack. *Conversations with a Pocket Gopher.* West.

Seaman, Donna, ed. *In Our Nature: Stories of Wildness.* Animals.

◊ **Silko, Leslie Marmon. *Ceremony.* Native.**

Smiley, Jane. *A Thousand Acres.* Ecofeminist.

Smith, Lawrence R. *Annie's Soup Kitchen.* Environmental Action/Ecodefense.

Stabenow, Dana. *A Cold Day for Murder.* Mystery.

Stadler, John, ed. *Eco-Fiction.* History.

✓Steinbeck, John. *The Grapes of Wrath.* History.

Sterchi, Beat. *Cow.* Switzerland.

✓**Stewart, George Rippey. *Earth Abides.* History.**

Straley, John. *The Woman Who Married a Bear.* Mystery.

Sucharitkul, Somtow. *Starship and Haiku.* Thailand.

Theroux, Paul. *The Mosquito Coast.* Cautionary.

Tolkien, J. R. R. *Lord of the Rings.* History.

Traven, B. *The Bridge in the Jungle.* Mexico.

Turner, George. *Drowning Towers.* Cautionary.

Varley, John. Gaean trilogy. Speculative.

Warner, Irving. *Wagner Descending.* Environmental Action/Ecodefense.

Waters, Frank. *The Woman at Otowi Crossing.* History.

Welch, James. *Winter in the Blood.* Native.

Weller, Anthony. *The Siege of Salt Cove.* Environmental Action/Ecodefense.

Wilhelm, Kate. *Where Late the Sweet Birds Sang.* Speculative.

Wongar, B. Nuclear trilogy. Native.

NOTES

1 | ECOCRITICISM AND ECOFICTION: DEFINITIONS AND ANALYSES

1. Cheryll Glotfelty and Harold Fromm, eds., *The Ecocriticism Reader: Landmarks in Literary Ecology* (Athens: University of Georgia Press, 1996), 16.

2. For ecocritical approaches to these naturalists' work, see David Mazel's *A Century of Early Ecocriticism* (Athens: University of Georgia Press, 2001).

3. William Rueckert, "Literature and Ecology: An Experiment in Ecocriticism," *Iowa Review* 9, no. 1 (Winter 1978): 72–73.

4. William Howarth, "Some Principles of Ecocriticism," in *The Ecocriticism Reader: Landmarks in Literary Ecology*, ed. Cheryll Glotfelty and Harold Fromm (Athens: University of Georgia Press, 1996), 69.

5. Mike Vasey. E-mail discussion, Bioregional Studies, Feb. 20, 1996.

6. Patrick D. Murphy, *Further Afield in the Study of Nature-Oriented Literature* (Charlottesville: University Press of Virginia, 2000), 1.

7. Ibid., 4–5.

8. Ibid., 42.

9. Diane Ackerman, preface to *In Our Nature: Stories of Wildness* (Athens: University of Georgia Press, 2002), 3.

10. Gabriel Navarre, "Toward a Definition of Environmental Fiction," in *Earthworks: Ten Years on the Environmental Front* (San Francisco: Friends of the Earth, 1980), 218–19.

11. Patricia Greiner, "Radical Environmentalism in Recent Literature Concerning the American West," *Rendezvous* 19, no. 1 (Fall 1983): 8 (emphasis mine).

12. Ibid., 10.

13. Lawrence Buell, *Writing for an Endangered World: Literature, Culture, and Environment in the U.S. and Beyond* (Cambridge: Harvard University Press, 2001), 7.

14. Patricia Netzley, *Environmental Literature: An Encyclopedia of Works, Authors, and Themes* (Santa Barbara, CA: ABC-Clio, 1991), 78.

15. Ibid., 79.

16. Donna Seaman, ed., "Many Shades of Green, or Ecofiction Is in the Eye of the Reader," *TriQuarterly* 118:9–28.

17. Elizabeth Englehardt, *The Tangled Roots of Feminism, Environmentalism, and Appalachian Literature* (Athens: Ohio University Press, 2003), 4.

18. Karen J. Warren, *Ecofeminism: Women, Culture, Nature* (Bloomington: Indiana University Press, 1997), xi.

19. Garry Peterson, "Ecological Fiction." http://www.geog.mcgill.ca/faculty/peterson/ecofiction/ (accessed August 24, 2004).

20. Donna Seaman, ed., *In Our Nature: Stories of Wildness* (Athens: University of Georgia Press, 2002), 10.

21. Jonathan Bate, *The Song of the Earth* (Cambridge: Harvard University Press, 2000), 38.

22. Buell, *Writing for an Endangered World,* 2.

23. Barbara Kingsolver, *High Tide in Tucson* (New York: Harper Collins, 1995), 228.

24. Ibid., 234.

2 | ECOFICTION'S ROOTS AND HISTORICAL DEVELOPMENT

1. Glen Love, "Ecocriticism and Science: Toward Consilience?" *New Literary History* 30, no. 3 (1999): 562–63.

2. Willa Cather, introduction to *The Best Stories of Sarah Orne Jewett* (Boston: Houghton Mifflin, 1925), x.

3. "John Fox, Jr.," *Contemporary Authors Online* (Farmington Hills, MI: Gale Group, 2004).

4. Paul Goodman, introduction to *Metamorphosis,* by Franz Kafka (New York: Vanguard, 1946), 5.

5. Ursula Heise, "The Virtual Crowd," in *The ISLE Reader: Ecocriticism, 1993–2003* (Athens: University of Georgia Press, 2003), 79.

6. George R. Stewart, *A Little of Myself* (Berkeley, CA: Bancroft Library, 1972), 189.

7. Frederick Waage. E-mail message from ASLE discussion list, July 28, 2007.

8. Robert Silverberg, in *Jack Vance,* ed. Tim Underwood and Chuck Miller (New York: Taplinger, 1980), 184.

9. John Stadler, *Eco-Fiction* (New York: Washington Square Press, 1971), ix–x.

10. Gerald Haslam, "Present Trends," in *A Literary History of the American West* (Fort Worth: Texas Christian University, 1987), 1162.

11. Susanne Bounds and Patti Capel Swartz, "Women's Resistance in the Desert West," in *The Literature of Nature: An International Sourcebook* (Chicago: Fitzroy Dearborn, 1998), 80.

3 | CONTEMPORARY ECOFICTION

1. Alan Weltzien, *Rick Bass* (Boise: Boise State University, 1998), 44.

2. Elizabeth Marshall Thomas, *Certain Poor Shepherds* (New York: Simon and Schuster, 1996), 2.

3. Ibid., 128.

4. Sybil S. Steinberg, "Review, Wherever That Great Heart May Be," *Publishers Weekly* 243, no. 5 (Jan. 29, 1996): 83.

5. Donna Seaman, ed., *In Our Nature: Stories of Wildness* (Athens: University of Georgia Press, 1992), 6.

6. Barry Lopez, "Interview with Jim Aton," *Western American Literature* 21, no. 1 (Spring 1986): 16.

7. Paul Goodman, introduction to *Metamorphosis*, by Franz Kafka (New York, Vanguard Press, 1946), 5.

8. Patrick Murphy, e-mail correspondence, July 8, 2004.

9. J. G. Ballard, *Best Science Fiction from "New Worlds 3"* (London: Panther, 1968), 38.

4 | NATIVE AMERICAN AND CANADIAN ECOFICTION

1. Paula Gunn Allen, "American Indian Fiction, 1968–1983," in *A Literary History of the American West,* 1058.

2. William Brandon, *The Last Americans: The Indian in American Culture* (New York: McGraw-Hill, 1974), 57.

3. Joseph Bruchac, "Contemporary Native American Writing: An Overview," in *Dictionary of Native American Literature* (New York: Garland, 1994), 312.

4. "Wayne Johnson," *Contemporary Authors Online* (Farmington Hills, MI: Gale Group, 2004).

5 | ECOFICTION FROM ALL AROUND THE WORLD

1. Seodial Deena, "The Caribbean," in *The Literature of Nature: An International Sourcebook* (Chicago: Fitzroy Dearborn, 1998), 367–38.

2. Karl Guthke, *B. Traven: The Lives Behind the Legend* (Chicago: Lawrence Hill, 1991).

3. Richard Kerridge, "Nature in the English Novel," in *The Literature of Nature,* 151.

4. Linden Peach, "The Environment in Twentieth-Century Welsh Writing in English," in *The Literature of Nature,* 191.

5. Richard Kerridge, "Nature in the English Novel," 155.

6. Montserrat López Mújica, "La esperanza de Jean Giono," *Cedille: Revista de Estudios Franceses* 4 (2008): 151.

7. Yuri Vedenin, "Nature and Environment in Russian Literary Prose," in *The Literature of Nature*, 224.

8. Ibid., 226.

9. Takashi Kinoshita and Masataka Ota, "Nature in Modern Japanese Literature," in *The Literature of Nature*, 286.

10. S. Murali, "A Booklist of International Environmental Literature," *World Literature Today* 83, no. 1 (Jan. 1, 2009): 56.

11. Maysa Abou-Youssef, "Symbolic and Intersubjective Representations in Arab Environmental Writing," in *The Literature of Nature*, 355.

12. "Russell Foreman," *Contemporary Authors Online*.

13. C. Christopher Norden, "Ecological Restoration and the Australian Aboriginal Novel," in *The Literature of Nature*, 270.

14. C. Christopher Norden, *Native and Non-native: A Rhetoric of the Contemporary Fourth World Novel* (Madison: University of Wisconsin, 1991), 270.

6 | ECOROMANCE: DOIN' THE WILD THING

1. "Harold Bell Wright," *Contemporary Authors Online*.

2. Marilyn French, "Margaret Atwood," *New York Times Book Review*, Feb. 3, 1980, 8.

3. Daniel Barth, "Review of Your Name Here," *Review of Contemporary Fiction* 15, no. 2 (Summer 1995): 225.

7 | THE REAL WEST

1. Gerald Haslam, "Present Trends," in *A Literary History of the American West*, 1162.

2. Mark Siegel, "Contemporary Trends in Western American Fiction," *A Literary History of the American West*, 1182.

3. Michael Cleary, *Fifty Western Writers* (Westport, CT: Greenwood, 1982), 427.

4. Louis L'Amour, *Hondo* (New York: Gold Medal, 1953), 59.

5. Nathaniel Lewis, review of *Nothing but Blue Skies*, *Western American Literature* 28, no. 3 (Fall 1993): 283.

6. Jerome Klinkowitz, *The Practice of Fiction in America: Writers from Hawthorne to the Present* (Ames: Iowa State University Press, 1980), 64.

7. Mark Siegel, "Contemporary Trends in Western American Fiction," 1182.

8. "Frank Bergon," *Contemporary Authors Online*.

9. Mark Siegel, "Contemporary Trends in Western American Fiction," 1182.

1. Andre Norton, interview by Charles Platt, in *The Dream Makers: The Uncommon Men and Women Who Write Science Fiction*, vol. 2 (New York: Berkley, 1983), 206.

2. Veronica Hollinger, "Feminist Theory and Science Fiction," in *The Cambridge Companion to Science Fiction* (Cambridge: Cambridge University, 2003), 128 (emphasis mine).

3. Marlene S. Barr, *Lost in Space: Probing Feminist Science Fiction and Beyond* (Chapel Hill: University of North Carolina, 1993), 3–4.

4. Marge Piercy, "Marge Piercy," in *Women's Culture: The Women's Renaissance of the Seventies* (Lanham, MD: Scarecrow, 1981), 78.

5. Stephen A. Norwick, *Bibliography of Environmental Literature* (Rohnert Park: Sonoma State University, 1988), 32.

9 | MYSTERIES

1. Kimberly Dilley, *Busybodies, Meddlers, and Snoops: The Female Hero in Contemporary Women's Mysteries* (Westport, CT: Greenwood, 1988), xii.

2. Marion Shaw, "The New Avengers," *London Times*, March 12, 1995, Feature section, 3.

3. Ibid., 4,

4. Carrie Spector, "Hellraiser!" *Mother Jones* 20, no. 1 (Jan.–Feb., 1995): 17.

BIBLIOGRAPHY

Abbey, Edward. 1971. *Black Sun.* Boulder, CO: Johnson Books, 2003.

———. 1956. *The Brave Cowboy: An Old Tale in a New Time.* New York: Avon, 1992.

———. 1962. *Fire on the Mountain.* New York: Avon, 1992.

———. 1988. *The Fool's Progress: An Honest Novel.* New York: Holt, 1998.

———. 1980. *Good News.* New York: Plume, 1991.

———. *Hayduke Lives!* Boston: Little, Brown, 1990.

———. *Jonathan Troy.* New York: Dodd, Mead, 1954.

———. 1975. *The Monkey Wrench Gang.* New York: Perennial Classics, 2000.

Abbey, Lloyd Robert. *The Last Whales.* New York: Grove Weidenfeld, 1989.

Abbey, Sue, and Sandra Phillips, eds. *Fresh Cuttings: A Celebration of Fiction and Poetry from UQP's Black Writing Series.* St. Lucia: University of Queensland Press, 2003.

Abrahams, Peter. 1946. *Mine Boy.* London: Heinemann, 1989.

Abramov, Fedor. *The Swans Flew By and Other Stories.* Moscow: Raduga, 1986.

Acokamittiran. 1973. *Water.* Oxford: Heinemann, 1993.

Adams, Douglas. *Dirk Gently's Holistic Detective Agency.* New York: Simon & Schuster, 1987.

———. 1979. *The Hitchhiker's Guide to the Galaxy.* New York: Ballantine, 1997.

———. 1982. *Life, the Universe and Everything.* New York: Ballantine, 1995.

———. 1988. *The Long Dark Tea-Time of the Soul.* New York: Pocket Books, 1990.

———. 1980. *The Restaurant at the End of the Universe.* New York: Ballantine, 1997.

———. 1985. *So Long, and Thanks for All the Fish.* New York: Ballantine, 1999.

Adams, Richard. 1977. *The Plague Dogs.* New York: Fawcett Columbine, 1997.

———. 1974. *Shardik.* New York: Overlook Press, 2002.

———. *Tales from Watership Down.* New York: Knopf, 1996.

———. *Traveler.* New York: Knopf, 1988.

———. 1972. *Watership Down.* New York: Perennial, 2001.

Agee, Jonis. *Bend This Heart.* Minneapolis: Coffee House Press, 1989.

———. *South of Resurrection.* New York: Viking, 1997.

———. 1993. *Strange Angels.* New York: Penguin, 2000.

Aguilera Malta, Demetrio. 1933. *Don Goyo.* Clifton, NJ: Humana Press, 1980.

———. 1970. *Seven Serpents & Seven Moons.* Austin: University of Texas Press, 1979.

Albert, Susan Wittig. *Hangman's Root*. New York: Scribner's, 1994.

———. *The Tale of Cuckoo Brow Wood*. New York: Berkley, 2006.

———. *The Tale of Hawthorn House: The Cottage Tales of Beatrix Potter*. New York: Berkley Prime Crime, 2007.

———. *The Tale of Holly How*. New York: Berkley, 2005.

———. *The Tale of Hill Top Farm*. New York: Berkley, 2004.

———. *Thyme of Death*. New York: Scribner's, 1992.

Alcalá, Kathleen. *The Flower in the Skull*. San Francisco: Chronicle Books, 1998.

———. *Mrs. Vargas and the Dead Naturalist*. Corvallis, OR: CALYX Books, 1992.

———. *Spirits of the Ordinary: A Tale of Casas Grandes*. San Francisco: Chronicle Books, 1997.

———. *Treasures in Heaven*. San Francisco: Chronicle Books, 2000.

Aldiss, Brian Wilson. 1965. *Earthworks*. New York: Avon, 1980.

———. *Greybeard*. New York: Harcourt Brace, 1964.

———. *Helliconia*. London: HarperCollins, 1996.

———. 1962. *Hothouse*. New York: Baen, 1984.

———. 1969. *Neanderthal Planet*. New York: Avon, 1969.

Aldiss, Brian Wilson, and Roger Penrose. 1999. *White Mars, or, the Mind Set Free: A 21st Century Utopia*. New York: St. Martin's, 2000.

Alexander, Rosanne. *Selkie*. London: Andre Deutsch, 1991.

Alexie, Sherman. *The Lone Ranger and Tonto Fistfight in Heaven*. New York: Atlantic Monthly Press, 1993.

———. *Reservation Blues*. New York: Atlantic Monthly Press, 1995.

———. *Ten Little Indians*. New York: Grove Press, 2004.

Alison, Jane. *Natives and Exotics*. Orlando: Harcourt, 2006.

Allan, Margaret. *Keeper of the Stone*. New York: Penguin, 1994.

———. *The Last Mammoth*. New York: Signet, 1995.

———. *The Mammoth Stone*. New York: Signet, 1993.

Allen, Paula Gunn. 1983. *The Woman Who Owned the Shadows*. San Francisco: Aunt Lute Books, 1994.

———, ed. *Song of the Turtle: American Indian Literature, 1974–1994*. New York: Ballantine, 1996.

———, ed. *Spider Woman's Granddaughters: Traditional Tales and Contemporary Writing by Native American Women*. Boston: Beacon Press, 1989.

Allen, Paula Gunn, and Carolyn Dunn Anderson, eds. *Hozho: Walking in Beauty: Native American Stories of Inspiration, Humor, and Life*. Chicago: Contemporary Books, 2001.

Allende, Isabel. *City of the Beasts*. New York: HarperCollins, 2002.

———. 1989. *Eva Luna.* New York: HarperLibros, 1995.

———. 1986. *The House of the Spirits.* New York: Everyman's Library, 2005.

Alther, Lisa. 1975. *Kinflicks.* New York: Plume, 1996.

Amado, Jorge. 1977. *Tieta.* Madison: University of Wisconsin Press, 2003.

Amis, Martin. 1989. *London Fields.* London: Vintage, 1999.

Anaya, Rudolfo A. *Alburquerque.* Albuquerque: University of New Mexico Press, 1992.

———. 1972. *Bless Me, Ultima.* New York: Warner Books, 1994.

———. *Jemez Spring.* Albuquerque: University of New Mexico Press, 2005.

———. *Rio Grande Fall.* New York: Warner Books, 1996.

———. *Shaman Winter.* New York: Warner Books, 1999.

———. *Zia Summer.* New York: Warner Books, 1995.

Anderson, Alison. *Darwin's Wink: A Novel of Nature and Love.* New York: Thomas Dunne Books, 2004.

Anderson, Kevin J. 1988. *Resurrection, Inc.* London: Voyager, 1998.

Anderson, Kevin J., and Doug Beason. *Ill Wind.* New York: Forge, 1995.

Anderson, Lorraine, ed. 1991. *Sisters of the Earth: Women's Prose and Poetry About Nature.* New York: Vintage Books, 2003.

Andreae, Christine. *Grizzly, a Mystery.* New York: St. Martin's, 1994.

———. *A Small Target.* New York: St. Martin's, 1996.

———. *Trail of Murder.* New York: St. Martin's, 1992.

Andrews, Sarah. *Bone Hunter.* New York: St. Martin's, 1999.

———. *Dead Dry.* New York: St. Martin's, Minotaur, 2005.

———. *Earth Colors.* New York: St. Martin's, Minotaur, 2004.

———. *An Eye for Gold.* New York: St. Martin's, 2000.

———. *A Fall in Denver.* New York: Scribner, 1995.

———. *Fault Line.* New York: St. Martin's, 2002.

———. *Killer Dust.* New York: St. Martin's, Minotaur, 2003.

———. *Mother Nature.* New York: St. Martin's, 1997.

———. *Only Flesh and Bones.* New York: St. Martin's Press, 1998.

———. *Tensleep.* New York: Signet, 1995.

Anthony, Michael. *Green Days by the River.* Boston: Houghton Mifflin, 1967.

———. *The Year in San Fernando.* London: Andre Deutsch, 1965.

Anthony, Piers. *Being a Green Mother.* New York: Ballantine, 1987.

———. *Hope of Earth.* New York: Tor, 1997.

———. *Neq the Sword.* London: Corgi Books, 1975.

———. 1968. *Omnivore.* Cincinnati: Mundania, 2004.

———. *Orn.* New York: Avon, 1971.

———. *Ox.* New York: Avon, 1976.

———. 1968. *SOS the Rope.* London: Faber and Faber, 1970.

———. 1972. *Var the Stick.* New York: Bantam, 1973.

Arana, Marie. *Cellophane.* New York: Dial Press, 2006.

Aridjis, Homero. 1985. *1492: The Life and Times of Juan Cabezón of Castile.* New York: Summit Books, 1991.

———. 1967. *Persephone.* New York: Vintage Books, 1986.

Armstrong, Jeannette C. *Slash.* Penticton, BC: Theytus Books, 1988.

———. *Whispering in Shadows.* Penticton, BC: Theytus Books, 2000.

Arnow, Harriette Louisa Simpson. 1954. *The Dollmaker.* New York: Perennial, 2003.

Arthur, Elizabeth. *Antarctic Navigation.* New York: Knopf, 1995.

———. *Bad Guys.* New York: Knopf, 1986.

———. *Beyond the Mountain.* New York: Harper & Row, 1983.

———. *Binding Spell.* New York: Doubleday, 1988.

Arvin, Nick. *In the Electric Eden.* New York: Penguin, 2003.

Asimov, Isaac. 1951. *Foundation.* New York: Bantam, 2004.

———. 1986. *Foundation and Earth.* Garden City: Doubleday, 1986.

———. 1952. *Foundation and Empire.* New York: Bantam, 2004.

———. 1982. *Foundation's Edge.* New York: Bantam, 1991.

———. 1953. *Second Foundation.* New York: Bantam, 2004.

Assiniwi, Bernard. *The Beothuk Saga.* New York: Thomas Dunne, 2002.

Astaf'ev, Viktor Petrovich. *Queen Fish: A Story in Two Parts and Twelve Episodes.* Moscow: Progress Publishers, 1982.

Astley, Thea. *An Item from the Late News.* St. Lucia: University of Queensland Press, 1982.

———. *It's Raining in Mango: Pictures from a Family Album.* New York: Putnam, 1987.

Atwood, Margaret Eleanor. 1969. *The Edible Woman.* New York: Anchor Books, 1998.

———. 1985. *The Handmaid's Tale.* New York: Anchor Books, 1998.

———. 1979. *Life Before Man.* New York: Anchor Books, 1998.

———. 2003. *Oryx and Crake.* New York: Anchor Books, 2004.

———. 1972. *Surfacing.* New York: Anchor Books, 1998.

———. 1991. *Wilderness Tips.* New York: Bantam, 1993.

Auel, Jean M. 1980. *The Clan of the Cave Bear.* New York: Crown, 2001.

———. 1985. *The Mammoth Hunters.* New York: Crown, 2001.

———. 1990. *The Plains of Passage.* New York: Crown, 2001.

———. 2002. *The Shelters of Stone.* New York: Crown, 2002.

———. 1982. *The Valley of Horses.* New York: Crown, 2001.

Auster, Paul. *In the Country of Last Things.* New York: Penguin, 1988.

Austin, Mary Hunter. *The Basket Woman: A Book of Indian Tales.* Reno: University of Nevada Press, 1999.

———. *Cactus Thorn.* Reno: University of Nevada Press, 1988.

———. 1917. *The Ford.* Berkeley: University of California Press, 1997.

———. *Isidro.* Upper Saddle River, NJ: Literature House, 1970.

———. 1950. *Mother of Felipe, and Other Early Stories.* San Francisco: Book Club of California, 1950.

———. *One-Smoke Stories.* Athens: Ohio University Press, 2003.

———. 1931. *Starry Adventure.* Boston: Houghton Mifflin, 1931.

———. 1909. *Stories from the Country of Lost Borders.* New Brunswick, NJ: Rutgers University Press, 1987.

———. 1918. *The Trail Book.* Reno: University of Nevada Press, 2004.

———. *Western Trails.* Reno: University of Nevada Press, 1987.

Aylworth, Susan. *A Rainbow in Paradise.* New York: Avalon Books, 1999.

Ayres, E. C. *Eye of the Gator.* New York: St. Martin's, 1995.

———. *Night of the Panther.* New York: St. Martin's, 1997.

Badran, Margot, and Miriam Cooke, eds. *Opening the Gates: An Anthology of Arab Feminist Writing.* Bloomington: Indiana University Press, 2004.

Baker, Will. *Shadow Hunter.* New York: Pocket Books, 1993.

Bakker, Robert T. *Raptor Red.* New York: Bantam, 1995.

Baldacci, David. *Wish You Well.* New York: Warner Books, 2000.

Ball, Pamela. *Lava.* New York: Norton, 1997.

Ballard, J. G. 1974. *Concrete Island.* New York: Picador, 2001.

———. 1973. *Crash.* New York: Picador, 2001.

———. 1966. *The Crystal World.* London: Flamingo, 1993.

———. 1962. *The Drowned World.* London: Millennium, 1999.

———. 1975. *High-Rise.* London: Flamingo, 2003.

———. *Rushing to Paradise.* New York: Picador, 1995.

Bancroft, Griffing. *Vanishing Wings; a Tale of Three Birds of Prey.* New York: Watts, 1972.

Bardhan, Kalpana, ed. *Of Women, Outcastes, Peasants, and Rebels: A Selection of Bengali Short Stories.* Berkeley: University of California Press, 1990.

Barker, Clive. *Sacrament.* New York: HarperCollins, 1996.

Barker, Jane Valentine. *Mari.* Niwot: University Press of Colorado, 1997.

Barnes, Julian. *England, England.* New York: Knopf, 1999.

———. 1989. *A History of the World in 10 1/2 Chapters.* Cambridge: Cambridge University Press, 1995.

Barr, Nevada. 1998. *Blind Descent.* New York: Putnam, 2001.

———. 2001. *Blood Lure.* New York: Berkley, 2002.

———. 1997. *Endangered Species.* New York: Berkley, 2008.

———. 1996. *Firestorm.* New York: Avon, 1997.

———. *Hard Truth.* New York: Berkley, 2006.

———. 2004. *High Country.* New York: Berkley, 2005.

———. 1995. *Ill Wind.* New York: Berkley, 2004.

———. ed. *Naked Came the Phoenix: A Serial Novel.* New York: St. Martin's, 2002.

———. 1994. *A Superior Death.* New York: Berkley, 2003.

———. 1993. *Track of the Cat.* New York: Berkley, 2003.

———. *Winter Study.* New York: Putnam, 2008.

Barrett, Andrea. 1993. *The Forms of Water.* London: Flamingo, 2002.

———. 1988. *Lucid Stars.* New York: Simon & Schuster, 1989.

———. 1991. *The Middle Kingdom.* London: Flamingo, 2001.

———. 1989. *Secret Harmonies.* New York: Washington Square Press, 1991.

———. 2002. *Servants of the Map.* New York: Norton, 2003.

———. 1996. *Ship Fever.* London: Flamingo, 2000.

———. 1998. *The Voyage of the Narwhal.* London: Flamingo, 2000.

Barron, T. A. 1992. *The Ancient One.* New York: Harcourt Brace, 2004.

———. 1990. *Heartlight.* New York: Ace, 2003.

———. 1994. *The Merlin Effect.* New York: Harcourt Brace, 2004.

Barth, John. 1960. *The Sot-Weed Factor.* Garden City, NY: Doubleday, 1987.

———. 1987. *The Tidewater Tales.* Baltimore: Johns Hopkins University Press, 1997.

Barton, Emily. *The Testament of Yves Gundron.* New York: Farrar, Straus, and Giroux, 2000.

Bass, Rick. *The Diezmo.* Boston: Houghton Mifflin, 2005.

———. *Fiber.* Athens: University of Georgia Press, 1998.

———. *The Hermit's Story.* Boston: Houghton Mifflin, 2002.

———. *In the Loyal Mountains.* Boston: Houghton Mifflin, 1995.

———. *The Lives of Rocks.* Boston: Houghton Mifflin, 2006.

———. 1994. *Platte River.* New York: Ballantine, 1995.

———. 1997. *The Sky, the Stars, the Wilderness.* Boston: Houghton Mifflin, 1998.

———. 1989. *The Watch.* New York: Norton, 1994.

———. *Where the Sea Used to Be.* Boston: Houghton Mifflin, 1998.

Bawarchi, Ray. *The Dirt People.* Asheville, NC: Blue Throat Press, 2007.

Baxter, Charles. *Shadow Play.* New York: Norton, 1993.

Baykurt, Fakir. *A Report from Kuloba and Other Stories.* Holladay, UT: Southmoor Press, 2000.

Bear, Greg. 1992. *Anvil of Stars*. New York: Warner, 1993.

———. 1985. *Blood Music*. New York: Simon & Schuster, 2002.

———. 2003. *Darwin's Children*. New York: Ballantine, 2004.

———. 1999. *Darwin's Radio*. New York: Ballantine, 2003.

———. 1985. *Eon*. London: Gollancz, 2002.

———. 1988. *Eternity*. London: Millennium, 1999.

———. 1987. *The Forge of God*. New York: Tor, 2001.

———. *Legacy*. New York: Tor, 1995.

Beard, Patricia, ed. *The Voice of the Wild: An Anthology of Animal Stories*. New York: Viking, 1992.

Behrendt, Larissa. 2000. *Home*. St Lucia: University of Queensland Press, 2004.

Belfer, Lauren. *City of Light*. New York: Dial Press, 1999.

Bell, Clare. 1984. *Clan Ground*. New York: Grafton, 1988.

———. 1993. *Jaguar Princess*. New York: Pan, 1995.

———. 1989. *People of the Sky*. New York: Tor, 1990.

———. *Ratha's Challenge*. New York: McElderry, 1994.

———. *Ratha and Thistle-Chaser*. New York: McElderry, 1990.

———. 1983. *Ratha's Creature*. New York: Grafton, 1988.

———. 1986. *Tomorrow's Sphinx*. New York: Dell, 1988.

Bell, Neal. 1972. *Gone to Be Snakes Now*. New York: Popular Library, 1974.

Belli, Gioconda. *Infinity in the Palm of Her Hand: A Novel of Adam and Eve*. New York: Harper, 2009.

———. *The Inhabited Woman*. Willamantic, CT: Curbstone Press, 1994.

Bellow, Saul. 1959. *Henderson, the Rain King*. New York: Pengiun, 1996.

Belov, Vasilii. 1953. *Morning Rendezvous*. Moscow: Raduga, 1983.

Benford, Gregory. 1980. *Timescape*. London: Millennium, 2000.

Benson, Ann. *The Plague Tales*. New York: Delacorte Press, 1997.

Berger, Thomas. *Robert Crews*. New York: Morrow, 1994.

Bergon, Frank. 1987. *Shoshone Mike*. Reno: University of Nevada Press, 1994.

———. *The Temptations of St. Ed & Brother S*. Reno: University of Nevada Press, 1993.

———. *Wild Game*. Reno: University of Nevada Press, 1995.

Berry, Don. 1962. *Moontrap*. Corvallis: Oregon State University Press, 2004.

———. 1963. *To Build a Ship*. Corvallis: Oregon State University Press, 2004.

———. 1960. *Trask*. Corvallis: Oregon State University Press, 2004.

Berry, R. M. *Leonardo's Horse*. Normal, IL: FC2, 1997.

Berry, Wendell. *Andy Catlett*. Washington DC: Counterpoint, 2007.

———. *Hannah Coulter*. Washington DC: Shoemaker & Hoard, 2004.

————. *Jayber Crow.* Washington DC: Counterpoint, 2000.

————. 1960. *Nathan Coulter.* San Francisco: North Point Press, 1985.

————. *A Place on Earth.* San Francisco: North Point Press, 1983.

————. *Remembering.* San Francisco: North Point Press, 1988.

————. *That Distant Land: The Collected Stories.* Washington DC: Shoemaker & Hoard, 2004.

————. *Watch with Me: And Six Other Stories of the Yet-Remembered Ptolemy Proudfoot and His Wife, Miss Minnie, Née Quinch.* New York: Pantheon, 1994.

————. *The Wild Birds: Six Stories of the Port William Membership.* San Francisco: North Point Press, 1986.

Billheimer, John W. *Dismal Mountain.* New York: St. Martin's, 2001.

————. *Drybone Hollow.* New York: St. Martin's, 2003.

————. *Highway Robbery.* New York: St. Martin's, 2000.

Billman, Jon. *When We Were Wolves.* New York: Random House, 1999.

Bird, Carmel. *The Bluebird Cafe.* New York: New Directions, 1991.

Bishop, Michael. *Count Geiger's Blues.* New York: T. Doherty, 1992.

————. *Unicorn Mountain.* New York: Morrow, 1988.

Bisson, Terry. 1993. *Bears Discover Fire and Other Stories.* New York: Orb, 1995.

————. 2000. *In the Upper Room and Other Likely Stories.* New York: Tom Doherty Associates, 2001.

————. 1995. *Pirates of the Universe.* New York: Tor, 1996.

————. 1986. *Talking Man.* New York: Avon, 1987.

Bitov, Andrei. *The Monkey Link.* New York: Farrar, Straus, and Giroux, 1995.

Black, Cara. *Murder on the Île Saint-Louis.* New York: Soho, 2007.

Blake, Jennifer. 1994. *Shameless.* New York: Fawcett Gold Medal, 1997.

Blew, Mary Clearman. 1977. *Lambing Out, and Other Stories.* Norman: University of Oklahoma Press, 2001.

————. *Runaway: A Collection of Stories.* Lewiston, ID: Confluence Press, 1990.

————. *Sister Coyote: Montana Stories.* New York: Lyons Press, 2000.

Bohjalian, Christopher A. 1995. *Water Witches.* New York: Simon & Schuster, 1997.

Bova, Ben. *Brothers.* New York: Bantam, 1996.

————. 1978. *Colony.* New York: Avon, 1999.

————. *Empire Builders.* New York: Tor, 1993.

————. 1996. *Moonrise.* New York: Avon, 1998.

————. *Moonwar.* New York: Avon, 1998.

————. *The Precipice.* New York: Tor, 2001.

————. 1985. *Privateers.* New York: Eos, 2000.

————. 1973. *The Winds of Altair.* New York: Tom Doherty Associates, 1988.

Bowen, 'Asta. *Hungry for Home: A Wolf Odyssey.* New York: Simon & Schuster, 1997.

Bowen, Peter. 2000. *The Stick Game.* New York: St. Martin's, 2004.

————. *Wolf, No Wolf; and, Notches.* New York: St. Martin's, 2002.

Box, C. J. 2001. *Open Season.* London: Robert Hale, 2002.

————. 2002. *Savage Run.* New York: Berkley, 2003.

————. 2004. *Trophy Hunt.* New York: Berkley, 2005.

————. 2003. *Winterkill.* New York: Berkley, 2004.

Boyd, John. *The Doomsday Gene.* New York: Weybright and Talley, 1973.

————. 1970. *The Organ Bank Farm.* New York: Bantam, 1972.

————. 1969. *The Pollinators of Eden.* New York: Penguin, 1978.

Boyd, William. *Brazzaville Beach.* New York: Morrow, 1990.

Boyle, T. Coraghessan. *Drop City.* New York: Viking, 2003.

————. *A Friend of the Earth.* New York: Viking, 2000.

————. *The Road to Wellville.* New York: Viking, 1993.

————. *Tooth and Claw.* New York: Viking, 2005.

Brackett, Leigh. 1955. *The Long Tomorrow.* New York: Ballantine, 1974.

Bradbury, Ray. 1953. *Fahrenheit 451.* New York: Simon & Schuster, 2003.

————. 1950. *The Martian Chronicles.* New York: Avon, 1997.

Bradfield, Scott. *Animal Planet.* New York: Picador, 1995.

————. *Greetings from Earth: New and Collected Stories.* New York: Picador USA, 1996.

Bradley, Marion Zimmer. 1983. *The Mists of Avalon.* New York: Ballantine, 2001.

————. 1962. *The Planet Savers; the Sword of Aldones.* New York: Ace, 1982.

————. 1976. *The Shattered Chain.* London: Severn House, 1985.

Bradley, Will. *Ark Liberty.* New York: ROC, 1992.

Bradshaw, Gillian. *Bloodwood.* Sutton: Severn House, 2007.

Brandeis, Gayle. *The Book of Dead Birds.* New York: HarperCollins, 2003.

Brandt, Ann. *Crowfoot Ridge.* New York: HarperCollins, 1999.

Brant, Beth. *Food & Spirits.* Ithaca, NY: Firebrand Books, 1991.

————, ed. *A Gathering of Spirit: A Collection by North American Indian Women.* Ithaca, NY: Firebrand Books, 1988.

Brautigan, Richard. *A Confederate General from Big Sur.* New York: Grove Press, 1968.

————. *Trout Fishing in America.* New York: Dell, 1967.

Braver, Gary. *Elixir.* New York: Forge, 2000.

Brin, David. *Brightness Reef.* New York: Bantam, 1995.

————. 1990. *Earth.* New York: Bantam, 1994.

————. *Glory Season.* New York: Bantam, 1993.

————. 1998. *Heaven's Reach: The Final Book of the New Uplift Trilogy.* New York: Bantam, 1999.

————. 1996. *Infinity's Shore.* London: Orbit, 1998.

————. *Kiln People.* New York: Tor, 2002.

————. 1985. *The Postman.* London: Orbit, 1998.

————. 1984. *The Practice Effect.* New York: Bantam, 1994.

————. 1983. *Startide Rising.* New York: Bantam, 1995.

————. 1980. *Sundiver.* New York: Bantam, 1995.

————. 1987. *The Uplift War.* New York: Bantam, 1995.

Brissenden, R. F. *Poor Boy.* New York: St. Martin's, 1987.

————. *Wildcat.* North Sydney, NSW: Allen & Unwin, 1991.

Broder, Bill. *The Sacred Hoop: A Cycle of Earth Tales.* San Francisco: Sierra Club Books, 1992.

Broderick, Damien. *The Dreaming Dragons: A Time Opera.* New York: Pocket Books, 1980.

————. *Transcension.* New York: Tor, 2002.

Brooks, Adrian. *Roulette.* San Francisco: Suspect Thoughts, 2007.

Brown, George Mackay. *Beside the Ocean of Time.* London: J. Murray, 1994.

————. *Vinland.* London: J. Murray, 1992.

Browner, Jesse. *Turnaway.* New York: Villard, 1996.

Bruchac, Joseph. *Dawn Land.* Golden, CO: Fulcrum, 1993.

————. *Long River.* Golden, CO: Fulcrum, 1995.

————. *The Waters Between: A Novel of the Dawn Land.* Hanover, NH: University Press of New England, 1998.

Brunner, John. 1972. *The Sheep Look Up.* Dallas: BenBella Books, 2003.

————. 1968. *Stand on Zanzibar.* London: Millennium, 1999.

Bryant, Dorothy. 1971. *The Kin of Ata Are Waiting for You.* New York: Random House, 1997.

Buckler, Ernest. 1963. *The Cruelest Month.* Toronto: McClelland and Stewart, 1977.

————. 1952. *The Mountain and the Valley.* Toronto: McClelland and Stewart, 1993.

Buckley, Christopher. *Thank You for Smoking.* New York: Random House, 1994.

Buell, Lawrence. *The Environmental Imagination.* Cambridge: Harvard University Press, 1995.

Bunin, Ivan Alekseevich. 1910. *The Village.* New York: Knopf, 1923.

Bunkley, Anita R. *Balancing Act.* New York: Dutton, 1997.

Burke, Terrill Miles. *Dolphin Magic: Adepts Vs. Inepts.* Fiddletown, CA: Alpha-Dolphin Press, 1993.

———. *Dolphin Magic: The Ancient Knowledge*. Fiddletown, CA: Alpha-Dolphin Press, 1994.

———. *Dolphin Magic: The First Encounter*. Fiddletown, CA: Alpha-Dolphin Press, 1992.

———. *Dolphin Magic: The Unexpected Stranger*. Fiddletown, CA: Alpha-Dolphin Press, 1995.

———. *Dolphin Magic: Unobstructed Universes*. Fiddletown, CA: Alpha-Dolphin Press, 1996.

Burroughs, William S. *Ghost of Chance*. New York: High Risk Books, 1995.

Bush, Catherine. 1993. *Minus Time*. Toronto: HarperCollins, 2000.

Butala, Sharon. *Fever*. Toronto: HarperCollins, 1990.

———. 1985. *Queen of the Headaches*. Regina, SK: Coteau Books, 1994.

Butler, Octavia E. 1988. *Adulthood Rites*. New York: Warner Books, 1997.

———. *Bloodchild and Other Stories*. New York: Seven Stories Press, 2005.

———. 1984. *Clay's Ark*. New York: Warner Books, 1996.

———. 1987. *Dawn*. New York: Warner Books, 1997.

———. *Fledgling*. New York: Seven Stories Press, 2005.

———. 1989. *Imago*. New York: Warner Books, 1997.

———. *Kindred*. Boston: Beacon Press, 2003.

———. 1977. *Mind of My Mind*. New York: Warner Books, 1994.

———. 1993. *Parable of the Sower*. New York: Warner Books, 2000.

———. 1998. *Parable of the Talents*. New York: Warner Books, 2001.

———. 1976. *Patternmaster*. New York: Warner Books, 1995.

———. 1978. *Survivor*. London: Sphere, 1981.

———. 1980. *Wild Seed*. New York: Popular Library, 1988.

———. *Xenogenesis*. New York: Warner Books, 1988.

Byatt, A. S. *Angels & Insects: Two Novellas*. New York: Random House, 1992.

———. *Babel Tower*. New York: Random House, 1996.

Cady, Jack. *Inagehi*. Seattle: Broken Moon Press, 1994.

Callahan, S. Alice. 1891. *Wynema: A Child of the Forest*. Lincoln: University of Nebraska Press, 1997.

Callenbach, Ernest. 1975. *Ecotopia: The Notebooks and Reports of William Weston*. Berkeley: Banyan Tree Books/Heyday Books, 2004.

———. *Ecotopia Emerging*. Berkeley: Banyan Tree Books, 1981.

Calvino, Italo. 1979. *If on a Winter's Night a Traveler*. San Diego: Harcourt Brace, 1999.

———. 1963. *Marcovaldo, or, the Seasons in the City*. San Diego: Harcourt Brace, 1983.

Cameron, Anne. 1980. *Daughters of Copper Woman*. Madeira Park, BC: Harbour, 2002.

———. *Tales of the Cairds*. Madeira Park, BC: Harbour, 1989.

Cameron, Sara. *Natural Enemies*. New York: Bantam, 1993.

Canary, Brenda Brown. 1975. *Home to the Mountain*. New York: Avon, 1982.

Canter, Mark. *Ember from the Sun*. New York: Delacorte Press, 1996.

Carey, Peter. *Bliss*. New York: Vintage, 1996.

Carpentier, Alejo. 1979. *The Harp and the Shadow*. San Francisco: Mercury House, 1990.

———. 1956. *The Lost Steps*. Minneapolis: University of Minnesota Press, 2001.

Carr, Terry, ed. *Dream's Edge: Science Fiction Stories About the Future of Planet Earth*. San Francisco: Sierra Club Books, 1980.

Carswell, Catherine MacFarlane. 1920. *Open the Door!* New York: Penguin, 1986.

Casey, John. *Spartina*. New York: Vintage, 1998.

Castillo, Ana. 1993. *So Far from God*. New York: Norton, 2005.

Cather, Willa. 1912. *Alexander's Bridge*. New York: Barnes & Noble Books, 2005.

———. 1918. *My Ántonia*. New York: Oxford University Press, 2006.

———. 1913. *O Pioneers!* New York: Signet, 2004.

———. 1932. *Obscure Destinies*. Lincoln: University of Nebraska Press, 1998.

———. 1925. *The Professor's House*. London: Virago, 2006.

———. 1915. *The Song of the Lark*. New York: Oxford University Press, 2000.

Chalfoun, Michelle. *The Width of the Sea*. London: Doubleday, 2001.

Chant, Joy. 1977. *The Grey Mane of Morning*. Toronto: Bantam, 1982.

———. 1970. *Red Moon and Black Mountain: The End of the House of Kendreth*. Toronto; New York: Bantam, 1983.

———. *When Voiha Wakes*. New York: Bantam, 1983.

Charbonneau, Louis. *The Ice: A Novel of Antarctica*. New York: D. I. Fine, 1991.

———. *The Magnificent Siberian*. New York: D.I. Fine, 1995.

———. *White Harvest*. New York: D.I. Fine, 1994.

Charnas, Suzy McKee. *The Conqueror's Child*. New York: Tor, 1999.

———. 1994. *The Furies*. New York: Orb, 2001.

———. *Motherlines*. New York: Berkley, 1978.

———. 1974. *Walk to the End of the World*. Sevenoaks, Kent: Hodder and Stoughton, 1981.

Cheever, John. *Oh, What a Paradise It Seems*. New York: Knopf, 1982.

Chief Eagle, D. 1967. *Winter Count*. Lincoln: University of Nebraska Press, 2003.

Child, Lincoln. *Terminal Freeze*. New York: Doubleday, 2009.

Chizmar, Richard T., ed. *The Earth Strikes Back: An Anthology of Ecological Horror*. Clarkston, GA: White Wolf Publishing, 1996.

Cho, Se-hui. 1976. *The Dwarf.* Honolulu: University of Hawaii Press, 2006.

Chock, Eric Edward, ed. *Talk Story: An Anthology of Hawaii's Local Writers.* Honolulu: Petronium Press/Talk Story, 1978.

Choyce, Lesley. *Coming Up for Air.* St. John's, NF: Creative Publishers, 1988.

———. *Downwind.* St. John's, NF: Creative Publishers, 1984.

———. 1994. *The Republic of Nothing.* Fredericton, NB: Goose Lane, 1999.

———. *Sea of Tranquility.* Toronto: Dundurn Group, 2003.

———. *The Second Season of Jonas MacPherson.* Saskatoon, SK: Thistledown Press, 1989.

Christensen, Mark. *Aloha.* New York: Simon & Schuster, 1994.

Christofferson, April. *Buffalo Medicine.* New York: Tor, 2004.

———. *Clinical Trial.* New York: Forge, 2000.

———. *Edgewater.* New York: Tom Doherty Associates, 1998.

———. *The Protocol.* New York: Forge, 1999.

Christopher, John. 1957. *No Blade of Grass.* New York: Avon, 1980.

Clark, Walter Van Tilburg. 1945. *The City of Trembling Leaves.* Reno: University of Nevada Press, 1991.

———. 1949. *The Track of the Cat.* Reno: University of Nevada Press, 1993.

Clarke, Brian. 2000. *The Stream.* Woodstock, NY: Overlook Press, 2004.

Clarkson, Ewan. *The Flight of the Osprey.* New York: St. Martin's, 1996.

———. *Ice Trek.* New York: St. Martin's, 1987.

Cleeves, Ann. 1987. *Come Death and High Water.* New York: Ballantine, 1988.

———. *High Island Blues.* New York: Fawcett Gold Medal, 1996.

———. *The Mill on the Shore.* New York: Ballantine, 1994.

———. *A Prey to Murder.* New York: Ballantine, 1989.

Clement, Peter. *Mutant.* New York: Ballantine, 2001.

Coe, David B. 1997. *Children of Amarid.* New York: Tor, 1998.

———. *Eagle-Sage.* New York: Tor, 2000.

———. *The Outlanders.* New York: Tor, 1998.

Coel, Margaret. *The Dream Stalker.* New York: Berkley, 1997.

———. *Killing Raven.* New York: Berkley, 2003.

———. *The Thunder Keeper.* New York: Berkley, 2001.

Coetzee, J. M. *Disgrace.* New York: Viking, 1999.

———. *Elizabeth Costello.* New York: Viking, 2003.

———. *The Lives of Animals.* Princeton, NJ: Princeton University Press, 1999.

Coldsmith, Don. *South Wind.* New York: Bantam, 1998.

———. *Tallgrass: A Novel of the Great Plains.* New York: Bantam, 1997.

Coleman, Jane Candia. *Borderlands: Western Stories.* Unity, ME: Five Star, 2000.

————. *Stories from Mesa Country.* Athens, OH: Swallow Press, 1991.

Collis, Brad. *The Soul Stone.* Rydalmere, NSW: Sceptre, 1993.

Conrad, Barnaby, and Niels Mortensen. *Endangered.* New York: Berkley, 1980.

Conrad, James. *Making Love to the Minor Poets of Chicago.* New York: St. Martin's, 2000.

Cook, Donald Fuller. *Reservation Nation.* Albany, CA: Boaz, 2007.

Cooke, Grace MacGowan. 1910. *The Power and the Glory.* Boston: Northeastern University Press, 2003.

Cook-Lynn, Elizabeth. *From the River's Edge.* New York: Arcade, 1991.

Corpi, Lucha. *Delia's Song.* Houston: Arte Publico Press, 1989.

Coupland, Douglas. *Generation X: Tales for an Accelerated Culture.* New York: St. Martin's, 1991.

————. *Microserfs.* New York: ReganBooks, 1995.

Cox, Richard Hubert Francis. *Eclipse.* New York: St. Martin's, 1996.

Crace, Jim. 1991. *Arcadia.* London: Penguin, 1998.

————. 1999. *Being Dead.* New York: Picador, 2001.

————. 1986. *Continent.* London: Penguin, 2001.

————. 1988. *The Gift of Stones.* London: Penguin, 2003.

————. 1995. *Signals of Distress.* New York: Picador, 2005.

Craddock, Charles Egbert. *His Vanished Star.* Boston: Houghton, Mifflin and Company, 1894.

Craig, Philip R. 1994. *Off Season: A Martha's Vineyard Mystery.* New York: Avon, 1996.

Craig, Philip R., and William G. Tapply. 2001. *First Light.* New York: Scribner, 2002.

Craven, Margaret. 1973. *I Heard the Owl Call My Name.* New York: Dell, 2003.

————. *Walk Gently This Good Earth.* New York: Putnam, 1977.

Cresswell, Jasmine. *The Disappearance.* Richmond, Surrey, UK: MIRA, 1999.

Crider, Bill. *The Prairie Chicken Kill.* New York: Walker, 1996.

Cummins, Ann. *Yellowcake.* Boston: Houghton Mifflin, 2007.

Cunningham, Elizabeth. *Daughter of the Shining Isles.* Barrytown, NY: Station Hill Arts, 2000.

————. *How to Spin Gold: A Woman's Tale.* Barrytown, NY: Station Hill Arts, 1997.

————. *The Return of the Goddess: A Divine Comedy.* Barrytown, NY: Station Hill Press, 1992.

————. *The Wild Mother.* Barrytown, NY: Station Hill Press, 1993.

Cussler, Clive. *Flood Tide.* New York: Simon & Schuster, 1997.

————. *Sahara.* New York: Pocket Books, 2005.

————. *Shock Wave: A Dirk Pitt Adventure.* New York: Pocket Books, 2002.

D'Alpuget, Blanche. *White Eye*. New York: Simon & Schuster, 1994.

Dann, John R. *Song of the Axe*. New York: Forge, 2001.

Danvers, Dennis. *Circuit of Heaven*. New York: Avon, 1998.

———. *End of Days*. New York: Avon, 1999.

———. *Wilderness*. New York: Eos, 2000.

Dara, Evan. *The Lost Scrapbook*. Normal, IL: FC2, 1995.

Date, S. V. *Smokeout*. New York: Putnam, 2000.

Daugherty, Tracy. *What Falls Away*. New York: Norton, 1996.

Dauncey, Guy. *Earthfuture: Stories from a Sustainable World*. Gabriola Island, BC: New Society Publishers, 1999.

Davenport, Kiana. *House of Many Gods*. New York: Ballantine, 2006.

———. *Shark Dialogues*. New York: Maxwell Macmillan, 1994.

———. *Song of the Exile*. New York: Ballantine, 1999.

Davidson, Diane Mott. 1995. *Killer Pancake*. New York: Bantam, 2002.

Davies, Martin. *The Conjuror's Bird*. London: Hodder & Stoughton, 2005.

Davies, Rhys. *A Time to Laugh*. New York: Stackpole Sons, 1938.

Davis, Claire. *Winter Range*. New York: Picador, 2000.

Davis, Jack, ed. *Paperbark: A Collection of Black Australian Writings*. St Lucia: University of Queensland Press, 1990.

Dawson, Janet. *Don't Turn Your Back on the Ocean*. New York: Fawcett Columbine, 1994.

DeLillo, Don. *Underworld*. New York: Scribner, 1997.

———. 1986. *White Noise*. New York: Penguin, 1999.

DeMille, Nelson. *Plum Island*. New York: Warner Books, 1997.

DesRochers, Diane. *Walker Between the Worlds*. St. Paul, MN: Llewellyn Publications, 1995.

Detweiler, M. David. *The Guide and the CEO*. Mechanicsburg, PA: Stackpole Books, 2001.

Devi, Mahasweta. *Imaginary Maps: Three Stories*. New York: Routledge, 1995.

Dezago, Todd, and Shane Davis. *Spider-Man and Fantastic Four: The Menace of Monster Isle!* Edina, MN: Spotlight, 2006.

Dick, Philip K. 1968. *Do Androids Dream of Electric Sheep?* New York: Ballantine, 1996.

———. 1964. *The Man in the High Castle*. New York: Vintage Books, 1992.

Dickey, James. 1970. *Deliverance*. London: Bloomsbury, 2005.

———. 1993. *To the White Sea*. New York: Scribner, 2002.

Dillard, Annie. 1992. *The Living*. New York: HarperPerennial, 1999.

Diski, Jenny. 1987. *Rainforest*. London: Penguin, 1988.

Doane, Michael. *Bullet Heart.* New York: Knopf, 1994.

Dodge, Jim. 1983. *Fup.* Edinburgh: Canongate, 2004.

―――. 1990. *Stone Junction: An Alchemical Potboiler.* New York: Grove Press, 1997.

Doerr, Anthony. *The Shell Collector.* New York: Scribner, 2002.

Doig, Ivan. 1996. *Bucking the Sun.* New York: Scribner, 2003.

―――. 1987. *Dancing at the Rascal Fair.* New York: Scribner, 2003.

―――. 1984. *English Creek.* New York: Scribner, 2005.

―――. *Mountain Time.* New York: Scribner, 1999.

―――. *Prairie Nocturne.* New York: Scribner, 2005.

―――. 1990. *Ride with Me, Mariah Montana.* New York: Scribner, 2005.

Donovan, Vince. *The Californiad: A Novel of Life, Love, and Endangered Species.* Los Angeles: Vincent Donovan, 2006.

Doolittle, Jerome. *Half Nelson.* New York: Pocket Books, 1994.

Dorris, Michael. 1987. *A Yellow Raft in Blue Water.* New York: Picador, 2003.

Dorris, Michael, and Louise Erdrich. *The Crown of Columbus.* New York: Harper-Collins, 1991.

Doss, James D. *The Shaman Laughs.* New York: St. Martin's, 1995.

―――. *The Shaman Sings.* New York: St. Martin's, 1994.

―――. *The Shaman's Bones.* New York: Avon, 1997.

―――. *The Shaman's Game.* New York: Avon, 1998.

Dostoyevsky, Fyodor. 1846. *Poor People.* London: Baker and Taylor, 2002.

Douglas, Carole Nelson. *Cup of Clay.* New York: T. Doherty Associates, 1991.

―――. *Seed upon the Wind.* New York: Tor, 1992.

Douglas, L. Warren. *Glaice: An Arbiter Tale.* New York: ROC, 1996.

―――. *A Plague of Change.* New York: Ballantine, 1992.

―――. *The Sacred Pool.* New York: Baen, 2001.

―――. *Stepwater: An Arbiter Tale.* New York: ROC, 1995.

―――. *The Veil of Years.* New York: Baen, 2001.

Douglas, Marjory Stoneman. *Nine Florida Stories.* Jacksonville: University of North Florida Press, 1990.

―――. *A River in Flood, and Other Florida Stories.* Gainesville: University Press of Florida, 1998.

Downs, Robert Bingham, ed. *The Bear Went Over the Mountain: Tall Tales of American Animals.* New York: Macmillan, 1964.

Doyle, Arthur Conan, Sir. *The Complete Professor Challenger Stories.* London: Wordsworth Editions, 1989.

―――. 1912. *The Lost World: Being an Account of the Recent Amazing Adventures of*

Professor George E. Challenger, Lord John Roxton, Professor Summerlee, and Mr. E.D. Malone of the "Daily Gazette." New York: Modern Library, 2004.

———. 1912. *The Poison Belt: Being an Account of Another Amazing Adventure of Professor Challenger.* Lincoln: University of Nebraska Press, 2001.

Dozois, Gardner R., ed. *Isaac Asimov's Earth.* New York: Ace, 1992.

Drinkard, Michael. *Disobedience.* New York: Norton, 1993.

Duane, Daniel. *Looking for Mo.* New York: Farrar, Straus, and Giroux, 1998.

Ducornet, Rikki. 1984. *Entering Fire.* San Francisco: City Lights, 1987.

———. 1989. *The Fountains of Neptune.* Normal, IL: Dalkey Archive Press, 1997.

———. 1993. *The Jade Cabinet.* Normal, IL: Dalkey Archive Press, 1994.

———. *Phosphor in Dreamland.* Normal, IL: Dalkey Archive Press, 1995.

———. 1984. *The Stain.* Normal, IL: Dalkey Archive Press, 1995.

Dufresne, John. *Deep in the Shade of Paradise.* New York: Norton, 2002.

———. *Louisiana Power & Light.* London: Vintage, 1999.

———. 1991. *The Way That Water Enters Stone.* New York: Plume, 1997.

Dunant, Sarah. 1995. *Fatlands.* New York: Scribner, 2004.

Duncan, David James. *River Teeth: Stories and Writings.* New York: Doubleday, 1995.

———. 1983. *The River Why.* San Francisco: Sierra Club Books, 2002.

Durrell, Gerald. *The Mockery Bird.* New York: Simon & Schuster, 1982.

Dykeman, Wilma. 1973. *Return the Innocent Earth.* Newport, TN: Wakestone Books, 1994.

Dymmoch, Michael Allen. *The Death of Blue Mountain Cat.* New York: St. Martin's, 1996.

Dyson, Cindy. *And She Was.* New York: William Morrow, 2005.

Eastlake, William. 1958. *The Bronc People.* Los Angeles: Seven Wolves Publishing, 1991.

———. *Dancers in the Scalp House.* New York: Viking, 1975.

———. 1956. *Go in Beauty.* Los Angeles: Seven Wolves Publishing, 1991.

———. 1963. *Portrait of an Artist with Twenty-Six Horses.* Los Angeles: Seven Wolves Publishing, 1991.

Echlin, Kim. *Elephant Winter.* Toronto: Viking, 1997.

Eckert, Allan W. *The Silent Sky: The Incredible Extinction of the Passenger Pigeon.* Boston: Little Brown, 1965.

———. *Song of the Wild.* Boston: Little Brown, 1980.

Edgerton, Clyde. *Redeye.* Chapel Hill, NC: Algonquin Books, 1995.

Ehrenreich, Barbara. *Kipper's Game.* New York: Farrar, Straus, and Giroux, 1993.

Ekman, Kerstin. *The Angel House.* Norwich, England: Norvik Press, 2002.

————. 1993. *Blackwater.* New York: Picador USA, 1997.

————. *City of Light.* Norwich, England: Norvik Press, 2003.

————. 1988. *The Forest of Hours.* London: Vintage, 1999.

————. *The Spring.* Norwich, England: Norvik Press, 2001.

————. *Witches' Rings.* Norwich, England: Norvik Press, 1997.

Elder, John, and Hertha Dawn Wong, eds. *Family of Earth and Sky: Indigenous Tales of Nature from Around the World.* Boston: Beacon Press, 1994.

Elgin, Suzette Haden. 1994. *Earthsong.* New York: Feminist Press, 2002.

————. 1987. *The Judas Rose.* New York: Feminist Press, 2002.

————. 1984. *Native Tongue.* New York: Feminist Press, 2000.

Elwood, Roger, and Virginia Kidd, eds. *Saving Worlds: A Collection of Original Science Fiction Stories.* Garden City, NY: Doubleday, 1973.

Elze, Winifred. *The Changeling Garden.* New York: St. Martin's, 1995.

————. *Here, Kitty, Kitty.* New York: St. Martin's, 1996.

Ende, Michael. 1979. *The Neverending Story.* New York: Penguin, 2005.

Endrezze, Anita. *Throwing Fire at the Sun, Water at the Moon.* Tucson: University of Arizona Press, 2000.

Engel, Marian. 1976. *Bear.* Boston: David R. Godine, 2003.

Erdrich, Louise. *The Antelope Wife.* New York: HarperFlamingo, 1998.

————. 1986. *The Beet Queen.* New York: HarperFlamingo, 1998.

————. 1994. *The Bingo Palace.* New York: HarperPerennial, 2006.

————. *Four Souls.* New York: Harper Perennial, 2005.

————. *The Last Report on the Miracles at Little No Horse.* New York: HarperCollins, 2001.

————. *Love Medicine: New and Expanded Version.* New York: H. Holt, 1993.

————. *The Painted Drum.* New York: HarperCollins, 2005.

————. *The Plague of Doves.* New York: HarperCollins, 2008.

————. *The Red Convertible: Selected and New Stories, 1978–2008.* New York: HarperCollins, 2009.

————. *Tales of Burning Love.* New York: HarperPerennial, 1997.

————. 1988. *Tracks.* New York: Harper Flamingo, 1998.

Eulo, Ken, and Joe Mauck. *Claw.* New York: Simon & Schuster, 1994.

Eustasio Rivera, José. *The Vortex.* London: Putnam, 1935.

Evans, Nicholas. 1995. *The Horse Whisperer.* London: Time Warner, 2006.

————. 1998. *The Loop.* London: Time Warner, 2006.

————. 2002. *The Smoke Jumper.* London: Time Warner, 2006.

Even, Aaron Roy. *Bloodroot.* New York: Thomas Dunne, 2000.

Everett, Percival L. *Grand Canyon, Inc.* San Francisco: Versus Press, 2001.

————. 1996. *Watershed.* Boston: Beacon Press, 2003.

————. 1989. *Zulus.* Sag Harbor, NY: Permanent Press, 1990.

Fall, Aminata Sow. 1981. *The Beggars' Strike, or, The Dregs of Society.* Harlow, Essex: Longman, 1986.

Farmer, Beverley. *The Seal Woman.* St. Lucia: University of Queensland Press, 1992.

Farmer, Philip José. 1977. *The Lavalite World.* New York: Berkley, 1985.

Fârnoagă, Georgiana, and Sharon King, trans. and eds. *The Phantom Church and Other Stories from Romania.* Pittsburgh: University of Pittsburgh Press, 1996.

Faulkner, William. 1955. *Big Woods: The Hunting Stories.* New York: Vintage Books, 1994.

————. 1942. *Go Down, Moses.* New York: Modern Library, 1995.

————. *Three Famous Short Novels; Spotted Horses, Old Man, the Bear.* New York: Vintage, 1966.

Fergusson, Harvey. 1927. *Wolf Song.* Lincoln: University of Nebraska Press, 1981.

Findley, Timothy. 1984. *Not Wanted on the Voyage.* Toronto: Penguin, 1996.

Fink, Jon Stephen. *Long Pig.* London: Vintage, 1997.

Flanagan, Richard. *Death of a River Guide.* New York: Grove Press, 2001.

————. *Gould's Book of Fish: A Novel in Twelve Fish.* New York: Grove Press, 2001.

Florman, Samuel C. *The Aftermath: A Novel of Survival.* New York: Thomas Dunne Books, 2001.

Follett, Ken. 1992. *The Hammer of Eden.* New York: Crown, 1998.

————. *The Third Twin.* New York: Ballantine, 1997.

Forbes, Edith. *Exit to Reality.* Seattle: Seal Press, 1997.

Ford, G. M. 1995. *Who in Hell Is Wanda Fuca?* London: Pan, 2006.

Ford, Peter Shann. *The Keeper of Dreams.* New York: Simon & Schuster, 2000.

Foreman, Dave. *The Lobo Outback Funeral Home.* Boulder: University Press of Colorado, 2000.

Foreman, Russell. 1958. *Long Pig.* London: Granada, 1981.

————. *The Ringway Virus.* Boston: Little, Brown, 1977.

————. *Sandalwood Island.* London: Heinemann, 1961.

Foster, Chris. *Winds Across the Sky.* Lower Lake, CA: Aslan, 1992.

Fowler, Connie May. *Remembering Blue.* New York: Doubleday, 2000.

Fox, John. 1913. *The Heart of the Hills.* Lexington: University Press of Kentucky, 1996.

————. 1903. *The Little Shepherd of Kingdom Come.* Lexington: University Press of Kentucky, 1987.

————. 1908. *The Trail of the Lonesome Pine.* Lexington: University Press of Kentucky, 1984.

Fox, Stuart. *The Back of Beyond.* New York: Forge, 1994.

———. *Black Fire.* New York: Tor, 1992.

Frank, Pat. 1959. *Alas, Babylon.* New York: HarperPerennial, 2005.

Franzen, Jonathan. 1992. *Strong Motion.* New York: Picador, 2001.

Freeman, Castle. *The Bride of Ambrose and Other Stories.* New York: Soho, 1987.

———. *Judgment Hill.* Hanover, NH: University Press of New England, 1997.

———. *My Life and Adventures.* New York: St. Martin's, 2002.

Freeman, Charlotte McGuinn. *Place Last Seen.* New York: Picador, 2000.

Froese, Robert. *The Hour of Blue.* Unity, ME: North Country Press, 1990.

Fromm, Pete. *Blood Knot.* New York: Lyons Press, 1998.

———. *Dry Rain.* New York: Lyons & Burford, 1997.

———. *King of the Mountain: Sporting Stories.* Mechanicsburg, PA: Stackpole Books, 1994.

———. 1999. *Night Swimming.* New York: Picador, 2000.

———. 1991. *The Tall Uncut: Lives amid the Landscapes of the American West.* New York: Lyons Press, 1998.

Fulton, Len. *Dark Other Adam Dreaming.* Paradise, CA: Dustbooks, 1975.

———. *The Grassman.* Berkeley, CA: Thorp Springs Press, 1974.

Furlong, Monica. 1991. *Juniper.* New York: Random House, 2002.

———. 1987. *Wise Child.* New York: Dell, 2001.

Gabaldon, Diana. *Outlander.* New York: Dell, 2005.

Gadd, Ben. *Raven's End.* San Francisco: Sierra Club Books, 2003.

Gaiman, Neil. *American Gods.* New York: W. Morrow, 2001.

Gaiman, Neil, and Terry Pratchett. 1990. *Good Omens: The Nice and Accurate Prophecies of Agnes Nutter, Witch.* New York: HarperTorch, 2006.

Galeano, Eduardo H. *The Book of Embraces.* New York: Norton, 1991.

———. *Memory of Fire.* New York: Pantheon, 1985–1988.

———. *Voices of Time: A Life in Stories.* New York: Metropolitan Books, 2006.

Galford, Ellen. *The Fires of Bride.* Ithaca, NY: Firebrand Books, 1988.

Gallegos, Rómulo. 1935. *Canaima.* Pittsburgh: University of Pittsburgh Press, 1996.

———. 1931. *Doña Barbara.* New York: Peter Smith, 1948.

Galloway, Les. 1984. *The Forty Fathom Bank.* San Francisco: Chronicle Books, 1994.

Galvin, James. *Fencing the Sky.* New York: Holt, 1999.

———. 1992. *The Meadow.* New York: Holt, 1993.

Gannett, Lewis. *Magazine Beach.* New York: HarperPrism, 1996.

Gansworth, Eric, ed. *Sovereign Bones: New Native American Writing.* New York: Nation Books, 2007.

Garber, Eugene K. *The Historian: Six Fantasies of the American Experience.* Minneapolis: Milkweed, 1993.

García Calderón, Ventura. 1924. *The White Llama: Being La Venganza Del Condor of V.G. Calderon*. London: Golden Cockerel Press, 1938.

García Márquez, Gabriel. 1970. *One Hundred Years of Solitude*. New York: Harper Perennial, 2006.

Gardner, John. 1971. *Grendel*. New York: Vintage Books, 2001.

Garland, Hamlin. 1910. *Cavanagh, Forest Ranger*. Sunset ed. St. Clair Shores, MI: Scholarly Press, 1974.

———. 1891. *Main-Travelled Roads*. Lincoln: University of Nebraska Press, 1995.

Garreau, Joel. *The Nine Nations of North America*. Boston: Houghton Mifflin, 1981.

Gary, Romain. 1956. *The Roots of Heaven*. New York: Time, 1964.

Gearhart, Sally Miller. 1978. *Wanderground: Stories of the Hill Women*. Denver: Spinsters Ink Books, 2002.

Ghosh, Amitav. *The Hungry Tide*. Boston: Houghton Mifflin, 2005.

Gibbon, Lewis Grassic. 1932–34. *A Scots Quair*. Edinburgh: Canongate Books, 1995.

Gibbons, Stella. 1932. *Cold Comfort Farm*. London: New York: Penguin, 1994.

Gilkes, Michael. *Couvade: A Dream-Play of Guyana*. London: Longman Caribbean, 1974.

Gill, Bartholomew. *Death on a Cold, Wild River*. New York: Morrow, 1993.

Gilling, Tom. *The Sooterkin*. New York: Viking, 2000.

Gilman, Charlotte Perkins. 1915. *Herland*. Mineola, NY: Dover, 1998.

———. 1916. *With Her in Ourland: Sequel to Herland*. Westport, CT: Greenwood Press, 1997.

———. 1892. *The Yellow Wall-Paper*. Athens: Ohio University Press, 2006.

Giono, Jean. 1929. *Colline*. Oxford: Blackwell, 1986.

———. 1937. *Joy of Man's Desiring*. Washington DC: Counterpoint, 1999.

———. 1954. *The Man Who Planted Trees*. White River Junction, VT: Chelsea Green, 2005.

———. 1934. *The Song of the World*. Washington DC: Counterpoint, 2000.

Gish, Robert. *Bad Boys and Black Sheep: Fateful Tales from the West*. Reno: University of Nevada Press, 1996.

———. *First Horses: Stories of the New West*. Reno: University of Nevada Press, 1993.

———. *When Coyote Howls*. Albuquerque: University of New Mexico Press, 1994.

Glancy, Diane. *Pushing the Bear: A Novel of the Trail of Tears*. New York: Harcourt Brace, 1996.

Gloss, Molly. *The Dazzle of Day*. New York: Tor, 1997.

———. *The Jump-Off Creek*. Boston: Houghton Mifflin, 1989.

———. *Wild Life*. New York: Simon & Schuster, 2000.

Goddard, J. R. *The Night Crew*. Boston: Little, Brown, 1970.

Goddard, Kenneth W. *Double Blind*. New York: Forge, 1997.

———. *Prey*. New York: Tor, 1992.

———. *Wildfire*. New York: Forge, 1994.

Gogol, Nikolai Vasilievich. 1842. *Dead Souls*. New York: Barnes & Noble Classics, 2005.

———. 1835/1842. *Taras Bulba*. New York: Modern Library, 2004.

Golding, William. 1955. *The Inheritors*. London: Faber, 2005.

———. 1954. *Lord of the Flies*. New York: Penguin, 2003.

Gómez-Vega, Ibis. *Send My Roots Rain*. San Francisco: Aunt Lute Books, 1991.

GoodWeather, Hartley. *DreadfulWater Shows Up*. New York: Scribner, 2003.

———. *The Red Power Murders: A DreadfulWater Mystery*. Toronto: HarperCollins, 2006.

Goonan, Kathleen Ann. *Crescent City Rhapsody*. New York: Avon, 2000.

———. *Mississippi Blues*. New York: Tor, 1997.

———. *Queen City Jazz*. 1994. New York: Orb, 2003.

Gordimer, Nadine. *Get a Life*. New York: Farrar, Straus, and Giroux, 2005.

Gould, Steven. 1996. *Wildside*. New York: Tom Doherty Associates, 2003.

Gould, Steven, and Laura J. Mixon. *Greenwar*. New York: Tom Doherty Associates, 1997.

Gowdy, Barbara. *The White Bone*. New York: Metropolitan Books, 1999.

Grace, Patricia. *Dogside Story*. Honolulu: University of Hawaii Press, 2001.

———. *Mutuwhenua: The Moon Sleeps*. Aukland, New Zealand; New York: Penguin, 1986.

———. 1986. *Potiki*. Honolulu: University of Hawaii Press, 1995.

Grahame, Kenneth. 1908. *The Wind in the Willows*. New York: Penguin, 2006.

Grahn, Judy. *Mundane's World*. Freedom, CA: Crossing Press, 1988.

Grant, Linda. *Lethal Genes*. New York: Scribner, 1996.

Grant, Richard. *In the Land of Winter*. New York: Avon, 1997.

———. *Rumors of Spring*. Toronto: Bantam, 1987.

———. *Tex and Molly in the Afterlife*. New York: Avon, 1996.

Grass, Günter. *The Rat*. San Diego: Harcourt Brace, 1987.

Gray, Muriel. *The Trickster*. New York: Doubleday, 1995.

Grimes, Martha. *Biting the Moon*. New York: Holt, 1999.

Grimwood, Ken. *Into the Deep*. New York: Morrow, 1995.

Güiraldes, Ricardo. 1926. *Don Segundo Sombra*. Pittsburgh: University of Pittsburgh Press, 1995.

Gunesekera, Romesh. *Heaven's Edge*. New York: Grove Press, 2002.

———. *Monkfish Moon*. New York: New Press, 1992.

————. *Reef.* New York: New Press, 1994.

————. *The Sandglass.* New York: New Press, 1998.

Guterson, David. 1999. *East of the Mountains.* New York: Vintage, 2003.

————. *The Other.* New York: Knopf, 2008.

————. 2003. *Our Lady of the Forest.* New York: Vintage, 2004.

————. *Snow Falling on Cedars.* San Diego: Harcourt Brace, 1994.

Guthrie, A. B., Jr. 1947. *The Big Sky.* Boston: Houghton Mifflin, 2002.

————. 1982. *Fair Land, Fair Land.* Boston: Houghton Mifflin, 1995.

————. 1960. *Mountain Medicine.* Eugene, OR: Comstock, 1991.

————. 1949. *The Way West.* Boston: Houghton Mifflin, 1993.

Haake, Katharine. *The Height and Depth of Everything.* Reno: University of Nevada Press, 2001.

————. *That Water, Those Rocks.* Reno: University of Nevada Press, 2002.

Hague, Michael. *In the Small.* New York: Little, Brown Young Readers, 2008.

Hale, Janet Campbell. *The Jailing of Cecelia Capture.* New York: Random House, 1985.

Hall, Dana Naone, ed. *Malama: Hawaiian Land and Water.* Honolulu: Bamboo Ridge Press, 1985.

Hall, James W. *Blackwater Sound.* New York: St. Martin's, 2002.

————. 1993. *Bones of Coral.* New York: St. Martin's, 2004.

————. *Gone Wild.* New York: Delacorte Press, 1995.

————. *Mean High Tide.* New York: Delacorte Press, 1994.

————. *Red Sky at Night.* New York: Delacorte Press, 1997.

————. *Under Cover of Daylight.* New York: Norton, 2001.

Hall, Patricia. *The Dead of Winter.* New York: St. Martin's, 1997.

————. *The Poison Pool.* New York: St. Martin's, 1993.

Hansen, Derek. *Sole Survivor.* New York: Simon & Schuster, 1999.

Harrigan, Stephen. *Aransas.* New York: Knopf, 1980.

Harris, Wilson. 1960–63. *The Guyana Quartet.* Boston: Faber and Faber, 1985.

Harrison, Harry. 1966. *Make Room! Make Room!* New York: Bantam, 1994.

————. 1980. *One Step from Earth.* New York: Tom Doherty Associates, 1985.

————. 1988. *Return to Eden.* New York: Ibooks, 2001.

————. 1984. *West of Eden.* New York: Ibooks, 2004.

————. 1986. *Winter in Eden.* New York: Ibooks, 2001.

Harrison, Jamie. *Going Local.* New York: Hyperion, 1996.

Harrison, Jim. *The Beast God Forgot to Invent.* New York: Atlantic Monthly Press, 2000.

————. *Dalva.* New York: Dutton, 1988.

————. 1976. *Farmer.* New York: Dell, 1989.

————. 1973. *A Good Day to Die.* New York: Delta/Seymour Lawrence, 1989.

————. *Julip.* Boston: Houghton Mifflin/Seymour Lawrence, 1994.

————. 1979. *Legends of the Fall.* New York: Delta, 1994.

————. *The Road Home.* New York: Atlantic Monthly Press, 1998.

————. *The Summer He Didn't Die.* New York: Atlantic Monthly Press, 2005.

————. 1984. *Sundog: The Story of an American Foreman, Robert Corvus Strang, as Told to Jim Harrison.* New York: Washington Square, 1989.

————. *True North.* New York: Grove Press, 2004.

————. 1981. *Warlock.* New York: Delta/S. Lawrence, 1989.

————. 1971. *Wolf: A False Memoir.* New York: Delta/Seymour Lawrence, 1989.

————. *The Woman Lit by Fireflies.* Boston: Houghton Mifflin/Seymour Lawrence, 1990.

Harrison, Payne. *Thunder of Erebus.* New York: Crown, 1991.

Harrison, Stuart. *The Snow Falcon.* New York: St. Martin's, 1999.

Harrison, Sue. *Brother Wind.* New York: Morrow, 1994.

————. *Call Down the Stars.* New York: Morrow, 2001.

————. 1995. *Cry of the Wind.* New York: Avon, 1998.

————. *Mother Earth, Father Sky.* New York: Doubleday, 1990.

————. *My Sister the Moon.* New York: Doubleday, 1992.

————. *Song of the River.* New York: Avon, 1998.

Haslam, Gerald W., ed. *California Heartland: Writing from the Great Central Valley.* Santa Barbara, CA: Capra Press, 1978.

————. *Condor Dreams & Other Fictions.* Reno: University of Nevada Press, 1994.

————, ed. 1992. *Many Californias: Literature from the Golden State.* Reno: University of Nevada Press, 1999.

————. *Okies.* Santa Barbara, CA: Peregrine Smith, 1975.

————. *That Constant Coyote: California Stories.* Reno: University of Nevada Press, 1990.

Hawkes, John. *Adventures in the Alaskan Skin Trade.* New York: Simon & Schuster, 1985.

————. *Sweet William: A Memoir of Old Horse.* New York: Simon & Schuster, 1993.

Hawthorne, Nathaniel. 1852. *The Blithedale Romance.* New York: Modern Library, 2001.

Heacox, Kim. *Caribou Crossing.* Santa Barbara, CA: Winter Wren Books, 2001.

Head, Bessie. 1971. *Maru.* Oxford: Heinemann, 1995.

————. 1973. *A Question of Power.* London: Penguin, 2002.

————. 1969. *When Rain Clouds Gather.* Oxford: Heinemann, 1995.

Healy, J. F. *Foursome.* New York: Pocket Books, 1993.

Hegland, Jean. 1996. *Into the Forest.* New York: Bantam, 1998.

Henderson, Davie. *Tomorrow's World.* United States: Medallion Press, 2008.

Henderson, William Haywood. *Native.* New York: Dutton, 1993.

Herbert, Brian. *The Garbage Chronicles: Being an Account of the Adventures of Tom Javik and Wizzy Malloy in the Faraway Land of Catapulted Garbage.* New York: Berkley, 1985.

———. *The Race for God.* New York: Ace, 1990.

———. *Sidney's Comet: Being an Account of the Remarkable Events Which Occurred During the Approach of the Great Garbage Comet.* New York: Berkley, 1983.

Herbert, Brian, and Kevin J. Anderson. *The Battle of Corrin.* London: Hodder & Stoughton, 2005.

———. *Dune: The Butlerian Jihad.* New York: Tor, 2002.

———. *Dune: House Atreides.* New York: Bantam, 1999.

———. *Dune: House Corrino.* New York: Bantam, 2002.

———. *Dune: House Harkonnen.* New York: Bantam, 2000.

———. *Dune: The Machine Crusade.* New York: Tor, 2003.

———. *Hunters of Dune.* New York: Tor, 2006.

Herbert, Frank. 1985. *Chapter House: Dune.* London: Gollancz, 2003.

———. 1976. *Children of Dune.* London: New English Library, 1999.

———. 1956. *The Dragon in the Sea.* New York: Tom Doherty Associates, 2008.

———. 1965. *Dune.* New York: Ace, 2005.

———. 1970. *Dune Messiah.* New York: Ace, 1999.

———. 1981. *God Emperor of Dune.* London: Gollancz, 2003.

———. 1984. *Heretics of Dune.* London: Gollancz, 2003.

———. 1972. *Soul Catcher.* New York: Ace, 1987.

———. *Under Pressure.* New York: SFBC Science Fiction, 2003.

Herbert, Frank, and Brian Herbert. *Man of Two Worlds.* New York: Putnam, 1986.

Herbert, Frank, Brian Herbert, and Kevin J. Anderson. *The Road to Dune.* London: Hodder, 2006.

Herbert, Frank, and B. Ransom. *The Ascension Factor.* New York: Putnam, 1988.

———. 1979. *The Jesus Incident.* London: Millennium, 2000.

———. 1983. *The Lazarus Effect.* New York: Ace, 1987.

Herbert, James. *Portent.* New York: HarperPrism, 1996.

Herbert, Xavier. 1939. *Capricornia.* North Ryde, NSW: Angus & Robertson, 1990.

———. 1975. *Poor Fellow My Country.* New York: St. Martin's Press, 1980.

Hersey, John. *Blues.* New York: Knopf, 1987.

———. *Key West Tales.* New York: Knopf, 1994.

———. 1954. *The Marmot Drive*. New York: Bantam, 1976.

———. *My Petition for More Space*. New York: Knopf, 1974.

Herzog, Arthur. *The Craving*. New York: Dell, 1982.

———. *Earth Sound*. London: Pan Books, 1977.

———. *Heat*. New York: Tudor, 1989.

———. *IQ 83*. New York: Simon & Schuster, 1978.

———. *Orca*. New York: Pocket Books, 1977.

———. *The Swarm*. New York: New American Library, 1978.

Heuler, Karen. *Journey to Bom Goody*. Livingston: Livingston Press at the University of West Alabama, 2005.

Heywood, Joseph. *Blue Wolf in Green Fire*. Guilford, CT: Lyons Press, 2005.

———. *Chasing a Blond Moon*. Guilford, CT: Lyons Press, 2003.

———. 2001. *Ice Hunter*. Guilford, CT: Lyons Press, 2005.

———. *Running Dark*. Guilford, CT: Lyons Press, 2005.

———. 2000. *The Snowfly*. Guilford, CT: Lyons Press, 2002.

Hiaasen, Carl. *Basket Case*. New York: Knopf, 2002.

———. 1987. *Double Whammy*. New York: Warner Books, 2005.

———. *Flush*. New York: Knopf, 2005.

———. 2002. *Hoot*. New York: Knopf, 2004.

———. 1997. *Lucky You*. New York: Warner Books, 2005.

———, ed. *Naked Came the Manatee*. New York: Putnam, 1996.

———. 1991. *Native Tongue*. New York: Warner Books, 2005.

———. *Nature Girl*. New York: Knopf, 2006.

———. *Scat*. New York: Knopf, 2009.

———. 2000. *Sick Puppy*. New York: Warner Books, 2005.

———. 1989. *Skin Tight*. New York: Warner Books, 2005.

———. 2004. *Skinny Dip*. New York: Warner Books, 2006.

———. 1995. *Stormy Weather*. New York: Warner Books, 2001.

———. 1993. *Strip Tease*. New York: Warner Books, 1996.

———. 1986. *Tourist Season*. New York: Warner Books, 2005.

Highwater, Jamake. *Dark Legend*. New York: Grove Press, 1994.

Highway, Tomson. *Kiss of the Fur Queen*. Norman: University of Oklahoma Press, 2000.

Hill, Lloyd E. *The Village of Bom Jesus*. Chapel Hill, NC: Algonquin Books, 1993.

Hill, Russell. *The Edge of the Earth*. New York: Ballantine, 1992.

Hillerman, Tony. 1993. *Sacred Clowns*. New York: HarperCollins, 2003.

Hillmer, Timothy. 1994. *The Hookmen*. New York: Scribner, 1996.

Hillsbery, Kief. *War Boy*. London: Picador, 2001.

Hirschfeld, Corson. *Aloha, Mr. Lucky.* New York: Forge, 2000.

Hoban, Russell. 1980. *Riddley Walker.* Bloomington: Indiana University Press, 1998.

———. 1975. *Turtle Diary.* London: Bloomsbury, 2000.

Hobbet, Anastasia. *Pleasure of Believing.* New York: Soho Press, 1997.

Hobson, Geary. *The Last of the Ofos.* Tucson: University of Arizona Press, 2000.

———, ed. *The Remembered Earth: An Anthology of Contemporary Native American Literature.* Albuquerque: University of New Mexico Press, 1991.

Hockenberry, John. *A River Out of Eden.* New York: Doubleday, 2001.

Høeg, Peter. 1992. *Smilla's Sense of Snow.* New York: Farrar, Straus, and Giroux, 1993.

———. *The Woman and the Ape.* New York: Farrar, Straus, and Giroux, 1996.

Hoffman, Alice. *Angel Landing.* New York: Berkley, 1999.

———. 1994. *Second Nature.* New York: Berkley, 1998.

Hoffman, Arthur L. *Tail Tigerswallow and the Great Tobacco War.* Albuquerque: Amador, 1988.

Hogan, Linda. *Mean Spirit.* New York: Atheneum; Toronto: Collier Macmillan Canada, 1990.

———. *Power.* New York: Norton, 1998.

———. *Solar Storms.* New York: Scribner, 1995.

Hope, Christopher. *Darkest England.* New York: Norton, 1996.

Hopper, Richard Inglis. *Strong Feather: The Story of the Last Covey in Indian Bend Wash.* Longwood, FL: Xulon Press, 2006.

Horsley, Kate. *The Changeling of Finnistuath.* Boston: Shambhala, 2003.

———. *Confessions of a Pagan Nun.* Boston: Shambhala, 2001.

Hospital, Janette Turner. *Oyster.* New York: Norton, 1998.

Houbein, Lolo. *Walk a Barefoot Road.* Bridgewater, SA: Middle Hill Books, 1990.

Hough, Emerson. 1905. *Heart's Desire: The Story of a Contented Town, Certain Peculiar Citizens, and Two Fortunate Lovers.* Lincoln: University of Nebraska Press, 1981.

Houston, James A. *Confessions of an Igloo Dweller.* Boston: Houghton Mifflin, 1995.

———. *Spirit Wrestler.* Toronto: McClelland & Stewart, 1997.

———. *The White Dawn: An Eskimo Saga.* San Diego: Harcourt Brace, 1983.

Houston, James D. 1978. *Continental Drift.* Berkeley: University of California Press, 1996.

———. *The Last Paradise.* Norman: University of Oklahoma Press, 1998.

———. *Love Life.* New York: Knopf, 1985.

———. *A Native Son of the Golden West.* New York: Dial Press, 1971.

Houston, Pam. 1988. *Cowboys Are My Weakness.* New York: Norton, 2005.

———. *Sight Hound.* New York: Norton, 2005.

———. *Waltzing the Cat.* New York: Norton, 1998.

Hoyt, Richard. *Bigfoot*. New York: Tor, 1993.

———. *Fish Story*. New York: Viking, 1985.

———. *Snake Eyes*. New York: Forge, 1995.

———. 1996. *Tyger! Tyger!* New York: Forge, 1999.

———. 1991. *Whoo?* New York: Tor, 2000.

Hudson, W. H. 1887. *A Crystal Age*. New York: Dutton, 1970.

———. 1904. *Green Mansions*. New York: Oxford University Press, 1998.

———. 1885. *The Purple Land: Being the Narrative of One Richard Lamb's Adventures in the Banda Orientál, in South America, as Told by Himself*. Madison: University of Wisconsin Press, 2002.

Hulme, Keri. 1984. *The Bone People*. Baton Rouge: Louisiana State University Press, 2005.

Hunger, B. *Clearcut: A Novel of Bio-Consequences*. Charlottesville, VA: Hampton Roads, 1996.

Hunt, D. Trinidad. *The Operator's Manual for Planet Earth*. New York: Hyperion, 1997.

Hurston, Zora Neale. 1937. *Their Eyes Were Watching God*. New York: Harper, 2006.

Huxley, Aldous. 1940. *Ape and Essence*. London: Vintage, 2005.

———. 1932, 1958. *Brave New World: And, Brave New World Revisited*. New York: HarperCollins, 2004.

———. 1962. *Island*. New York: Perennial, 2002.

Hyde, Eleanor. *Animal Instincts*. New York: Fawcett Gold Medal, 1996.

Icaza, Jorge. 1934. *Huasipungo. The Villagers*. Carbondale: Southern Illinois University Press, 1973.

Ihimaera, Witi Tame. *Tangi*. Auckland: Heinemann Reed, 1989.

———. 1987. *The Whale Rider*. Orlando: Harcourt, 2003.

Isaacs, Jorge. 1890. *María: A South American Romance*. New York: Gordon Press, 1981.

Ishimure, Michiko. 1997. *Lake of Heaven*. Lanham, MD: Lexington Books, 2008.

Jackson, Melanie. *The Selkie*. New York: Dorchester, 2003.

Jefferies, Richard. 1885. *After London: Or, Wild England*. Oxford; New York: Oxford University Press, 1980.

Jekel, Pamela. *River Without End: A Novel of the Suwannee*. New York: Kensington, 1997.

———. *She Who Hears the Sun*. New York: Kensington Books, 1999.

Jennings, Dana Andrew. *Lonesome Standard Time*. New York: Harcourt Brace, 1995.

Jensen, Liz. 1998. *Ark Baby*. London: Bloomsbury, 2006.

———. 1995. *Egg Dancing*. London: Bloomsbury, 2006.

Jersild, P. C. 1973. *The Animal Doctor.* Lincoln: University of Nebraska Press, 1988.

———. 1980. *A Living Soul.* Norwich, England: Norvik, 1988.

Jewett, Sarah Orne. 1925. *Best Stories of Sarah Orne Jewett.* Augusta, ME: Tapley, 1988.

———. 1896. *The Country of the Pointed Firs, and Selected Short Fiction.* New York: Barnes & Noble Classics, 2005.

———. 1877. *Deephaven, and Other Stories.* New Haven, CT: College & University Press, 1966.

———. *Novels and Stories.* New York: Library of America, 1996.

———. *The Uncollected Short Stories of Sarah Orne Jewett.* Waterville, ME: Colby College Press, 1971.

———. 1886. *A White Heron, and Other Stories.* Mineola, NY: Dover, 1999.

Jiang, Rong. *Wolf Totem.* New York: Penguin, 2008.

Johnson, E. Pauline. *Legends of Vancouver.* Vancouver: Douglas & McIntyre, 1997.

———. *The Moccasin Maker.* Norman: University of Oklahoma Press, 1998.

———. *The Shagganappi.* Toronto: Ryerson Press, 1913.

Johnson, Josephine Winslow. 1934. *Now in November.* New York: Feminist Press, 1991.

Johnson, Rand D. *Arcadia Falls: A Fable.* Canada: Gloria Mundi Press, 2001.

Johnson, Wayne. *The Devil You Know.* New York: Shaye Areheart Books, 2004.

———. *Don't Think Twice.* New York: Harmony Books, 1999.

———. *Six Crooked Highways.* New York: Harmony Books, 2000.

———. *The Snake Game.* New York: Knopf, 1990.

Johnston, Dorothy. *Maralinga, My Love.* Fitzroy, Vic.: McPhee Gribble/Penguin, 1988.

Jones, Gwyn. 1936. *Times Like These.* London: V. Gollancz, 1979.

Jones, Jack. *Rhondda Roundabout.* London: Faber and Faber, 1934.

Jones, Lewis. 1937, 1939. *Cwmardy; &, We Live.* Cardigan, Wales: Parthian, 2006.

Jones, Stan. 1999. *White Sky, Black Ice.* New York: Soho, 2003.

Jones, Stephen Graham. *The Bird Is Gone: A Manifesto.* Normal, IL: FC2, 2003.

Jose, Nicholas. *The Rose Crossing.* Woodstock, NY: Overlook Press, 1996.

Kafka, Franz. 1915. *The Metamorphosis and Other Stories.* New York: Charles Scribner's Sons, 1993.

Kafka, Kimberly. *True North.* New York: Dutton, 2000.

Kagan, Janet. *Mirabile.* New York: Tor, 1991.

Kahn, Stan. *Y3K.* Livermore, CA: WingSpan Press, 2007.

Kantner, Seth. *Ordinary Wolves.* Minneapolis: Milkweed, 2004.

Katz, Daniel R., and Miles Chapin, eds. *Tales from the Jungle: A Rainforest Reader.* New York: Crown Trade Paperbacks, 1995.

Keeble, John. *Broken Ground.* New York: Harper & Row, 1987.

———. *Nocturnal America.* Lincoln: University of Nebraska Press, 2006.

———. 1981. *Yellowfish.* New York: Harper & Row, 1987.

Kelly, M. T. *Breath Dances Between Them.* Toronto: Stoddart, 1991.

———. 1987. *A Dream Like Mine.* New York: Bantam, 1992.

———. *Out of the Whirlwind.* Toronto: Stoddart, 1995.

———. *The Ruined Season.* Windsor, ON: Black Moss Press, 1982.

Kenmuir, Dale. *Sing of Black Gold.* Pretoria: De Jager-HAUM, 1991.

Kenny, Maurice, ed. *Stories for a Winter's Night: Short Fiction by Native Americans.* Buffalo, NY: White Pine Press, 2000.

———. *Tortured Skins, and Other Fictions.* East Lansing: Michigan State University Press, 2000.

Kenyon, Kay. *The Braided World.* New York: Bantam, 2003.

———. *Bright of the Sky.* Amherst, NY: Pyr, 2007.

———. *Leap Point.* New York: Bantam, 1998.

———. *Maximum Ice.* New York: Bantam, 2002.

———. *Rift.* New York: Bantam, 1999.

———. *The Seeds of Time.* New York: Bantam, 1997.

———. *Tropic of Creation.* New York: Bantam, 2000.

———. *A World Too Near.* Amherst, NY: Pyr, 2008.

Kerouac, Jack. 1962. *Big Sur.* London: HarperPerennial, 2006.

———. 1958. *The Dharma Bums.* London: Penguin, 2000.

Kerr, Philip. *Esau.* New York: Holt, 1997.

———. *The Grid.* New York: Warner Books, 1996.

———. *The Second Angel.* New York: Holt, 1999.

Kersey, Colin. *Soul Catcher.* New York: St. Martin's, 1995.

Kesey, Ken. 1962. *One Flew Over the Cuckoo's Nest.* New York: Penguin, 2003.

———. *Sailor Song.* New York: Viking, 1992.

———. 1964. *Sometimes a Great Notion.* New York: Penguin, 1988.

Kieffer, Janet. *Food Chain.* Sandpoint, ID: Lost Horse Press, 2004.

Kilcup, Karen L., ed. *Native American Women's Writing, 1800–1924: An Anthology.* Oxford: Blackwell, 2000.

Kilian, Crawford. *Icequake.* New York: Bantam, 1980.

———. *Tsunami.* New York: Bantam, 1984.

Kilworth, Garry. *The Foxes of Firstdark.* New York: Doubleday, 1990.

Kincaid, Jamaica. 1983. *At the Bottom of the River.* New York: Farrar, Straus, and Giroux, 2000.

———. 1990. *Lucy.* New York: Farrar, Straus, and Giroux, 2002.

King, Thomas, ed. *All My Relations: An Anthology of Contemporary Canadian Native Fiction.* Norman: University of Oklahoma Press, 1992.

————. 1998. *Coyote Sings to the Moon.* Portland, OR: WestWinds Press, 2001.

————. 1993. *Green Grass, Running Water.* Toronto: HarperPerennial Canada, 1999.

————. 1990. *Medicine River.* Toronto: Penguin, 2005.

————. 1993. *One Good Story, That One.* Toronto: HarperPerennial Canada, 2000.

————. *A Short History of Indians in Canada.* Toronto: HarperPerennial, 2006.

————. *Truth & Bright Water.* New York: Atlantic Monthly Press, 1999.

Kingsolver, Barbara. 1990. *Animal Dreams.* New York: HarperPerennial, 2003.

————. 1988. *The Bean Trees.* New York: HarperPerennial, 2003.

————. *Homeland and Other Stories.* New York: Harper & Row, 1989.

————. 1993. *Pigs in Heaven.* New York: HarperPerennial, 2003.

————. 1998. *The Poisonwood Bible.* New York: HarperPerennial, 2005.

————. *Prodigal Summer.* New York: HarperCollins, 2000.

Kinsella, W. P. *Dance Me Outside: More Tales from the Ermineskin Reserve.* Boston: D. R. Godine, 1986.

————. *The Moccasin Telegraph and Other Indian Tales.* Boston: D. R. Godine, 1984.

Kirby, T. J. *Dangerous Nature.* New York: Zebra Books, 1993.

Kiteley, Brian. *Still Life with Insects.* New York: Ticknor & Fields, 1989.

Kittredge, William. *The Willow Field.* New York: Knopf, 2006.

Klein, Olaf G. *Aftertime.* Evanston, IL: Northwestern University Press, 1999.

Klinkenborg, Verlyn. *Timothy, Or, Notes of an Abject Reptile.* New York: Knopf, 2006.

Knight, Damon Francis. *Why Do Birds.* New York: Tor, 1992.

Knighton, Gary. *Isles of Omega.* Hungington, WV: University Editions, 1993.

Kramer, Peter D. *Spectacular Happiness.* New York: Scribner, 2001.

Krupat, Arnold. *Woodsmen, Or, Thoreau and the Indians.* Norman: University of Oklahoma Press, 1994.

Kube-McDowell, Michael P. 1990. *The Quiet Pools.* New York: Ibooks, 2004.

Kumin, Maxine. *Quit Monks or Die!* Ashland, OR: Story Line Press, 1999.

Kunstler, James Howard. *World Made by Hand.* New York: Atlantic Monthly Press, 2008.

Kurtz, Don. *South of the Big Four.* San Francisco: Chronicle Books, 1995.

La Farge, Oliver. 1929. *Laughing Boy.* Boston: Houghton Mifflin, 2004.

La Farge, Tom. *The Crimson Bears.* Los Angeles: Sun & Moon Press, 1993.

————. *Zuntig.* København: Green Integer, 2001.

Lake, David J. *The Right Hand of Dextra.* New York: Daw Books, 1977.

————. *The Wildings of Westron.* New York: Daw Books, 1977.

Lambert, Page. *Shifting Stars: A Novel of the West.* New York: Forge, 1997.

L'Amour, Louis. 1953. *Hondo.* New York: Bantam, 2004.

Landers, Gunnard. *The Deer Killers.* New York: Walker, 1990.

———. *Eskimo Money.* Minocqua, WI: Willow Creek Press, 1999.

———. *The Hunting Shack.* New York: Arbor House, 1979.

———. *Rite of Passage.* New York: Arbor House, 1980.

———. *The Violators.* New York: Walker, 1991.

Lang, Simon. *All the Gods of Eisernon.* New York: Avon, 1973.

Lang, Susan. *Small Rocks Rising.* Reno: University of Nevada Press, 2002.

Lange, Oliver. *The Land of the Long Shadow.* New York: Seaview, 1981.

Langton, Jane. *God in Concord.* New York: Viking, 1992.

Laurence, Margaret. 1974. *The Diviners.* Chicago: University of Chicago Press, 1993.

Lauritzen, Elizabeth M. *Shush'Ma.* Caldwell, ID: Caxton Printers, 1964.

Lawrence, D. H. 1923. *Kangaroo.* London: Penguin, 1997.

———. 1928. *Lady Chatterley's Lover.* New York: New American Library, 2003.

———. 1926. *The Plumed Serpent.* London: Penguin, 1995.

———. 1915. *The Rainbow.* New York: Random House, 2002.

———. 1911. *The White Peacock.* Oxford: Oxford University Press, 1997.

———. 1921. *Women in Love.* New York: Modern Library, 2002.

Lawrence, Louise. *The Patchwork People.* New York: Clarion Books, 1994.

———. *The Warriors of Taan.* New York: Harper & Row, 1988.

Lawrence, R. D. 1991. *Cry Wild.* New York: Pinnacle, 1992.

———. *The White Puma.* New York: Holt, 1990.

Lawson, Mary. *Crow Lake.* New York: Dial Press, 2002.

Le Guin, Ursula K. 1985. *Always Coming Home.* Berkeley: University of California Press, 2001.

———. *The Birthday of the World and Other Stories.* New York: HarperCollins, 2002.

———. *Buffalo Gals and Other Animal Presences.* Santa Barbara, ca: Capra Press, 1987.

———. *Changing Planes.* Orlando: Harcourt, 2003.

———. 1967. *City of Illusions.* London: Vista, 1996.

———. 1982. *The Compass Rose.* New York: Perennial, 2005.

———. 1974. *The Dispossessed.* London: Orion, 2006.

———. 1983. *The Eye of the Heron.* New York: Tom Doherty, 2003.

———. 1972. *The Farthest Shore.* New York: Pocket Books, 2004.

———. 1994. *A Fisherman of the Inland Sea.* New York: Perennial, 2005.

———. *Four Ways to Forgiveness.* New York: Perennial, 2004.

———. 1971. *The Lathe of Heaven.* New York: Perennial Classics, 2003.

———. 1969. *The Left Hand of Darkness.* New York: Barnes & Noble Books, 2004.

————. 2001. *The Other Wind.* New York: Harcourt Brace, 2003.

————. 1966. *Planet of Exile.* New York: Harper & Row, 1978.

————. 1966. *Rocannon's World.* New York: Ace, 1980.

————. 1991. *Searoad.* Boston: Shambhala, 2004.

————. 2001. *Tales from Earthsea.* New York: Ace, 2003.

————. 1990. *Tehanu: The Last Book of Earthsea.* New York: Simon & Schuster, 2001.

————. 2000. *The Telling.* New York: Harcourt Brace, 2003.

————. 1970. *The Tombs of Atuan.* New York: Pocket Books, 2004.

————. *Unlocking the Air and Other Stories.* New York: HarperCollins, 1996.

————. 1975. *The Wind's Twelve Quarters.* New York: Perennial, 2004.

————. 1968. *A Wizard of Earthsea.* New York: Bantam, 2004.

————. 1972. *The Word for World Is Forest.* New York: Ace, 1989.

Leigh, Julia. *The Hunter.* New York: Four Walls, Eight Windows, 2000.

Leithauser, Brad. *The Friends of Freeland.* New York: Knopf, 1997.

Lem, Stanislaw. *Fiasco.* San Diego: Harcourt Brace, 1987.

————. 1974. *The Futurological Congress: From the Memoirs of Ijon Tichy.* New York: Avon, 1981.

————. *The Invincible.* New York: Seabury Press, 1973.

————. 1970. *Solaris.* San Diego: Harcourt Brace, 2002.

L'Engle, Madeleine. 1989. *An Acceptable Time.* New York: Bantam, 1997.

————. 1965. *The Arm of the Starfish.* New York: Farrar, Straus, and Giroux, 1988.

————. 1976. *Dragons in the Waters.* New York: Dell, 1982.

————. 1980. *A Ring of Endless Light.* New York: Bantam, 1995.

Leon, Donna. 1993. *Death in a Strange Country.* New York: Penguin, 2005.

Leonov, Leonid. 1924. *The Badgers.* Westport, CT: Hyperion Press, 1973.

————. 1966. *The Russian Forest.* Moscow: Progress, 1976.

————. 1932. *Soviet River.* Westport, CT: Hyperion Press, 1973.

Léourier, Christian. 1971. *The Mountains of the Sun.* New York: Berkley, 1974.

Lerman, Rhoda. *Animal Acts.* New York: Holt, 1994.

Lerner, Andrea, ed. *Dancing on the Rim of the World: An Anthology of Contemporary Northwest Native American Writing.* Tucson: University of Arizona, 1990.

Lesley, Craig. *River Song.* New York: Picador, 1999.

————. *The Sky Fisherman.* New York: Picador, 1996.

————. *Storm Riders.* New York: Picador, 2000.

————, ed. *Talking Leaves: Contemporary Native American Short Stories.* New York: Laurel, 1991.

————. 1984. *Winterkill.* New York: Picador, 1997.

Lessing, Doris May. *Canopus in Argos: Archives.* New York: Vintage Books, 1992.

Lethem, Jonathan. *Girl in Landscape.* New York: Doubleday, 1998.

Lips, Christie Hart. *The White Stone.* Berkeley: Creative Arts, 2000.

Llewellyn, Richard. 1939. *How Green Was My Valley.* New York: Scribner, 1997.

London, David. *Sun Dancer.* New York: Simon & Schuster, 1996.

London, Jack. 1906. *Before Adam.* Lincoln: University of Nebraska Press, 2000.

———. 1903. *The Call of the Wild: Complete Text with Introduction, Historical Contexts, Critical Essays.* Boston: Houghton Mifflin, 2004.

———. 1902. *Children of the Frost.* Doylestown, PA: Wildside Press, 2005.

———. 1902. *A Daughter of the Snows.* Oakland: Star Rover House, 1987.

———. 1901. *The God of His Fathers, and Other Stories.* Freeport, NY: Books for Libraries Press, 1969.

———. 1909. *Martin Eden.* New York: Modern Library, 2002.

———. 1915. *The Scarlet Plague.* New York: Arno Press, 1975.

———. 1904. *The Sea-Wolf.* New York: Modern Library, 2000.

———. 1912. *Smoke Bellew.* New York: Dover, 1992.

———. 1900. *The Son of the Wolf: Tales of the Far North.* New York: Oxford University Press, 1996.

———. 1913. *The Valley of the Moon.* Berkeley: University of California Press, 1998.

———. 1906. *White Fang.* New York: Puffin, 2003.

Lopez, Barry Holstun. 1990. *Crow and Weasel.* New York: Farrar, Straus, and Giroux, 1998.

———. 1976. *Desert Notes: Reflections in the Eye of a Raven.* New York: Avon, 1981.

———. 1994. *Field Notes: The Grace Note of the Canyon Wren.* New York: Vintage Books, 2004.

———. 1976. *Giving Birth to Thunder, Sleeping with His Daughter: Coyote Builds North America.* New York: Avon, 1990.

———. *Lessons from the Wolverine.* Athens: University of Georgia Press, 1997.

———. 2000. *Light Action in the Caribbean.* New York: Vintage Books, 2001.

———. *River Notes: The Dance of Herons.* Kansas City: Andrews and McMeel, 1979.

———. 1981. *Winter Count.* New York: Vintage Books, 1999.

Lord, Gabrielle. *Salt.* Rydalmere, NSW: Hodder, 1998.

Lord, Nancy. *The Compass Inside Ourselves.* Fairbanks: Fireweed, 1984.

———. *The Man Who Swam with Beavers.* Minneapolis: Coffee House Press, 2001.

———. *Survival.* Minneapolis: Coffee House Press, 1991.

Love, Ann. *Grizzly Dance.* Toronto: Key Porter, 1994.

Lunge-Larsen, Lise. *The Hidden Folk: Stories of Fairies, Dwarves, Selkies, and Other Secret Beings.* Boston: Houghton Mifflin, 2004.

———. *The Troll with No Heart in His Body and Other Tales of Trolls from Norway.* Boston: Houghton Mifflin, 1999.

Lynch, Jim. *The Highest Tide.* New York: Bloomsbury USA, 2005.

Mabie, Hamilton Wright. *A Child of Nature.* New York: Dodd, Mead, 1901.

MacAlister, V. A. *The Mosquito War.* New York: Forge, 2001.

MacDonald, John D. 1986. *Barrier Island.* New York: Ballantine, 1987.

———. 1977. *Condominium.* New York: Ballantine, 1985.

———. 1962. *A Flash of Green.* New York: Fawcett Gold Medal, 1984.

MacGill-Callahan, Sheila. *Forty Whacks.* New York: St. Martin's, 1994.

Mackey, Mary. *The Fires of Spring.* New York: Onyx, 1998.

———. *The Horses at the Gate.* New York: Penguin, 1996.

———. *The Last Warrior Queen.* New York: Seaview, 1983.

———. *The Year the Horses Came.* San Francisco: HarperSanFrancisco, 1993.

Maclean, Norman. 1976. *A River Runs Through It.* Chicago: University of Chicago Press, 1989.

MacLeod, Alistair. 1986. *As Birds Bring Forth the Sun and Other Stories.* Toronto: McClelland & Stewart, 1992.

———. 2000. *Island: The Complete Stories.* New York: Vintage Books, 2002.

———. 1976. *The Lost Salt Gift of Blood.* Toronto: McClelland & Stewart, 1989.

MacLeod, Ian. *The Great Wheel.* New York: Harcourt Brace, 1997.

———. *The Light Ages.* London: Earthlight, 2003.

Malmont, Valerie S. *Death, Lies, and Apple Pies.* New York: Simon & Schuster, 1997.

Manfred, Frederick Feikema. *Frederick Manfred Reader.* Duluth, MN: Holy Cow! Press, 1996.

———. 1944. *The Golden Bowl.* Albuquerque: University of New Mexico Press, 1976.

———. *Green Earth.* New York: Crown, 1977.

———. 1966. *King of Spades.* Lincoln: University of Nebraska Press, 1983.

———. 1954. *Lord Grizzly.* Lincoln: University of Nebraska Press, 1983.

———. 1975. *The Manly-Hearted Woman.* Lincoln: University of Nebraska Press, 1985.

———. *Of Lizards and Angels: A Saga of Siouxland.* Norman: University of Oklahoma Press, 1992.

———. 1964. *Scarlet Plume.* New York: Penguin, 1994.

Mann, Paul. *The Burning Ghats.* New York: Fawcett Columbine, 1996.

Manning, Laurence. *The Man Who Awoke.* New York: Ballantine, 1975.

Maracle, Lee. *Ravensong.* Vancouver: Press Gang Publishers, 1993.

———. *Sojourners and Sundogs: First Nations Fiction.* Vancouver: Press Gang Publishers, 1999.

Margolis, David. *Change of Partners*. Sag Harbor, NY: Permanent Press, 1997.

Markoosie. 1971. *Harpoon of the Hunter*. Kingston, ON: McGill-Queens University Press, 1982.

Maron, Margaret. *Shooting at Loons*. New York: Mysterious Press, 1994.

Maron, Monika. 1981. *Flight of Ashes*. London: Readers International, 1986.

Martin, David Lozell. *Crazy Love*. New York: Simon & Schuster, 2002.

Martin, George R. R. 1986. *Tuf Voyaging*. Atlanta: Meisha Merlin, 2003.

Martin, Marcia. *Southern Storms*. New York: Jove Books, 1992.

Martin, Valerie. 1994. *The Great Divorce*. New York: Vintage Contemporaries, 2003.

Mason, Bobbie Ann. *An Atomic Romance*. New York: Random House, 2005.

Masters, Dexter. 1955. *The Accident*. London: Faber, 1987.

Masumoto, David Mas. *Silent Strength*. Tokyo: New Currents International, 1985.

Mathews, John Joseph. *Sundown*. Norman: University of Oklahoma Press, 1988.

Matson, Suzanne. *The Tree-Sitter*. New York: Norton, 2006.

Matthee, Dalene. 1983. *Circles in a Forest*. London: Penguin, 2005.

Matthews, Greg. *The Wisdom of Stones*. New York: HarperCollins, 1994.

Matthiessen, Peter. 1965. *At Play in the Fields of the Lord*. New York: Vintage Books, 1991.

———. *Bone by Bone*. New York: Random House, 1999.

———. 1975. *Far Tortuga*. New York: Vintage, 1988.

———. *Killing Mister Watson*. New York: Random House, 1990.

———. *Lost Man's River*. New York: Random House, 1997.

———. *On the River Styx*. New York: Collins Harvill, 1989.

———. *Shadow County: A New Rendering of the Watson Legend*. New York: Modern Library, 2008.

May, Julian. *Intervention: A Root Tale to the Galactic Milieu and a Vinculum Between It and the Saga of Pliocene Exile*. Boston: Houghton Mifflin, 1987.

Mayhar, Ardath. *People of the Mesa*. New York: Diamond, 1992.

Mayor, Archer. *Occam's Razor*. New York: Mysterious Press, 1999.

Mazza, Cris. *Animal Acts: Fictions*. New York: Fiction Collective, 1988.

———. *Dog People*. Minneapolis: Coffee House Press, 1997.

———. *Girl Beside Him*. Normal, IL: FC2, 2001.

McBride, Regina. *The Nature of Air and Water*. New York: Scribner, 2001.

McCabe, Peter. *Wasteland*. New York: Scribner, 1994.

McCaffrey, Anne. 1968. *Dragonflight*. New York: Ballantine, 2005.

McCaffrey, Anne, and Elizabeth Ann Scarborough. *Power Lines*. New York: Ballantine, 1994.

———. *Power Play*. New York: Ballantine, 1995.

————. *Powers That Be.* New York: Ballantine, 1993.

McCarthy, Cormac. *The Road.* New York: Knopf, 2006.

McClendon, Lise. *Blue Wolf.* New York: Walker, 2001.

McCloskey, William B. *Breakers.* New York: Lyons Press, 2000.

————. 1979. *Highliners.* New York: Lyons Press, 2000.

McCrumb, Sharyn. 1992. *The Hangman's Beautiful Daughter.* New York: Signet, 2000.

————. *The Rosewood Casket.* New York: Dutton, 1996.

McDonald, Roger. *The Ballad of Desmond Kale.* New York: Random House Australia, 2007.

————. *Mr. Darwin's Shooter.* New York: Atlantic Monthly Press, 1998.

————. *Rough Wallaby.* Sydney: Bantam, 1989.

————. *Water Man.* Sydney: Picador, 1993.

McGahan, Jerry. *A Condor Brings the Sun.* San Francisco: Sierra Club Books, 1996.

McGarrity, Michael. *Hermit's Peak.* New York: Scribner, 1999.

————. *The Judas Judge.* New York: Dutton, 2000.

————. *Mexican Hat.* New York: Norton, 1997.

McGuane, Thomas. 1971. *The Bushwhacked Piano.* London: Vintage, 2003.

————. *The Cadence of Grass.* New York: Knopf, 2002.

————. *Gallatin Canyon.* New York: Knopf, 2006.

————. *Keep the Change.* Boston: Houghton Mifflin, 1989.

————. 1973. *Ninety-Two in the Shade.* London: Vintage, 2003.

————. *Nothing but Blue Skies.* Boston: Houghton Mifflin, 1992.

————. 1968. *The Sporting Club.* New York: Vintage, 1996.

McIntyre, Vonda N. 1978. *Dream Snake.* New York: Dell, 1986.

————. *The Moon and the Sun.* New York: Pocket Books, 1997.

————. *Star Trek IV: The Voyage Home.* New York: Pocket Books, 1986.

McLaren, Philip. *Scream Black Murder.* Philadelphia: Intrigue Press, 2002.

————. *Sweet Water . . . Stolen Land.* St. Lucia: University of Queensland Press, 1993.

McMullen, James P. *Cry of the Panther: Quest of a Species.* Sarasota, FL: Pineapple Press, 1996.

McMullen, Sean. 2001. *Eyes of the Calculor.* New York: Tor, 2004.

————. 2000. *The Miocene Arrow.* New York: Tor, 2003.

————. *Mirrorsun Rising.* North Adelaide, SA: Aphelion, 1995.

————. 1999. *Souls in the Great Machine.* New York: Tor, 2002.

————. *Voices in the Light.* North Adelaide, SA: Aphelion, 1994.

McNichols, Charles Longstreth. *Crazy Weather.* Lincoln: University of Nebraska Press, 1994.

McNickle, D'Arcy. *The Hawk Is Hungry & Other Stories.* Tucson: University of Arizona Press, 1993.

———. *The Surrounded.* New York: Quality Paperback Book Club, 1998.

———. 1977. *Wind from an Enemy Sky.* Albuquerque: University of New Mexico Press, 1988.

McQueen, James. *Hook's Mountain.* New York: Penguin, 1989.

McQuillan, Karin. *The Cheetah Chase.* London: Macmillan, 1995.

———. *Deadly Safari.* New York: St. Martin's, 1990.

———. *Elephants' Graveyard.* New York: Ballantine, 1994.

Mda, Zakes. *The Whale Caller.* New York: Farrar, Straus, and Giroux, 2005.

Melhem, D. H. *Blight.* New York: Riverrun Press, 1995.

Melville, Herman. 1849. *Mardi and a Voyage Thither.* New Haven, CT: College & University Press, 1973.

———. 1851. *Moby-Dick.* New York: Bantam, 2003.

———. 1847. *Omoo.* Mineola, NY: Dover, 2000.

———. 1856. *The Piazza Tales and Other Prose Pieces, 1839–1860.* Evanston, IL: Northwestern University Press, 1987.

———. 1846. *Typee: Complete Text with Introduction, Historical Contexts, Critical Essays.* Boston: Houghton Mifflin, 2004.

Mera, Juan León. 1879. *Cumandá: The Novel of the Ecuadorian Jungle.* Bloomington, IN: AuthorHouse, 2007.

Metz, Don. *King of the Mountain.* New York: Harper & Row, 1990.

Michelsen, G. F. *Hard Bottom.* Hanover, NH: University Press of New England, 2001.

Miles, Emma Bell. 1905. *The Spirit of the Mountains.* Knoxville: University of Tennessee Press, 1975.

Miller, Henry. 1957. *Big Sur and the Oranges of Hieronymus Bosch.* London: Flamingo, 1993.

Miller, Walter M. 1960. *A Canticle for Leibowitz.* New York: Eos, 2006.

———. *Saint Leibowitz and the Wild Horse Woman.* New York: Bantam, 1997.

Mitchell, Don. *The Nature Notebooks.* Hanover, NH: University Press of New England, 2004.

Mittelhölzer, Edgar. *Latticed Echoes: A Novel in the Leitmotiv Manner.* London: Secker & Warburg, 1960.

Moffat, Gwen. *Raptor Zone.* New York: McMillan, 1990.

———. *The Stone Hawk.* New York: St. Martin's, 1989.

Moffitt, Ian. *Gilt Edge.* Sydney: Pan Crime, 1991.

Mohin, Ann. *The Farm She Was.* Bridgehampton, NY: Bridge Works, 1998.

Momaday, N. Scott. *The Ancient Child.* New York: Doubleday, 1989.

————. 1968. *House Made of Dawn.* New York: HarperPerennial Classics, 1999.

Monroe, Mary Alice. 2002. *The Beach House.* Don Mills, ON: MIRA, 2006.

————. *Skyward.* Ontario: MIRA, 2003.

Montero, Mayra. 1995. *In the Palm of Darkness.* New York: HarperCollins, 1997.

Moody, Skye Kathleen. *Blue Poppy.* New York: St. Martin's, 1997.

————. *The Good Diamond.* New York: St. Martin's, 2004.

————. *Habitat.* New York: St. Martin's, 1999.

————. *K Falls.* New York: St. Martin's, 2001.

————. *Medusa.* New York: St. Martin's, 2003.

————. 1996. *Rain Dance.* Toronto: Worldwide, 1998.

————. *Wildcrafters.* New York: St. Martin's, 1998.

Moore, Barbara. *The Wolf Whispered Death.* New York: St. Martin's, 1986.

Moore, MariJo, ed. *Genocide of the Mind: New Native American Writing.* New York: Nation Books, 2003.

Moore, Ruth. 1946. *Spoonhandle.* Nobleboro, ME: Blackberry Books, 1986.

Moore, Ward. 1947. *Greener Than You Think.* New York: Crown, 1985.

Moran, Richard. *Cold Sea Rising.* New York: Berkley, 1987.

————. *Dallas Down.* New York: Arbor House, 1988.

————. *Earth Winter.* New York: Forge, 1995.

————. *The Empire of Ice.* New York: Forge, 1994.

Morgan, Robin. *The Mer-Child: A Legend for Children and Other Adults.* New York: Feminist Press, 1991.

Morris, Irvin. *From the Glittering World: A Navajo Story.* Norman: University of Oklahoma Press, 1997.

Morris, William. 1890. *News from Nowhere, Or, an Epoch of Rest: Being Some Chapters from a Utopian Romance.* New York: Oxford University Press, 2003.

Morrow, James. *Towing Jehovah.* New York: Harcourt Brace, 1994.

Morse, David E. *The Iron Bridge.* New York: Harcourt Brace, 1998.

Moses, Ed. *Nine Sisters Dancing.* Santa Barbara, CA: Fithian Press, 1996.

Mosley, Nicholas. *Children of Darkness and Light.* Normal, IL: Dalkey Archive Press, 1997.

Mourning Dove. 1927. *Cogewea, the Half Blood: A Depiction of the Great Montana Cattle Range.* Lincoln: University of Nebraska Press, 1981.

————. 1933. *Coyote Stories.* Lincoln: University of Nebraska Press, 1990.

————. *Mourning Dove's Stories.* San Diego: San Diego State University, 1991.

Mowat, Farley. *The Farfarers: Before the Norse.* South Royalton, VT: Steerforth Press, 2000.

————. 1975. *The Snow Walker.* Mechanicsburg, PA: Stackpole, 2004.

Mudrooroo. 1983. *Doctor Wooreddy's Prescription for Enduring the Ending of the World.* Melbourne: Hyland House, 1998.

———. *Doin Wildcat: A Novel Koori Script.* Melbourne: Hyland House, 1988.

———. *The Kwinkan.* Pymble, NSW: Angus & Robertson, 1993.

———. 1979. *Long Live Sandawara.* Melbourne: Hyland House, 1987.

———. 1991. *Master of the Ghost Dreaming.* North Ryde, NSW: Angus & Robertson, 1995.

———. *The Promised Land.* Pymble, NSW: Angus & Robertson, 2000.

———. *Underground.* Sydney: Angus & Robertson, 1999.

———. *Undying.* North Ryde, NSW: Angus & Robertson, 1998.

———. 1965. *Wild Cat Falling.* New York: HarperCollins, 1995.

———. 1992. *Wildcat Screaming.* Pymble, NSW: Angus & Robertson, 1995.

Mueller, Marnie. *Green Fires: Assault on Eden: A Novel of the Ecuadorian Rainforest.* Willimantic, CT: Curbstone Press, 1994.

Muir, Willa. 1931. *Imagined Corners.* Edinburgh: Canongate, 1987.

Muller, Marcia. *A Walk Through the Fire.* New York: Mysterious Press, 1999.

———. *Where Echoes Live.* New York: Mysterious Press, 1991.

———. *Wolf in the Shadows.* New York: Mysterious Press, 1993.

Munves, James. *Andes Rising.* New York: New Directions, 1999.

Murfree, Mary Noailles. *His Vanished Star.* Boston: Houghton, Mifflin, 1894.

———. 1884. *In the Tennessee Mountains.* Knoxville: University of Tennessee Press, 1988.

Murphy, Pat. *The City, Not Long After.* New York: Doubleday, 1989.

———. *Nadya: The Wolf Chronicles.* New York: Tor, 1996.

———. *Wild Angel.* New York: Tor, 2000.

Murray, Earl. *In the Arms of the Sky.* New York: Forge, 1998.

———. *Song of Wovoka.* New York: Tor, 1992.

———. *South of Eden.* New York: Forge, 2000.

Myers, Edward. *Fire and Ice.* New York: ROC, 1992.

———. *The Mountain Made of Light.* New York: ROC, 1992.

———. *The Summit.* New York: Penguin, 1994.

Nagatsuka, Takashi. 1910. *The Soil: A Portrait of Rural Life in Meiji Japan.* Berkeley: University of California Press, 1989.

Nasnaga. *Indians' Summer.* New York: Harper & Row, 1975.

Naylor, Gloria. 1988. *Mama Day.* New York: Vintage Books, 1993.

———. *The Men of Brewster Place.* New York: Hyperion, 1998.

———. 1982. *The Women of Brewster Place.* New York: Penguin, 1988.

Neihardt, John Gneisenau. 1952. *When the Tree Flowered: The Story of Eagle Voice, a Sioux Indian*. Lincoln: University of Nebraska Press, 1991.

Nelson, Dylan, and Kent Nelson, eds. *Birds in the Hand: Fiction and Poetry About Birds*. New York: North Point Press, 2004.

Nelson, Kent. *All Around Me Peaceful*. New York: Delta Books, 1989.

———. *Cold Wind River*. New York: Dodd, Mead, 1981.

———. *Discoveries: Short Stories of the San Juan Mountains*. Ouray, CO: Western Reflections, 1998.

———. *Land That Moves, Land That Stands Still*. New York: Viking, 2003.

———. *Language in the Blood*. Salt Lake City: Peregrine Smith Books, 1991.

———. *The Middle of Nowhere*. Salt Lake City: Peregrine Smith Books, 1991.

———. *The Touching That Lasts*. Boulder, CO: Johnson Books, 2006.

Ngugi wa Thiong'o. 1967. *A Grain of Wheat*. London: Penguin, 2002.

———. 1977. *Petals of Blood*. New York: Penguin, 2005.

———. 1965. *The River Between*. New York: Penguin, 2002.

———. 1964. *Weep Not, Child*. London: Heinemann, 1987.

Nichols, John Treadwell. 1978. *The Magic Journey*. New York: Holt, 2000.

———. 1974. *The Milagro Beanfield War*. New York: Holt, 2000.

———. *The Nirvana Blues*. New York: Holt, 1999.

Nichols, Robert. *Arrival*. New York: New Directions, 1977.

———. *Daily Lives in Nghsi-Altai*. New York: New Directions, 1977–79.

———. *Exile*. New York: New Directions, 1979.

———. *From the Steam Room: A Comic Fiction*. Gardiner, ME: Tilbury House, 1993.

———. *Garh City*. New York: New Directions, 1978.

———. *The Harditts in Sawna*. New York: New Directions, 1979.

———. *In the Air*. Baltimore: Johns Hopkins University Press, 1991.

Niven, Larry. *Rainbow Mars*. New York: Tor, 1999.

Nixon, Cornelia. *Angels Go Naked*. Washington DC: Counterpoint, 2000.

Nolan, Christopher. *The Banyan Tree*. New York: Arcade, 2000.

Noon, Jeff. *Pollen*. New York: Crown, 1996.

Norris, Frank. 1901. *The Octopus: A Story of California*. New York: Penguin, 1994.

Norton, Andre. 1972. *Breed to Come*. New York: Ace, 1980.

———. 1968. *Fur Magic*. New York: Godalming, 2006.

Norwood, Warren. *Shudderchild*. New York: Bantam, 1987.

O'Brien, Dan. *Brendan Prairie*. New York: Scribner, 1996.

———. *The Contract Surgeon*. Boston: Houghton Mifflin, 2001.

———. *Eminent Domain*. New York: Crown, 1990.

————. *In the Center of the Nation.* New York: Atlantic Monthly Press, 1991.

————. *The Indian Agent.* New York: HarperTorch, 2006.

————. *Spirit of the Hills.* New York: Crown, 1988.

Ohlin, Alix. *The Missing Person.* New York: Knopf, 2005.

Ojaide, Tanure. *The Activist.* Lagos: Farafina, 2006.

Ore, Rebecca. 1995. *Gaia's Toys.* New York: Tor, 1997.

Orotaloa, Rexford T. *Suremada: Faces from a Solomon Island Village.* Suva: Mana, 1989.

————. *Two Times Resurrection.* Honiari, Solomon Islands: University of the South Pacific, 1985.

Ortiz, Simon J. *Men on the Moon.* Tucson: University of Arizona Press, 1999.

Orwell, George. 1945. *Animal Farm: A Fairy Story.* New York: Plume, 2003.

————. 1939. *Coming Up for Air.* San Diego: Harcourt Brace, 1999.

————. 1949. *Nineteen Eighty-Four.* New York: Plume, 2003.

Oskison, John M. *Black Jack Davy.* New York: Appleton, 1926.

————. *Brothers Three.* New York: Macmillan, 1935.

————. *Wild Harvest: A Novel of Transition Days in Oklahoma.* New York: D. Appleton and Company, 1925.

Ostenso, Martha. *The Waters Under the Earth.* New York: Dodd, Mead & Company, 1930.

————. 1925. *Wild Geese.* Toronto: McClelland & Stewart, 1989.

Owens, Louis. *Bone Game.* Norman: University of Oklahoma Press, 1994.

————. *Dark River.* Norman: University of Oklahoma Press, 1999.

————. 1996. *Nightland.* Norman: University of Oklahoma Press, 2001.

————. 1992. *The Sharpest Sight.* Norman: University of Oklahoma Press, 1995.

————. 1991. *Wolfsong.* Norman: University of Oklahoma Press, 1995.

Ozeki, Ruth L. *All Over Creation.* New York: Viking, 2003.

————. *My Year of Meats.* New York: Viking, 1998.

Page, Jake. *Cavern.* Albuquerque: University of New Mexico Press, 2003.

Pak, Gary. *The Watcher of Waipuna and Other Stories.* Honolulu: Bamboo Ridge Press, 1992.

Palmer, David R. *Emergence.* New York: Bantam, 1990.

Palmer, Michael. 1996. *Critical Judgment.* New York: Bantam, 1998.

————. *Miracle Cure.* New York: Bantam, 1998.

————. *Natural Causes.* New York: Bantam, 1994.

Pancake, Ann. *Strange as This Weather Has Been.* Berkeley: Counterpoint, 2007.

Paretsky, Sara. *Blood Shot.* New York: Delacorte, 1988.

Pascoe, Bruce. *Fox.* Fitzroy, Vic.: Penguin, 1988.

Paton, Alan. 1948. *Cry, the Beloved Country.* New York: Scribner, 2003.

———. 1953. *Too Late the Phalarope.* New York: Scribner, 1995.

Paul, Barbara. *Under the Canopy.* New York: New American Library, 1980.

Pausewang, Gudrun. 1987. *Fall-out.* New York: Puffin, 1997.

———. 1982. *The Last Children.* New York: Walker, 1990.

Paustovsky, Konstantin. 1949. *Selected Stories.* Moscow: Progress, 1974.

Pavic, Milorad. *Landscape Painted with Tea.* New York: Knopf, 1990.

Paxson, Diana L., and Adrienne Martine-Barnes. 1993. *Master of Earth and Water.* New York: Avon, 1994.

———. *The Shield Between the Worlds.* New York: Morrow, 1994.

———. *Sword of Fire and Shadow.* New York: Morrow, 1995.

Peak, Michael. *Catamount.* New York: ROC, 1992.

———. *Cat House.* New York: New American Library, 1989.

Pelevin, Viktor. *The Life of Insects.* New York: Farrar, Straus, and Giroux, 1998.

Pellegrino, Charles R. *Dust.* New York: Avon, 1998.

Penn, W. S. *Killing Time with Strangers.* Tucson: University of Arizona Press, 2000.

Perry, Elaine. *Another Present Era.* New York: Farrar, Straus, and Giroux, 1990.

Perumalmurukan. 2000. *Seasons of the Palm.* Chennai, India: Tara, 2004.

Petersen, Ray. *Cowkind.* New York: St. Martin's, 1996.

Peterson, Brenda. *Animal Heart.* San Francisco: Sierra Club Books, 2004.

———. *Duck and Cover.* New York: HarperCollins, 1991.

———. 1978. *River of Light.* St. Paul, MN: Graywolf, 1986.

Peyer, Bernd. *The Singing Spirit: Early Short Stories by North American Indians.* Tucson: University of Arizona Press, 1989.

Phillips, Joseph J. *Operation Elbow Room: An Interplanetary Ecofiction.* Santa Barbara, CA: Fithian Press, 1995.

Pieczenik, Steve R. *State of Emergency.* New York: Putnam, 1997.

Piekarski, Vicki, ed. *Westward the Women: An Anthology of Western Stories by Women.* Albuquerque: University of New Mexico Press, 1988.

Pierce, Meredith Ann. 1985. *Birth of the Firebringer.* New York: Firebird, 2003.

———. 1992. *Dark Moon.* New York: Firebird, 2003.

———. 1996. *The Son of Summer Stars.* New York: Firebird, 2003.

———. 1985. *The Woman Who Loved Reindeer.* San Diego: Harcourt, 2000.

Piercy, Marge. 1991. *He, She, and It.* New York: Fawcett Columbine, 1997.

———. 1976. *Woman on the Edge of Time.* New York: Ballantine, 1997.

Pierre, George. *Autumn's Bounty.* San Antonio: Naylor, 1972.

Pilkington, Doris. *Caprice: A Stockman's Daughter.* St. Lucia: University of Queensland Press, 2002.

————. 1996. *Rabbit-Proof Fence*. New York: Hyperion, 2002.

————. *Under the Wintamarra Tree*. St. Lucia: University of Queensland Press, 2002.

Pipkin, John. *Woodsburner*. New York: Nan A. Talese, 2009.

Platt, Randall Beth. *Out of a Forest Clearing: An Environmental Fable*. Santa Barbara, CA: J. Daniel, 1991.

Pohl, Frederik. *Chernobyl*. New York: Bantam, 1987.

————. *Midas World*. New York: St. Martin's, 1983.

————. 1953. *The Space Merchants*. London: Gollancz, 2003.

————. 1984. *The Years of the City*. New York: Baen, 1995.

Pokagon, Simon. 1899. *O-gî-Mäw-Kwe Mit-i-Gwä-kî* [Queen of the Woods]. Barrien Springs, MI: Hardscrabble Books, 1972.

Popescu, Petru. *Almost Adam*. New York: William Morrow, 1996.

Popham, Melinda Worth. *Skywater*. St. Paul, MN: Graywolf, 1990.

Posey, Carl A. *Bushmaster Fall*. New York: Donald I. Fine, 1992.

Powe, B. W. *Outage: A Journey into Electric City*. Hopewell, NJ: Ecco Press, 1995.

Power, Susan. *The Grass Dancer*. New York: Berkley, 1997.

Powers, Richard. *Gain*. New York: Farrar, Straus, and Giroux, 1998.

————. *The Gold Bug Variations*. New York: W. Morrow, 1991.

Powlik, James. *Meltdown*. New York: Delacorte Press, 2000.

————. *Sea Change*. New York: Delacorte Press, 1999.

Powys, John Cowper. 1933. *A Glastonbury Romance*. London: Penguin, 1999.

Poyer, David. *As the Wolf Loves Winter*. New York: Forge, 1996.

————. *Bahamas Blue*. New York: St. Martin's, 1992.

————. *The Dead of Winter*. New York: Forge, 1995.

————. *Down to a Sunless Sea*. New York: St. Martin's, 1998.

————. *Hatteras Blue*. New York: St. Martin's, 1992.

————. *Louisiana Blue*. New York: St. Martin's, 1995.

————. *Thunder on the Mountain*. New York: Forge, 1999.

————. *Winter in the Heart*. New York: Tor, 1993.

Poyer, Joe. *Operation Malacca*. Garden City, NY: Doubleday, 1968.

Preda, Marin. *The Morometes*. Bucharest: Foreign Languages Pub. House, 1957.

Preston, Douglas J., and Lincoln Child. *Mount Dragon*. New York: Forge, 1996.

————. *Still Life with Crows*. New York: Warner Books, 2003.

Preuss, Paul. *Core*. London: HarperCollins, 1996.

Priest, Christopher. 1974. *Inverted World*. London: Gollancz, 1987.

Prishvin, Mikhail Mikhailovich. 1952. *The Lake and the Woods: Or, Nature's Calendar*. Westport, CT: Greenwood Press, 1975.

————. 1954. *Shiptimber Grove*. London: Lawrence & Wishart, 1957.

Proffitt, Nicholas. *Edge of Eden.* New York: Bantam, 1991.

Prose, Francine. 1995. *Hunters and Gatherers.* New York: Picador, 2003.

Proulx, Annie. *Bad Dirt: Wyoming Stories 2.* New York: Scribner, 2004.

———. 1999. *Close Range: Brokeback Mountain and Other Stories.* London: Harper-Perennial, 2006.

———. 1993. *The Shipping News.* New York: Scribner, 2003.

———. *That Old Ace in the Hole.* New York: Scribner, 2002.

Pugh, Marshall. *Last Place Left.* Harmondsworth: Penguin, 1972.

Pushkin, Aleksandr Sergeevich. 1831. *Tales of Belkin and Other Prose Writings.* New York: Penguin, 1998.

Quinn, Daniel. 1992. *Ishmael.* New York: Bantam, 1999.

———. *The Man Who Grew Young.* New York: Context Books, 2001.

———. 1997. *My Ishmael.* New York: Bantam, 1998.

———. *The Story of B.* New York: Bantam, 1996.

Quinn, Elizabeth. *Killer Whale.* New York: Pocket Books, 1997.

———. *Lamb to the Slaughter.* New York: Pocket Books, 1996.

———. *Murder Most Grizzly.* New York: Pocket Books, 1993.

———. *A Wolf in Death's Clothing.* New York: Pocket Books, 1995.

Quiroga, Horacio. *The Decapitated Chicken and Other Stories.* Madison: University of Wisconsin Press, 2004.

Rash, Ron. 2002. *One Foot in Eden.* New York: Picador, 2004.

Rasputin, Valentin Grigor'evich. 1979. *Farewell to Matyora.* Evanston, IL: Northwestern University Press, 1991.

———. 1978. *Live and Remember.* Evanston, IL: Northwestern University Press, 1992.

Rawlings, Marjorie Kinnan. 1942. *Cross Creek.* New York: Simon & Schuster, 1996.

———. 1938. *The Yearling.* New York: Simon & Schuster, 2002.

Ray, Charles. *The Tarheel Connection: An Environmental Romance.* Wyandotte, OK: Gregath, 2003.

Rebreanu, Liviu. *The Uprising.* London: P. Owen, 1964.

Redfield, Dana. *Jonah.* Charlottesville, VA: Hampton Roads, 2000.

Reid, William, and Robert Bringhurst. 1984. *The Raven Steals the Light.* Seattle: University of Washington Press, 1996.

Reiss, Bob. *Purgatory Road.* New York: Simon & Schuster, 1996.

Reyes, Alina. *The Butcher and Other Erotica.* New York: Grove Press, 1995.

Rhys, Jean. 1967. *Wide Sargasso Sea.* London: Penguin, 2001.

Rice, Patricia. *Carolina Girl.* New York: Ivy Books, 2004.

Richards, David Adams. *Mercy Among the Children.* New York: Arcade, 2001.

Richards, Thomas. *Zero Tolerance.* New York: Farrar, Straus, and Giroux, 1997.

Richter, Conrad. 1946. *The Fields.* Athens: Ohio University Press, 1991.

————. 1953. *The Light in the Forest.* New York: Knopf, 2005.

————. 1978. *The Rawhide Knot and Other Stories.* Lincoln: University of Nebraska Press, 1985.

————. 1937. *The Sea of Grass.* Athens: Ohio University Press, 1992.

————. 1950. *The Town.* Athens: Ohio University Press, 1991.

————. 1940. *The Trees.* Athens: Ohio University Press, 1991.

————. 1960. *The Waters of Kronos.* University Park: Pennsylvania State University Press, 2002.

Ridge, John Rollin. 1854. *The Life and Adventures of Joaquin Murieta, the Celebrated California Bandit.* Norman: University of Oklahoma Press, 1969.

Ripley, Ann. *The Christmas Garden Affair.* New York: Kensington Books, 2003.

————. *Death at the Spring Plant Sale.* New York: Kensington Books, 2003.

————. 1995. *Death of a Garden Pest.* New York: St. Martins Press, 1996.

————. *Death of a Political Plant.* New York: Bantam, 1998.

————. *The Garden Tour Affair.* New York: Bantam, 1999.

————. *Harvest of Murder.* New York: Kensington Books, 2002.

————. 1994. *Mulch.* New York: Bantam, 1998.

————. *The Perennial Killer.* New York: Bantam, 2000.

Rivera, José Eustasio. 1924. *The Vortex.* Translated by E. K. James. London: Putnam, 1935.

Rivera, Tomás. *And the Earth Did Not Part.* Berkeley: Quinto Sol, 1971.

Roads, Michael J. *Getting There.* Charlottesville, VA: Hampton Roads, 1998.

Robbins, Tom. 1971. *Another Roadside Attraction.* New York: Bantam, 2003.

————. 1976. *Even Cowgirls Get the Blues.* New York: Bantam, 2003.

————. 2000. *Fierce Invalids Home from Hot Climates.* New York: Bantam, 2003.

————. 2003. *Villa Incognito.* New York: Bantam, 2004.

Roberts, Nora. *Heaven and Earth.* New York: Jove Books, 2001.

————. *Montana Sky.* New York: Berkley, 1996.

Robinson, Eden. *Monkey Beach.* Boston: Houghton Mifflin, 2000.

————. *Traplines.* New York: Holt, 1996.

Robinson, Harry. *Write It on Your Heart: The Epic World of an Okanagan Storyteller.* Vancouver: Talonbooks, 2004.

Robinson, Kim Stanley. 1998. *Antarctica.* New York: Bantam, 1999.

————. 1996. *Blue Mars.* New York: Bantam, 1997.

————. 1989. *Escape from Kathmandu.* New York: T. Doherty Associates, 2000.

————. *Fifty Degrees Below.* New York: Bantam, 2005.

————. *Forty Signs of Rain.* New York: Bantam, 2004.

————, ed. *Future Primitive: The New Ecotopias.* New York: Tor, 1994.

————. 1988. *The Gold Coast.* New York: Orb, 1995.

————. 1994. *Green Mars.* London: HarperCollins, 2001.

————. *Icehenge.* New York: Orb, 1999.

————. *The Martians.* New York: Bantam, 1999.

————. *The Memory of Whiteness.* London: HarperCollins, 1999.

————. 1990. *Pacific Edge.* New York: Orb, 1995.

————. *The Planet on the Table.* New York: T. Doherty, 1986.

————. 1993. *Red Mars.* London: Voyager/HarperCollins, 2001.

————. 1991. *Remaking History and Other Stories.* New York: Orb, 1994.

————. 1990. *A Short, Sharp Shock.* London: Voyager, 2000.

————. *Sixty Days and Counting.* New York: Bantam Books, 2007.

————. 1984. *The Wild Shore.* New York: Orb, 1995.

————. 2002. *The Years of Rice and Salt.* New York: Bantam, 2003.

Roderus, Frank. *Mustang War.* New York: Doubleday, 1991.

Roessner, Michaela. *Vanishing Point.* New York: T. Doherty Associates, 1993.

Rogers, Jane. 1995. *Promised Lands.* Woodstock, NY: Overlook Press, 1997.

Romtvedt, David. *Crossing Wyoming.* Fredonia, NY: White Pine Press, 1992.

Rosemary. Kristine. *The War Against Gravity.* Seattle: Black Heron Press, 1993.

Rosen, Kenneth Mark, ed. *The Man to Send Rain Clouds: Contemporary Stories by American Indians.* New York: Penguin, 1992.

Rosen, Michael J., ed. *The Company of Animals: 20 Stories of Alliance and Encounter.* New York: Doubleday, 1993.

Roshwald, Mordecai. 1959. *Level 7.* Madison: University of Wisconsin Press, 2004.

Rosny, J.-H. 1920. *Quest for Fire: A Novel of Prehistoric Times.* New York: Ballantine, 1982.

Rossi, Anacristina. *The Madwoman of Gandoca.* Lewiston, NY: E. Mellen, 2006.

Rothenberg, Rebecca. *The Bulrush Murders.* New York: Carroll & Graf, 1991.

————. *The Dandelion Murders.* New York: Mysterious Press, 1994.

————. *The Shy Tulip Murders.* New York: Mysterious Press, 1996.

————. *The Tumbleweed Murders.* Santa Barbara, CA: Perseverance Press, 2001.

Rothschild, Michael. *Rhapsody of a Hermit, and Three Tales.* New York: Viking, 1973.

————. *Wondermonger.* New York: Viking, 1990.

Ruff, Matt. *Sewer, Gas & Electric: The Public Works Trilogy.* New York: Atlantic Monthly Press, 1997.

Ruhen, Olaf. *Naked Under Capricorn.* Sydney: Angus & Robertson, 1982.

Russ, Joanna. 1975. *The Female Man.* London: Women's, 2002.

————. *Picnic on Paradise.* New York: Berkley, 1979.

Russell, Alan. *The Forest Prime Evil.* New York: Walker, 1992.

Russell, Sharman Apt. *The Last Matriarch.* Albuquerque: University of New Mexico Press, 2000.

Sadoveanu, Mihail. *Ancuta's Inn.* Bucharest: "The Book" Pub. House, 1954.

———. 1983. *The Hatchet; The Life of Stephen the Great.* New York: East European Monographs, 1991.

Sait Faik. *A Dot on the Map.* Bloomington: Indiana University Press, 1983.

Sallot, Lynne, and Tom Peltier. *Bearwalk.* Don Mills, ON: Musson, 1977.

Salmon, M. H. *Home Is the River.* San Lorenzo, NM: High-Lonesome Books, 1989.

Sam'an, Anzhil Butrus, ed. *A Voice of Their Own: Short Stories by Egyptian Women.* Guizeh, Egypt: Foreign Cultural Information Dept., 1994.

Sanders, Scott R. 1986. *Bad Man Ballad.* Bloomington: Indiana University Press, 2004.

———. *The Engineer of Beasts.* New York: Orchard Books, 1988.

———. 1985. *Terrarium.* Bloomington: Indiana University Press, 1995.

———. 1983. *Wilderness Plots: Tales About the Settlement of the American Land.* Columbus: Ohio State University Press, 1988.

Sanders, William. *The Ballad of Billy Badass & the Rose of Turkestan.* United States: Yandro House, 1999.

———. *Blood Autumn.* New York: St. Martin's, 1995.

Sandoz, Mari. 1957. *The Horsecatcher.* Lincoln: University of Nebraska Press, 1986.

———. 1963. *The Story Catcher.* Lincoln: University of Nebraska Press, 1986.

Saramago, José. *The Cave.* New York: Harcourt Brace, 2002.

———. 1986. *The Stone Raft.* New York: Harcourt Brace, 1995.

Sarris, Greg. *Watermelon Nights.* New York: Hyperion, 1998.

———, ed. *The Sound of Rattles and Clappers: A Collection of New California Indian Writing.* Tucson: University of Arizona Press, 1994.

Saunders, George. *In Persuasion Nation.* New York: Riverhead Books, 2006.

———. *Pastoralia.* New York: Riverhead Books, 2000.

Savage, Sam. *Firmin: Adventures of a Metropolitan Lowlife.* Minneapolis: Coffee House Press, 2006.

Schaefer, Jack. *An American Bestiary.* Boston: Houghton Mifflin, 1975.

———. 1978. *Conversations with a Pocket Gopher.* Santa Barbara, CA: Capra, 1992.

———. *Mavericks.* Boston: Houghton Mifflin, 1967.

———. 1960. *Old Ramon.* New York: Walker, 1993.

Schätzing, Frank. 2004. *The Swarm.* New York: Regan Books, 2006.

Schmitz, Anthony. *Darkest Desire: The Wolf's Own Tale.* Hopewell, NJ: Ecco Press, 1998.

Schutte, James E. *The Bunyip Archives.* Dallas: Baskerville, 1992.

Scortia, Thomas N., and Frank M. Robinson. *The Prometheus Crisis.* Garden City, NY: Doubleday, 1975.

Seaman, Donna, ed. 2000. *In Our Nature: Stories of Wildness.* Athens: University of Georgia Press, 2002.

Searls, Hank. *Sounding.* New York: Ballantine, 1982.

Self, W. *Great Apes.* New York: Grove, 1997.

————. 1995. *Grey Area and Other Stories.* New York: Grove, 1996.

Senehi, Rose. *In the Shadows of Chimney Rock.* Boone, NC: Ingalls, 2008.

————. *Pelican Watch.* Boone, NC: Ingalls, 2007.

Sepúlveda, Luis. *The Old Man Who Read Love Stories.* London: Arcadia, 2001.

Serafini, Luigi. 1981. *Codex Seraphinianus.* New York: Abbeville Press, 1983.

Seton, Ernest Thompson. *The Best of Ernest Thompson Seton.* London: Hodder & Stoughton, 1974.

————. *Selected Stories of Ernest Thompson Seton.* Ottawa: University of Ottawa Press, 1977.

Sguiglia, Eduardo. *Fordlandia.* New York: T. Dunne Books, 2000.

Shacochis, Bob. 1993. *Swimming in the Volcano.* New York: Grove Press, 2004.

Shakespeare, L. M. *Poisoning the Angels.* New York: St. Martin's, 1993.

Shapero, Rich. *Wild Animus.* Woodside, CA: Too Far, 2004.

Sheffield, Charles, ed. 1995. *How to Save the World.* New York: Tor, 1999.

Sheffield, Charles, and David Bischoff. *The Selkie.* New York: Macmillan, 1982.

Shen, Congwen. 1934. *Border Town.* New York: Harper, 2009.

————. 1947. *The Chinese Earth.* New York: Columbia University Press, 1982.

————. *Imperfect Paradise.* Honolulu: University of Hawaii Press, 1995.

————. 1943. *The Long River.* Partial trans. by Lillian Chen Ming Chu. New York: Columbia University Press, 1966.

————. *Selected Stories of Shen Congwen.* Hong Kong: Chinese University Press, 2004.

Shepherd, Nan. 1928. *The Quarry Wood.* Edinburgh: Canongate, 1987.

Shono, Junzo. *Evening Clouds.* Berkeley: Stone Bridge Press, 2000.

Shuler, Linda Lay. *Let the Drum Speak: A Novel of Ancient America.* New York: Morrow, 1996.

————. *She Who Remembers.* New York: Morrow, 1988.

————. *Voice of the Eagle.* New York: Morrow, 1992.

Shute, Nevil. 1957. *On the Beach.* New York: Ballantine, 1997.

Sibal, Nina. *Yatra: The Journey.* London: Women's Press, 1987.

Siddons, Anne Rivers. 1990. *King's Oak.* New York: HarperTorch, 2001.

————. 1998. *Low Country.* New York: HarperTorch, 2004.

Siegel, Robert. *The Ice at the End of the World.* San Francisco: HarperSanFrancisco, 1994.

————. *Whalesong.* San Francisco: HarperSanFrancisco, 1991.

————. 1981. *White Whale.* San Francisco: HarperSanFrancisco, 1994.

Silko, Leslie. *Almanac of the Dead.* New York: Simon & Schuster, 1991.

————. 1977. *Ceremony.* New York: Penguin, 1986.

————. *Gardens in the Dunes.* New York: Simon & Schuster, 1999.

————. *Storyteller.* New York: Little, Brown, 1981.

————. *Yellow Woman.* New Brunswick, NJ: Rutgers University Press, 1993.

Silverberg, Robert. *Hot Sky at Midnight.* New York: Bantam, 1994.

————. 1971. *The World Inside.* New York: Ibooks, 2004.

Simak, Clifford D. 1972. *A Choice of Gods.* New York: Ballantine, 1982.

————. 1952. *City.* Baltimore: Old Earth Books, 2004.

————. 1963. *Way Station.* Baltimore: Old Earth Books, 2004.

Simmons, Dan. *Fires of Eden.* New York: Putnam, 1994.

Simons, Les. *Gila!* New York: New American Library, 1981.

Simons, Margaret. *The Ruthless Garden.* Melbourne, Vic.: Bookworld, 1993.

Simonson, Sheila. *Meadowlark.* New York: St. Martin's, 1996.

————. *Mudlark.* New York: St. Martin's, 1993.

Sinclair, Upton. 1907. *The Jungle.* New York: Penguin, 2006.

————. 1917. *King Coal.* New York: Bantam, 1994.

————. 1927. *Oil!* Berkeley: University of California Press, 1997.

Sivasankarapilla, Takali. 1956. *Chemmeen.* New York: Harper, 1962.

Sky, Gino. 1980. *Appaloosa Rising: The Legend of the Cowboy Buddha.* Berkeley: North Atlantic Books, 1988.

————. *Coyote Silk.* Berkeley: North Atlantic Books, 1987.

Slipperjack, Ruby. *Honour the Sun.* Winnipeg: Pemmican Publications, 1987.

Slonczewski, Joan. *The Children Star.* New York: Tor, 1998.

————. *Daughter of Elysium.* New York: Morrow, 1993.

————. 1986. *A Door into Ocean.* New York: Orb, 2000.

————. 1980. *Still Forms on Foxfield.* New York: Avon, 1988.

————. 1989. *The Wall Around Eden.* New York: Avon, 1990.

Smiley, Jane. *The All-True Travels and Adventures of Lidie Newton.* New York: Knopf, 1998.

————. 1980. *Barn Blind.* New York: Fawcett Columbine, 1993.

————. *Good Faith.* New York: Knopf, 2003.

————. 1988 *The Greenlanders.* New York: Anchor Books, 2005.

————. 2000. *Horse Heaven.* New York: Ballantine, 2003.

————. 1995. *Moo.* London: HarperPerennial, 2006.

————. 1991. *A Thousand Acres.* New York: Anchor, 2003.

Smith, Bill. *Tanaki on the Shore.* Washington DC: Portal Press, 2006.

Smith, Diane. *Letters from Yellowstone.* New York: Penguin, 2000.

————. *Pictures from an Expedition.* New York: Penguin, 2004.

Smith, Joseph. *The Wolf.* London: Jonathan Cape, 2008.

Smith, Lawrence R. *Annie's Soup Kitchen.* Norman: University of Oklahoma Press, 2003.

Smith, Martin Cruz. 1986. *Stallion Gate.* London: Pan, 1996.

Smith, Patrick D. *Forever Island; and, Allapattah.* Englewood, FL: Pineapple Press, 1987.

Smith, Stephanie A. *Other Nature.* New York: Tor, 1995.

Smith, Wilbur. *Elephant Song.* London: Macmillan, 1991.

————. *Hungry as the Sea.* New York: Doubleday, 1978.

————. 1964. *When the Lion Feeds.* London: Pan, 1998.

Sobin, Gustaf. *The Fly-Truffler.* New York: Norton, 2000.

Sojourner, Mary. *Delicate: Stories.* New York: Scribner, 2004.

————. *Sisters of the Dream.* Flagstaff, AZ: Northland, 1989.

Soloukhin, Vladimir Alekseevich. *Honey on Bread.* Moscow: Progress, 1982.

Somtow, S. P. *Moon Dance.* New York: T. Doherty, 1989.

Souza, Márcio. *The Emperor of the Amazon.* New York: Avon, 1980.

————. *Mad Maria.* New York: Avon, 1985.

Speart, Jessica. *Bird Brained.* New York: Avon, 1999.

————. *Black Delta Night.* New York: Avon, 2001.

————. *Blue Twilight.* New York: Avon, 2004.

————. *Border Prey.* New York: Avon, 2000.

————. *Coastal Disturbance.* New York: Avon, 2003.

————. *Gator Aide.* New York: Avon, 1997.

————. *A Killing Season.* New York: Avon, 2002.

————. *Restless Waters.* Sutton: Severn House, 2005.

————. 1998. *Tortoise Soup.* New York: Avon, 2000.

————. *Unsafe Harbor.* New York: Severn House, 2006.

Spinrad, Norman. *Pictures at 11.* New York: Bantam, 1994.

Spitzer, Mark. *Chum.* Cambridge, MA: Zoland, 2001.

St. Clair, Margaret. *The Dolphins of Altair.* New York: Dell, 1967.

Stabenow, Dana. *Better to Rest.* New York: New American Library, 2003.

————. *A Cold-Blooded Business.* New York: Berkley, 1994.

———. *A Cold Day for Murder.* New York: Berkley, 1992.

———. *Dead in the Water.* New York: Berkley, 1993.

———. *Hunter's Moon.* New York: Putnam, 1999.

———. *Killing Grounds.* New York: Putnam, 1998.

———. *Midnight Come Again.* New York: St. Martin's, 2000.

———. *The Singing of the Dead.* New York: St. Martin's, 2001.

Stadler, John, ed. *Eco-Fiction.* New York: Washington Square Press, 1971.

Stafford, Jean. 1947. *The Mountain Lion.* Austin: University of Texas Press, 1992.

Standiford, Les. *Black Mountain.* New York: Putnam, 2000.

———. *Spill.* New York: Atlantic Monthly Press, 1991.

Standing Bear, Luther. *Stories of the Sioux.* Lincoln: University of Nebraska Press, 2006.

Starhawk. *The Fifth Sacred Thing.* New York: Bantam, 1993.

Stebel, S. L. *Spring Thaw.* New York: Walker, 1989.

Stegner, Wallace Earle. 1967. *All the Little Live Things.* New York: Penguin, 1991.

———. 1971. *Angle of Repose.* New York: Modern Library, 2000.

———. 1943. *The Big Rock Candy Mountain.* New York: Penguin, 1991.

———. *Crossing to Safety.* New York: Random House, 1987.

———. 1979. *Recapitulation.* New York: Penguin, 1997.

———. 1961. *A Shooting Star.* New York: Penguin, 1996.

———. 1976. *The Spectator Bird.* New York: Penguin, 1990.

Steinbeck, John. 1945. *Cannery Row.* New York: Penguin, 2002.

———. 1936. *In Dubious Battle.* New York: Penguin, 2006.

———. 1939. *The Grapes of Wrath.* New York: Penguin, 2006.

———. 1947. *The Pearl.* New York: Penguin, 2002.

———. 1937. *The Red Pony.* London: Penguin, 2000.

———. 1954. *Sweet Thursday.* New York: Penguin, 1996.

———. 1933. *To a God Unknown.* New York: Penguin, 1995.

Stephenson, Neal. 1988. *Zodiac: The Eco-Thriller.* New York: Bantam, 1995.

Sterchi, Beat. 1983. *Cow.* London: Faber, 1999.

Stewart, George Rippey. 1949. *Earth Abides.* New York: Ballantine, 2006.

———. *East of the Giants.* New York: Ballantine, 1971.

———. 1948. *Fire.* Lincoln: University of Nebraska Press, 1984.

———. 1951. *Sheep Rock.* New York: Ballantine, 1971.

———. 1941. *Storm.* Berkeley: Heyday Books, 2003.

Stivens, Dal. *A Horse of Air.* Mitcham, Vic.: Whitehorse Press, 2008.

Stokes, Naomi Miller. *The Listening Ones.* New York: Forge, 1997.

———. *The Tree People.* New York: Forge, 1995.

Stone, George. *Blizzard*. New York: Grosset & Dunlap, 1977.

———. *A Legend of Wolf Song*. New York: Grosset & Dunlap, 1975.

Stovall, Linny, ed. *Extinction*. Hillsboro, OR: Blue Heron, 1992.

Stow, Randolph. *Tourmaline*. St. Lucia: University of Queensland Press, 2002.

Straley, John. 1998. *The Angels Will Not Care*. New York: Bantam, 2000.

———. *Cold Water Burning*. New York: Bantam, 2001.

———. 1993. *The Curious Eat Themselves*. New York: Bantam, 1995.

———. 1992. *The Woman Who Married a Bear*. New York: Signet, 1994.

Strieber, Whitley. *Wolf of Shadows*. New York: Knopf, 1985.

———. *The Wolfen*. New York: Morrow, 1978.

Strieber, Whitley, and James W. Kunetka. *Nature's End: The Consequences of the Twen-tieth Century*. New York: Warner Books, 1986.

———. *Warday and the Journey Onward*. New York: Holt, Rinehart, and Winston, 1984.

Strong, Albertine. *Deluge*. New York: Harmony Books, 1997.

Strong, Jonathan. *A Circle Around Her*. Cambridge, MA: Zoland Books, 2000.

———. *An Untold Tale*. Cambridge, MA: Zoland Books, 1993.

Sucharitkul, Somtow. 1981. *Starship & Haiku*. New York: Ballantine, 1988.

Sullivan, Mark T. *Ghost Dance*. New York: Avon, 1999.

———. *The Purification Ceremony*. New York: Avon, 1997.

Svoboda, Terese. *Cannibal*. New York: New York University Press, 1994.

———. *A Drink Called Paradise*. Washington DC: Counterpoint Press, 1999.

Swift, Graham. *Ever After*. New York: Knopf, 1992.

———. 1983. *Waterland*. New York: Vintage, 1992.

Swigart, Rob. *The Book of Revelations*. New York: Dutton, 1981.

———. *Little America*. Boston: Houghton Mifflin, 1977.

———. *Toxin*. New York: St. Martin's, 1989.

———. *Vector*. New York: Bluejay Books, 1986.

———. *Venom*. New York: St. Martin's, 1991.

Taniguchi, Jiro. *The Ice Wanderer and Other Stories*. Wisbech, England: Fanfare/Ponent Mon, 2007.

Taylor, Elizabeth Atwood. 1992. *The Northwest Murders*. New York: Ivy Books, 1994.

Tekin, Akin. *The Ownerless Planet*. Ankara: Dönence Basim Yayin Hizmetleri, 2003.

Tepper, Sheri S. *The Family Tree*. New York: Avon, 1997.

———. 1988. *The Gate to Women's Country*. London: HarperCollins, 1999.

———. 1989. *Grass*. London: Gollancz, 2002.

———. *Singer from the Sea*. New York: Avon, 1999.

———. *The Visitor*. New York: Eos, 2002.

Theroux, Paul. *Millroy the Magician*. New York: Random House, 1994.

———. *The Mosquito Coast*. New York: Avon, 1983.

———. *O-Zone*. New York: Putnam, 1986.

Thiele, Colin. *Fight Against Albatross Two*. New York: Harper & Row, 1974.

———. *Shadow Shark*. New York: Harper & Row, 1988.

Thomas, Elizabeth Marshall. *The Animal Wife*. Boston: Houghton Mifflin, 1990.

———. *Certain Poor Shepherds: A Christmas Tale*. New York: Simon & Schuster, 1996.

———. *Reindeer Moon*. Boston: Houghton Mifflin, 1987.

Thomas, Sue, ed. *Wild Women: Contemporary Short Stories by Women Celebrating Women*. Woodstock, NY: Overlook Press, 1994.

Thompson, Harry. *To the Edge of the World*. San Francisco: MacAdam/Cage, 2005.

Tobias, Michael. *Fatal Exposure*. New York: Pocket Books, 1991.

———. *Voice of the Planet*. New York: Bantam, 1990.

Tolkien, J. R. R. 1938. *The Annotated Hobbit: The Hobbit, Or, There and Back Again*. Boston: Houghton Mifflin, 2002.

———. 1954. *The Lord of the Rings*. Boston: Houghton Mifflin, 2005.

Tolstoy, Leo. 1866. *War and Peace*. New York: Modern Library, 2004.

Townsend, Lawrence G. *Secrets of the Wholly Grill: A Novel About Cravings, Barbecue, and Software*. New York: Carroll & Graf, 2002.

Trafzer, Clifford E., ed. *Blue Dawn, Red Earth: New Native American Storytellers*. New York: Anchor Books, 1996.

———. *Earth Song, Sky Spirit: Short Stories of the Contemporary Native American Experience*. New York: Doubleday, 1993.

Traven, B. 1938. *The Bridge in the Jungle*. Chicago: I. R. Dee, 1994.

———. 1935. *The Carreta*. Chicago: Elephant Paperbacks, 1994.

———. 1956. *The Cotton-Pickers*. Chicago: I. R. Dee, 1995.

———. 1934. *The Death Ship: The Story of an American Sailor*. Brooklyn: L. Hill, 1991.

———. 1940. *General from the Jungle*. Chicago: I. R. Dee, 1995.

———. 1931. *Government*. Chicago: I. R. Dee, 1993.

———. *The Kidnapped Saint and Other Stories*. Brooklyn: L. Hill, 1991.

———. 1933. *March to the Monteria*. Chicago: I. R. Dee, 1994.

———. *The Night Visitor and Other Stories*. Chicago: I. R. Dee, 1993.

———. *The Rebellion of the Hanged*. Chicago: I. R. Dee, 1994.

———. 1927. *The Treasure of the Sierra Madre*. New York: Samuel French, 2004.

———. 1936. *Trozas*. Chicago: I. R. Dee, 1994.

————. 1929. *The White Rose.* Brooklyn: L. Hill, 1979.

Turf and Joël Mouclier. *Ramparts: Unseeing Eyes.* Northampton, MA: Tundra, 1993.

Turner, George. 1978. *Beloved Son.* New York: Avon, 1996.

————. *The Destiny Makers.* New York: Morrow, 1992.

————. *Down There in Darkness.* New York: Tor, 1999.

————. *Drowning Towers.* New York: Avon, 1996.

————. *Vaneglory.* New York: Avon, 1996.

————. *Yesterday's Men.* New York: Avon, 1996.

Turtledove, Harry. *The Case of the Toxic Spell Dump.* New York: Baen, 1993.

Twain, Mark. 1884. *Adventures of Huckleberry Finn.* Mineola, NY: Dover, 2005.

————. 1872. *Roughing It.* New York: Oxford University Press, 1996.

Unger, Douglas. 1989. *Leaving the Land.* Lincoln: University of Nebraska Press, 1995.

Updike, John. *Toward the End of Time.* New York: Knopf, 1997.

Van Gieson, Judith. *Ditch Rider.* New York: HarperCollins, 1998.

————. 1996. *Hotshots.* New York: HarperPaperbacks, 1997.

————. *The Lies That Bind.* New York: HarperCollins, 1993.

————. 1988. *North of the Border.* Albuquerque: University of New Mexico Press, 2002.

————. 1991. *The Other Side of Death.* Albuquerque: University of New Mexico, 2003.

————. *Parrot Blues.* New York: HarperCollins, 1995.

————. *Raptor.* Albuquerque: University of New Mexico Press, 2002.

————. 1992. *The Wolf Path.* New York: HarperPaperbacks, 1993.

Van Winckel, Nance. *Curtain Creek Farm.* New York: Persea Books, 2000.

Vance, Jack. *Araminta Station.* New York: Tom Doherty Associates, 1988.

————. *Ecce and Old Earth.* New York: St. Martin's, 1991.

————. 1950. *Tales of the Dying Earth.* New York: Tom Doherty Associates, 2000.

————. 1992. *Throy.* New York: Tor, 1993.

Vargas Llosa, Mario. *Death in the Andes.* New York: Farrar, Straus, and Giroux, 1996.

————. 1961. *The Green House.* New York: Rayo, 2005.

————. 1989. *The Storyteller.* New York: Picador, 2001.

Varley, John. *Demon.* New York: Putnam, 1984.

————. *Mammoth.* New York: Ace, 2005.

————. 1983. *Millennium.* New York: Ace, 1999.

————. 1977. *The Ophiuchi Hotline.* London: Gollancz, 2003.

————. *Steel Beach.* New York: Putnam, 1992.

————. 1979. *Titan.* New York: Ace, 1987.

———. 1980. *Wizard.* New York: Berkley, 1981.

Velie, Alan R., ed. *The Lightning Within: An Anthology of Contemporary American Indian Fiction.* Lincoln: University of Nebraska Press, 1991.

Ventura, Michael. *The Zoo Where You're Fed to God.* New York: Simon & Schuster, 1994.

Vijayan, O. V. 1969. *The Legends of Khasak.* New Delhi: Penguin, 1994.

Vinge, Joan D. 1980. *The Snow Queen.* New York: Warner, 1989.

———. *The Summer Queen.* New York: Warner Books, 1991.

———. *World's End.* New York: Bluejay Books, 1984.

Viramontes, Helena María. *Their Dogs Came with Them.* New York: Dutton, 2000.

———. *Under the Feet of Jesus.* New York: Dutton, 1995.

Vizenor, Gerald Robert. *Bearheart: The Heirship Chronicles.* Minneapolis: University of Minnesota Press, 1990.

Voien, Steven. *Black Leopard.* New York: Knopf, 1997.

Vollmann, William T. *Argall: A Book of North American Landscapes.* New York: Viking, 2001.

———. 1992. *Fathers and Crows.* New York: Penguin, 1993.

———. 1990. *The Ice-Shirt.* New York: Penguin, 1993.

———. 1994. *The Rifles.* New York: Penguin, 1995.

———. *You Bright and Risen Angels: A Cartoon.* New York: Atheneum, 1987.

Vonarburg, Elisabeth. *In the Mothers' Land.* New York: Bantam, 1992.

———. *The Maerlande Chronicles.* Victoria, BC: Beach Holme, 1992.

———. *Reluctant Voyagers.* New York: Bantam, 1995.

———. 1988. *The Silent City.* New York: Bantam Books, 1992.

———. *Slow Engines of Time.* Edmonton: Tesseract Books, 2000.

Vonnegut, Kurt. *Cat's Cradle.* New York: Dial Press, 2006.

———. 1985. *Galapagos.* New York: Dell, 2006.

———. 1952. *Player Piano.* New York: Dell, 1999.

———. 1969. *Slaughterhouse-Five; or, The Children'sCrusade: A Duty-Dance with Death.* New York: Dial Press, 2005.

Voznesenskaia, Julia. *The Star Chernobyl.* London: Quartet Books, 1987.

Vreeland, Susan. *The Forest Lover.* New York: Viking, 2004.

Waldie, Scott. *Travers Corners.* New York: Lyons & Burford, 1997.

Walker, Alice. 1982. *The Color Purple.* Orlando: Harcourt, 2003.

———. 2004. *Now Is the Time to Open Your Heart.* New York: Ballantine, 2005.

———. 1992. *Possessing the Secret of Joy.* New York: Washington Square Press, 1997.

———. 1989. *The Temple of My Familiar.* New York: Washington Square Press, 1997.

Walker, Sage. *Whiteout.* New York: Tor, 1996.

Wallace, David Rains. *The Turquoise Dragon*. San Francisco: Sierra Club Books, 1985.

———. *The Vermilion Parrot*. San Francisco: Sierra Club Books, 1991.

Wallingford, Lee. *Clear-Cut Murder*. New York: Walker, 1993.

———. *Cold Tracks*. New York: Walker, 1991.

Walters, Charles. *A Beast of Muddy Brain*. Austin, TX: Acres U.S.A., 2009.

Wambaugh, Joseph. *Finnegan's Week*. New York: W. Morrow, 1993.

Warner, Irving. *Wagner, Descending: The Wrath of the Salmon Queen*. New York: Pleasure Boat Studio, 2004.

Warner, Susan. 1850. *The Wide, Wide World*. New York: Feminist Press, 1987.

Warren, Spring. *Turpentine*. New York: Black Cat, 2007.

Waters, Frank. 1937. *Below Grass Roots*. Athens: Swallow Press/Ohio University Press, 2002.

———. 1940. *The Dust Within the Rock*. Athens: Swallow Press/Ohio University Press, 2002.

———. *Flight from Fiesta*. Athens: Swallow Press/Ohio University Press, 1987.

———. 1984. *The Lizard Woman*. Athens: Swallow Press/Ohio University Press, 1995.

———. 1942. *The Man Who Killed the Deer*. Athens: Swallow Press/Ohio University Press, 1989.

———. 1941. *People of the Valley*. Athens: Swallow Press/Ohio University Press, 1984.

———. 1971. *Pike's Peak: A Mining Saga*. Athens: Swallow Press/Ohio University Press, 1987.

———. 1935. *The Wild Earth's Nobility*. Athens: Swallow Press/Ohio University Press, 2002.

———. 1988. *The Woman at Otowi Crossing*. Athens: Swallow Press/Ohio University Press, 1997.

Watkins, Paul. *Archangel*. New York: Random House, 1995.

Watson, Ian. *The Book of Being*. London: Gollancz, 1985.

———. *The Book of the River*. London: Gollancz, 1984.

———. *The Book of the Stars*. London: Gollancz, 1984.

———. *The Fallen Moon*. London: Gollancz, 1994.

———. 1976. *The Jonah Kit*. London: Gollancz, 2002.

———. *Lucky's Harvest*. London: Gollancz, 1993.

———. *Yaleen*. Dallas: BenBella Books, 2004.

Watson, Shiela. 1959. *The Double Hook*. Toronto: McClelland & Stewart, 1992.

Watts, Peter. *Maelstrom*. New York: Tor, 2001.

———. *Starfish*. New York: Tor, 1999.

Weatherford, Joyce. *Heart of the Beast*. New York: Scribner, 2001.

Weaver, Will. *Red Earth, White Earth.* St. Paul, mn: Borealis Books, 2006.

Webb, Mary. 1917. *Gone to Earth.* Leicester: Charnwood, 1982.

———. 1924. *Precious Bane.* London: Landsborough Publications, 1958.

Weger, G. M. *East Garrison.* Austin: Bridgeway Books, 2009.

Welch, James. 1986. *Fools Crow.* New York: Quality Paperback Book Club, 1995.

———. *The Heartsong of Charging Elk.* New York: Anchor, 2001.

———. *The Indian Lawyer.* New York: Norton, 1990.

———. 1974. *Winter in the Blood.* New York: Penguin, 1986.

Weld, William F. *Stillwater.* New York: Simon & Schuster, 2002.

Weller, Anthony. *The Siege of Salt Cove.* New York: Norton, 2004.

Weller, Archie. *The Day of the Dog.* Sydney; Boston: Allen & Unwin, 1981.

Wells, H. G. 1896. *The Island of Dr. Moreau.* New York: Bantam, 2005.

Wendt, Albert. 1986. *The Birth and Death of the Miracle Man and Other Stories.* Honolulu: University of Hawaii Press, 1999.

———. *Leaves of the Banyan Tree.* Honolulu: University of Hawaii Press, 1994.

———, ed. *Nuanua: Pacific Writing in English Since 1980.* Honolulu: University of Hawaii Press, 1995.

———. 1973. *Sons for the Return Home.* Honolulu: University of Hawaii Press, 1996.

Werber, Bernard. 1991. *Empire of the Ants.* New York: Bantam, 1998.

West, Paul. *The Place in Flowers Where Pollen Rests.* Rutherford, nj: Voyant Pub, 2002.

Weston, Susan B. *Children of the Light.* New York: St. Martin's, 1985.

Wetherell, W. D. *Hyannis Boat and Other Stories.* Boston: Little, Brown, 1989.

———. *Wherever that Great Heart May Be.* Hanover, nh: University Press of New England, 1996.

———. *The Wisest Man in America.* Hanover, nh: University Press of New England, 1995.

Wharton, Herb. 1992. *Unbranded.* St. Lucia: University of Queensland Press, 2000.

Wharton, Thomas. *Icefields.* New York: Washington Square Press, 1995.

———. 2001. *Salamander.* New York: Washington Square Press, 2002.

Wharton, William. 1978. *Birdy.* New York: Vintage Books, 1992.

———. *Franky Furbo.* New York: Holt, 1989.

Wheeler, Jordan. *Brothers in Arms.* Winnipeg: Pemmican Publications, 1989.

Wheeler, Kate. *When Mountains Walked.* Boston: Houghton Mifflin, 2000.

White, Patrick. 1957. *Voss.* London: Vintage, 1994.

White, Randy Wayne. *Captiva.* New York: Putnam, 1996.

———. *Dead of Night.* New York: Putnam, 2005.

———. *Everglades.* New York: Putnam, 2003.

————. *The Heat Islands.* New York: St. Martin's, 1992.

————. 1993. *The Man Who Invented Florida.* New York: St. Martin's, 1997.

————. *The Mangrove Coast.* New York: Putnam, 1998.

————. *North of Havana.* New York: Putnam, 1997.

————. *Sanibel Flats.* New York: St. Martin's, 1990.

————. *Shark River.* New York: Putnam, 2001.

————. *Tampa Burn.* New York: Putnam, 2004.

————. *Ten Thousand Islands.* New York: Putnam, 2000.

————. *Twelve Mile Limit.* New York: Putnam, 2002.

White, Robin. *Siberian Light.* New York: Viking, 1997.

Whitty, Julia. *A Tortoise for the Queen of Tonga.* Boston: Houghton Mifflin, 2002.

Wilbur, Richard, ed. *A Bestiary.* New York: Pantheon Books, 1993.

Wiley, Richard. *Ahmed's Revenge.* New York: Random House, 1998.

Wilhelm, Kate. *Children of the Wind: Five Novellas.* New York: St. Martin's, 1989.

————. *Juniper Time.* New York: Harper & Row, 1979.

————. 1976. *Where Late the Sweet Birds Sang.* New York: Orb, 1998.

Willard, Nancy. *Sister Water.* Detroit: Wayne State University Press, 2005.

Williams, Joy. *The Quick and the Dead.* New York: Knopf, 2000.

Williams, Liz. *The Ghost Sister.* New York: Bantam Books, 2001.

Williams, Raymond. 1960. *Border Country.* Cardiff, UK: Parthian, 2006.

————. 1979. *The Fight for Manod.* London: Hogarth, 1988.

————. 1979–80. *People of the Black Mountains.* London: Chatto & Windus, 1989.

————. 1964. *Second Generation.* London: Hogarth Press, 1988.

Williams, Walter Jon. *Days of Atonement.* New York: Tor, 1991.

Williamson, Penelope. *Heart of the West.* New York: Simon & Schuster, 1995.

Willis, Paul J. 1991. *No Clock in the Forest.* New York: Avon, 1993.

————. 1992. *The Stolen River.* New York: Avon, 1993.

Wilson, Kelpie. *Primal Tears.* Berkeley: Frog, Ltd., 2005.

Winterson, Jeanette. 1989. *Sexing the Cherry.* London: Vintage, 2001.

————. *The Stone Gods.* Toronto: Knopf Canada, 2008.

Winton, Tim. *Blueback: A Contemporary Fable.* New York: Scribner, 1997.

————. *Dirt Music.* New York: Scribner, 2003.

————. 1993. *Shallows.* London: Picador, 2003.

————. 1987. *That Eye, the Sky.* New York: Simon & Schuster, 2002.

Witt, Lana. *Slow Dancing on Dinosaur Bones.* New York: Scribner, 1996.

Wohl, Burton. *The China Syndrome.* New York: Bantam, 1979.

Wolf, Christa. 1989. *Accident: A Day's News.* Chicago: University of Chicago Press, 2001.

Wolf, Joan. *Daughter of the Red Deer.* New York: Dutton, 1991.

———. *The Horsemasters.* New York: Dutton, 1993.

———. *The Reindeer Hunters.* New York: Dutton, 1994.

Wolfe, Gene. 1989. *Endangered Species.* New York: Tor, 2004.

Wolfe, Swain. 1998. *The Lake Dreams the Sky.* New York: St. Martin's, 2004.

———. *The Woman Who Lives in the Earth.* New York: St. Martin's, 2003.

Wolk, Lauren. *Those Who Favor Fire.* New York: Random House, 1998.

Wolverton, Dave. *Path of the Hero.* New York: Bantam, 1993.

———. *Serpent Catch.* New York: Bantam, 1991.

Wongar, B. *Babaru.* Urbana: University of Illinois Press, 1982.

———. *Bilma.* Columbus: Ohio State University Press, 1984.

———. 1987. *Gabo Djara.* New York: Braziller, 1991.

———. *Karan.* New York: Braziller, 1991.

———. *The Last Pack of Dingoes.* Pymble, NSW: Angus & Robertson, 1993.

———. *Marngit.* North Ryde, NSW: Angus & Robertson, 1992.

———. 1994. *Raki.* London; New York: Marion Boyars, 1997.

———. 1978. *The Track to Bralgu.* Pymble, NSW: Angus & Robertson, 1992.

———. 1983. *Walg.* New York: Braziller, 1990.

Woolf, Virginia. 1927. *To the Lighthouse.* Orlando: Harcourt, 2005.

———. 1931. *The Waves.* Orlando: Harcourt, 2006.

Wray, John. *Lowboy.* New York: Farrar, Straus, and Giroux, 2009.

Wren, M. K. *A Gift upon the Shore.* New York: Ballantine, 1990.

———. *Wake Up, Darlin' Corey.* New York: Ballantine, 1990.

Wright, Alexis. *Carpentaria.* New York: Atria Books, 2009.

———. 1997. *Plains of Promise.* St. Lucia: University of Queensland Press, 2006.

Wright, Harold Bell. 1907. *The Shepherd of the Hills.* Doylestown, PA: Wildside Press, 2004.

———. 1911. *The Winning of Barbara Worth.* Gretna, LA: Pelican, 1999.

Wright, Nancy Means. *Mad Season.* New York: St. Martin's, 1996.

———. *Poison Apples.* New York: St. Martin's, 2000.

Wright, Ronald. *A Scientific Romance.* New York: Picador, 1998.

Wright, Steve. *A Drop in the Ocean.* Sydney: Pan, 1991.

Wrightson, Patricia. *Moon-Dark.* New York: Margaret K. McElderry Books, 1987.

———. *The Nargun and the Stars.* 1970. New York: M. K. McElderry Books, 1986.

Wyle, Dirk. *Amazon Gold.* Highland City, FL: Rainbow Books, 2003.

———. *Biotechnology Is Murder.* Highland City, FL: Rainbow Books, 2000.

———. *Medical School Is Murder.* Highland City, FL: Rainbow Books, 2001.

———. *Pharmacology Is Murder.* Highland City, FL: Rainbow Books, 1998.

Wylie, Philip. *The End of the Dream.* Garden City, NY: Doubleday, 1972.

———. *Triumph.* Garden City, NY: Doubleday, 1963.

Yamashita, Karen Tei. *Brazil-Maru.* Minneapolis: Coffee House Press, 1992.

———. *Circle K Cycles.* Minneapolis: Coffee House Press, 2001.

———. *Through the Arc of the Rain Forest.* Minneapolis: Coffee House Press, 1990.

———. *Tropic of Orange.* Minneapolis: Coffee House Press, 1997.

Yamauchi, Wakako. *Songs My Mother Taught Me: Stories, Plays, and Memoir.* New York: Feminist Press, 1994.

Yasar Kemal. 1974. *Iron Earth, Copper Sky.* London: Harvill, 1996.

———. *The Sea-Crossed Fisherman.* New York: Braziller, 1985.

———. 1977. *The Undying Grass.* London: Harvill Press, 1996.

———. 1963. *The Wind from the Plain.* London: Harvill Press, 1996.

Young Bear, Ray A. *Remnants of the First Earth.* New York: Grove Press, 1996.

Zabytko, Irene. *The Sky Unwashed.* Chapel Hill, NC: Algonquin Books, 2000.

Zachary, Hugh. *Tide: A Novel of Catastrophe.* New York: Putnam, 1974.

Zahava, Irene. *Hear the Silence: Stories by Women of Myth, Magic & Renewal.* Trumansburg, NY: Crossing Press, 1986.

Zaniewski, Andrzej. *Rat.* New York: Arcade, 1994.

Zettel, Sarah. *Kingdom of Cages.* New York: Warner Books, 2001.

———. *Playing God.* New York: Warner Books, 1998.

———. *The Quiet Invasion.* New York: Warner Books, 2000.

Zhang, Wei. 1987. *The Ancient Ship.* New York: HarperPerennial, 2008.

———. 1993. *September's Fable.* Paramus, NJ: Homa & Sekey Books, 2007.

Zigal, Thomas. 1996. *Hardrock Stiff.* New York: Delacorte Press, 1997.

Zimmerman, Marvin L. *The Ovum Factor.* Austin, TX: Synergy Books, 2008.

Zitkala-Sa. *Iktomi and the Ducks and Other Sioux Stories.* Lincoln: University of Nebraska Press, 2004.

———. 1901. *Old Indian Legends.* Lincoln: University of Nebraska Press, 1985.

INDEX

Africa, 25, 33, 39, 47, 56, 104, 145, 177; African
writers, 49, 99–101
African Americans, 22, 49, 120, 136; ecodefense and, 35, 56–57, 73; writers, 19, 70
air: air pollution, 30, 58, 67, 150, 170; biosphere, 152; fresh air, 46
Alaska, 34, 42, 61; Aleutian islands, 59–60, 161,
169; ecoromance and, 112, 113; mysteries
and, 168, 169, 178, 179–80; Native American
writers and, 74, 75; oil and, 53, 74; western
writing and, 118, 126, 127
alcohol, 59, 72, 165
alternative histories, 88, 139, 147–48, 149–50,
151
animal rights, 47, 92, 100; ecodefense and, 57,
58; in mid-twentieth-century fiction, 20,
23, 28; mysteries and, 166, 168, 169, 170;
research animals, 46, 59, 88, 113, 169, 173;
speculative fiction and, 134, 142
animals, 92, 95, 102, 104, 121; ecodefense and,
57–58, 59; ecoromance and, 112–13, 114; in
English fiction, 10, 20, 86, 87, 88–89; in
modern ecofiction, 33, 37, 38–47; mysteries and, 173, 181; Native Americans and,
72, 73, 75; speculative fiction and, 132,
139, 145, 146, 157–58, 159, 160, 162. *See also*
anthropomorphism
anthologies, 44, 56, 101; animal ecofiction, 40,
57; of Australian aboriginal writers, 105; of
cautionary fiction, 64; earliest, of ecofiction, 2, 130; of European ecofiction, 93; of
Hawaiian fiction, 107; of Indian writing,
97; of mid-twentieth century, 14, 26, 28; of
Native American/Canadian fiction, 70, 76;
of speculative fiction, 144–45, 149; of western writing, 123, 124
anthropology, 18, 33, 36, 148, 162, 181

anthropomorphism, 10, 20, 43, 121
apes, 20, 38, 58, 88–89, 93, 113, 135, 170
Appalachian region, 13, 15, 176
Arctic/Antarctica, 46, 60, 127; disaster fiction
and, 66, 67; ecodefense and, 53, 55; mysteries and, 168, 178; speculative fiction and,
147, 151, 155
Arizona, 30, 37, 46, 50, 51
Asian Americans, 123, 128
Asian ecofiction: India, 97–98; Japan, 95–96,
97; Korea and China, 96–97; Sri Lanka,
98–99
Australia, 25, 64; aboriginal culture, 87, 101,
103–6; ecofiction of, 101–7; speculative fiction and, 147

bears, 88, 112, 113, 128, 166, 171, 176, 178, 180
biologists, 56, 108, 112, 166, 178, 181, 182; biological warfare, 169, 177, 179; marine, 38,
54, 61, 98, 113, 157, 158, 168, 172, 180; wolf,
33, 138
biotechnology, 89, 116, 123, 133, 142; cloning,
35, 55, 81, 154, 155, 168; ecodefense and, 55,
57, 59; genetic engineering, 60, 132, 134–35,
136, 139, 141, 152, 154, 156, 168, 176–77; mysteries and, 168, 170, 176–77, 180, 183; nanotechnology, 133, 140. *See also* technology
birds, 12, 35, 37, 42, 58, 96, 126; endangered/
extinct species, 108–9, 112, 168, 169, 172,
180, 181; falcons, 57; hawks, 120; herons, 13;
oil spills and, 168; owls, 172, 173; parrots,
181; quails, 41; ravens, 41
botany, 14, 42, 82, 178
Buddhism, 35, 39, 125, 150
business/corporations, 5, 35, 39, 44, 67, 85;
agribusiness, 36, 52, 59, 123, 172; ecodefense
and, 50, 52, 53–54; fishing and, 55, 127; mys-

teries and, 171, 172, 174, 179; Native American writers and, 74, 75; pollution and, 38, 46–47, 53, 54, 55, 56, 75, 99, 143, 178, 183; speculative fiction and, 132, 133, 134, 136–37, 140, 143, 145, 149, 152, 155, 156. *See also* corruption; mining

California: Death Valley, 133; in early-twentieth century fiction, 12, 14; ecodefense and, 55, 58; ecoromance and, 110; green fiction of 1970s and, 31; in mid-twentieth-century fiction, 18, 19–20, 21, 27; mysteries and, 167, 177, 179, 181; San Joaquin valley, 123; speculative fiction and, 149–50; utopias and, 60, 61; Yosemite, 167

Canada: contemporary ecofiction, 81–82; Native Canadian writers, 71, 76–78; twentieth century ecofiction, 80–81

cannibalism, 11, 39, 76

capitalism, 14, 16

Caribbean, 35, 82–83

cats: cheetahs, 157–58; domestic cats, 43, 44, 159; wild cats, 157

cautionary fiction, 22, 35, 42, 63–68, 84, 89; vs. dystopian fiction, 5–6, 63; end of civilization, 16, 64–65, 67, 136, 156; nuclear power/weapons, 25, 64, 66, 139; politics and, 20, 66, 67; technology and, 23, 68, 133, 150. *See also* disaster fiction; speculative fiction

Celtic culture, 22, 72, 81, 87, 88, 89, 115, 159

Central America, 46, 67–68, 83, 85, 182

children: Canadian fiction for, 76, 82; early-twentieth-century fiction and, 14, 16; fantasy for, 157–60; mid-twentieth-century fiction and, 19, 20; modern ecofiction and, 41, 44, 58, 61, 93; speculative fiction and, 137, 142, 153, 158, 159; western writing and, 118, 120, 121, 124. *See also* family; young adults

Christianity, 6, 11, 47, 60, 90, 121; fundamentalism, 35, 39, 58, 82, 111, 138, 179; speculative fiction and, 134, 136, 138, 162

cities, 22, 23, 38, 95, 96, 116, 120; speculative fiction and, 25, 66, 67, 132, 144, 149, 151, 160

climate change, 58, 92, 168; cautionary fiction

and, 63, 64, 67; speculative fiction and, 134, 136, 140, 142, 146, 147, 149, 150, 151–52, 162

Colorado, 17, 30, 126, 183

communalism, 11, 55, 61, 85, 142, 150, 179

conservation, 12, 21, 41, 81–82, 98, 110, 113, 118; mysteries and, 168, 171, 173, 180, 182; speculative fiction and, 135, 149, 154. *See also* restoration

corruption, 53, 100, 101, 118; mysteries and, 167, 170, 171, 172, 174, 176, 179. *See also* business/corporations; politics

cougars, 120, 166, 176

Coyote (legendary character), 71, 76

coyotes, 27, 43, 57, 124

dams, 35, 36, 76, 96; ecodefense and, 51, 53, 55; green fiction of 1970s and, 30; mysteries and, 167, 177, 178; western writing and, 120, 121, 122

Darwin, Charles, 39, 102. *See also* evolution

death, 36, 39, 44, 72, 110, 126, 140, 144, 153, 159

deserts, 14, 43, 81, 115; speculative fiction and, 132, 141, 143; western writing and, 118, 126

disaster fiction, 4, 5–6, 12, 63–68, 87. *See also* cautionary fiction

dogs, 66, 105, 112; in early-to-mid-twentieth-century fiction, 15–16, 23; modern ecofiction and, 33, 34, 37, 39, 44

dolphins, 58, 61, 98, 125, 131, 135, 154, 158, 159, 170, 177

dowsers, 52, 81, 102, 103

drugs, 74, 142, 146, 152, 165, 176, 177, 181, 182, 183

dystopian fiction. *See* cautionary fiction; disaster fiction; speculative fiction

earthquakes, 55, 66, 67, 142, 144, 166, 182

ecocriticism: defined, 1; development, 1–2

ecodefense, 35, 49–59, 61, 73, 87, 90, 94, 148; ecoromance and, 111, 112, 114; in mid-twentieth-century fiction, 27, 30–31; mysteries and, 167, 173, 183; western writing and, 118, 121. *See also* environmental activism

New England and, 23, 115; speculative fiction and, 150, 155

floods, 64, 70, 76, 94, 96, 178

Florida, 18–19, 25, 36, 37, 59; ecoromance and, 109, 114; Florida panther, 57; mysteries and, 166, 171–72, 174, 175, 182

food, 59–60, 111, 140, 155, 157, 169, 180

forest rangers, 12, 22, 61, 114, 118, 122, 181; fish and wildlife rangers, 173, 176, 179; game wardens, 167–68; Native American, 74; park rangers, 53, 166–67

forests, 90, 94; activism and, 169, 179; clearcutting, 35, 52, 53; destruction of, 37, 53, 56, 143; fires, 11, 22, 127, 171, 181; in India, 97–98; mysteries and, 169, 171, 173, 179, 181; speculative fiction and, 136, 138, 139, 140, 143, 153, 157; western writing and, 119–20. *See also* logging; rain forests

Gaia hypothesis, 24, 39, 61, 145; Gaia planet, 148, 149. *See also* ecology

gay/lesbian, 108, 115–16, 126

global warming. *See* climate change

graphic novels, 38, 39, 96, 138, 140

Hawaii. *See* Polynesia

herbalism, 13, 46, 47, 53, 54, 110, 158, 165, 176

hippies, 21, 23, 27, 35, 183; speculative fiction and, 142, 150; utopias and, 61; western writing and, 121, 125

horses, 47, 88, 126–27, 161, 162, 182

hunting, 17–18, 19, 35, 57, 84; in Alaska, 74, 168; ivory, 56, 90, 168; mysteries and, 169, 170, 171, 173, 176, 179, 180; speculative fiction and, 132, 137, 139, 150, 162; western writing and, 120, 127

Idaho, 59

insects, 38, 39, 42, 44, 66, 67, 94–95, 171

Inuit, 42, 71, 93, 109, 126, 146, 161, 179

Inupiat, 75

islands, 11, 20, 32–33, 35, 57, 104, 114; Aleutians, 59–60, 161, 169; "Freeland," 61; mysteries and, 169, 174, 180; speculative fiction

and, 145, 158, 161; Sri Lanka, 98–99. *See also* Oceania; Polynesia

journalists, 18, 56, 118, 123, 139, 171, 172, 173

Kansas, 47

Kentucky, 23, 27, 133, 183

land development, 21, 26–27, 29, 30–31, 88, 106; in Australian fiction, 104, 107; ecodefense and, 51–53, 55; ecofeminism and, 45–46, 47–48; ecoromance and, 109, 115; mysteries and, 168, 169, 170–71, 172, 174, 175–76, 177, 179, 180, 181, 182, 183; Native Americans and, 75, 168, 169; speculative fiction and, 131, 138, 160; western writing and, 121, 125, 126

logging, 116, 126; in Alaska, 74; ecodefense and, 52, 53, 58; mysteries and, 167, 173, 176, 179, 181; in Pacific Northwest, 73; speculative fiction and, 153, 157. *See also* forests

magic, 4, 33, 57, 65, 72, 98, 124; dragons, 146; selkies, 89, 146; speculative fiction and, 130, 138, 139, 144, 153, 156, 158, 159

magic realism, 19, 33, 40, 98, 101, 138, 173; animal ecofiction, 41, 43; from Australia, 102, 103; ecodefense and, 54, 112; in European fiction, 90, 92; Native Americans and, 73, 76, 109, 120; nature of, 3; South American writers, 83–84; western writing and, 120, 121, 123, 124

Mars, 24, 60, 90, 116, 132, 148, 150–51

Mexican Americans, 29, 70, 123–24

Mexico, 14, 85–86, 87

Michigan, 37, 51, 161, 171

mining, 11, 17, 85; coal mines, 15, 50, 170, 183; copper, 75, 182–83; diamonds, 99, 109, 177; ecodefense and, 50, 51, 52, 53, 56; gold, 75, 137, 177, 180; mysteries and, 166, 177, 179, 180, 182–83; Native Americans and, 30, 70, 73; pollution from, 46–47, 75; silver, 183; speculative fiction and, 137, 146, 152; uranium, 51, 56, 74, 105

monsters, 43, 159

restoration, 70, 103–4, 106, 107, 121, 139. *See also* conservation

revolution, 31, 71, 85–86, 87, 94, 99, 100, 118, 145, 149

rivers, 16, 19, 34, 52, 155; Amazon, 48; in Asia, 96; Colorado, 48; Columbia, 177; mysteries and, 170, 176, 177; streams, 41; Swift River, 54; western writing and, 120, 122, 127

romance, 33, 73, 83, 87, 93, 103, 126; contemporary ecofiction and, 108–16; D. H. Lawrence and, 110; environmental activism and, 108–9, 114; intimate relations with animals, 113; Margaret Atwood and, 110–11; mysteries and, 169, 172, 176; nineteenth-century literature and, 110; philosophy and, 111–12, 113; speculative fiction and, 138, 139, 153, 161; Ursula K. Le Guin and, 110

Romanticism, 9, 86, 87

Russia, 68, 91, 93–95, 168, 177, 178, 182

Sasquatch, 42, 89, 150, 160, 173, 176

science fiction, 3, 11, 90, 98, 116; from Australia, 102, 103; of early-twentieth century, 13, 16, 18; in England, 86, 89; general contemporary fiction, 131–57; green fiction of 1970s and, 28, 30; of mid-twentieth century, 22–24, 65; nature of, 130–31; "New Wave" of, 129–30. *See also* speculative fiction

senior citizens, 21, 38, 42, 54, 82; aging, 134; Alzheimer's disease, 46; mysteries and, 174, 180, 182, 183; Native American writers and, 74, 75

sexism, 81, 115, 116, 131, 137–38, 143, 149, 165

shamans, 35, 61, 75, 109, 124, 137, 153

short stories, 84, 101; Asian ecofiction as, 96, 98; Canadian writers of, 80, 81; contemporary fiction, 38, 46, 57, 59, 61, 62, 67; of early-to-mid-twentieth century, 13–16, 17, 19, 26; of ecoromance, 112, 114, 115; European ecofiction as, 88, 91, 93, 95; of Native American writers, 71, 72, 73; of speculative fiction, 133, 135, 137, 140, 144, 149, 155, 156; of western writing, 119, 120, 123, 124, 126, 127

slavery, 11, 19, 47, 104, 132, 137–38, 156, 158

socialism, 11, 14–16, 86, 87, 88, 95, 101

social justice, 6, 15, 18, 178

soil, 30, 43, 95, 136, 155

South, 19, 62, 167, 174, 175

South America, 12, 56; Amazon region, 26, 43, 48, 83, 84, 123, 136, 183; Argentina, 83, 84; Brazil, 36, 60; Ecuador, 83, 115

South Dakota, 52, 126

Southwest, 14, 30, 58, 114, 158, 161; mysteries and, 176, 177, 180–81, 182–83; western writing and, 119, 120, 121, 124, 126

speculative fiction, 25, 44, 180; elements in, 3; fantasy, 82, 92, 109, 112, 113, 116, 125, 133, 135, 157–60; general contemporary fiction, 131–57; nature of, 129, 130–31; Ursula K. Le Guin, 110, 143–45. *See also* animals; business/corporations; cautionary fiction; cities; climate change; disaster fiction; endangered/extinct species; forests; magic; Native Americans; nature; oceans; overpopulation; philosophy; politics; pollution; prehistoric cultures; science fiction; survival; technology; war

spirituality, 12, 23, 81, 90, 100, 113; of Australian aborigines, 103, 105; contemporary fiction and, 32, 33, 37, 47, 58; ecofeminism and, 47, 180; in English fiction, 88, 89; Native Americans and, 72, 73, 74–75, 119, 124, 153, 161; nature in Russia and, 93; western writing and, 118, 119, 123, 124. *See also* philosophy

survival, 22, 25, 34, 42, 64, 65, 66, 74, 104, 126, 168; speculative fiction and, 135, 136, 137, 139–40, 141, 143, 145, 148, 151, 152, 155, 158, 161–62

sustainability, 13, 14, 61, 63, 65, 74, 99, 141; environmentalism and, 6, 49; speculative fiction and, 137, 146, 150, 151, 156

technology, 13, 16, 33, 47, 72, 91, 121; cautionary fiction and, 23, 68, 133, 150; in English fiction, 86–87, 89; in mid-twentieth-century fiction, 20, 23, 24, 26; mysteries and, 170, 171; nature vs., 34, 38, 39–40; nineteenth-century literature and, 86–87; speculative fiction and, 129–30, 132, 134, 135,